THE STOCK TOUR SWING

THE STOCK TOUR SWING

USE GOLF SCIENCE TO UNCOVER YOUR VERSION OF THE TOUR SWING.

The Stock Tour Swing

By Tyler Ferrell

ISBN: 978-0-9992437-0-1

www.GolfSmartAcademy.com

Dedication

This book is dedicated to my grandfather Owen "Obie" Williams, who introduced me to this great game. Those first few afternoons on the driving range sparked what has turned out to be a lifelong passion.

Foreword

I have been extremely blessed by many things in my life, but none more than our two children. Apparently, the old saying of apple trees and apples is true, as my children's favorite lines are, "How do you know?" and "Why?" I have spent a staggering amount of time asking those questions about my golf game. Like many of you out there, I am obsessed with getting better at golf. Frankly, our definition of better doesn't matter—so long as we are moving in the right direction.

I first met Tyler outside the Orlando International Airport baggage claim, driving around in circles until his AMM 3D Golf Electromagnetic System arrived on the belt. He hadn't even shut the door to my car when I started in on the golf questions. As he would now tell you with a smile, "How do you know?" and "Why?" were asked more than a few times! Even though we had an early morning start scheduled for the next day, we stayed up late into the night discussing general golf theory, golf swing ideas, golf training—if it had to do with golf, we addressed it. Those conversations spilled into the next three days on the driving range at Isleworth and inside the gym. I had *finally* met someone who got it. Tyler could explain not only what was happening in the golf swing, but why it was happening and how to train in the gym to support desired changes.

Over my 16 years of playing on the PGA Tour, I have come to appreciate the difficulty of the game of golf. People from all walks of life, other sports, all over the world are eaten up by this great game. But the endless challenge is improvement. Over this book, Tyler lays out a road map for how to organize your game for improvement. He will show you where the club should be, how to get it there, and offer some fitness ideas to help support it all. As we all know, fitness is important, but it is vital to know that our gym work is not hindering our golf goals.

As crazy as it sounds, my job is to chase a white Titleist around a massive field with holes in it. The difference between making a cut and winning is so small that I will do anything to improve. I have no choice. I have been to many teachers around the country, all of which I have learned from—but Tyler is unique in that he has the ability to tie it all together. He was able to clear my mind of useless clutter and get straight to the cause of my issues. He gave me range drills and a gym routine to help my body support what I do on the golf course. As a direct result, my mind is clearer on the course.

I wish I'd had access to this type of training my rookie year, but as Tyler would say, "The best time to plant a tree was 20 years ago; the second best time is now." His quote is a great reminder that all I can do is spend every day improving myself and my game. Or, as my favorite saying goes, "Find what you love and let it kill you."

As you move forward, read and reread certain chapters, and continually refer back to areas where you need improvement. Each golf swing and diagnosis is different—embrace your swing, your fix, and your journey. Remember, getting better is not a straight line—so enjoy the ride!

—*Charles Howell III*
PGA Tour Winner

CONTENTS

PART 3: Part 3 177

My Mission - Why this Program Is Special

Golf is a fascinating game that contains many clues to getting to know yourself and your swing. But the clues are subtle and take some detective work to recognize. This program will help you understand the subtle differences between being a great golfer, a hacker, or something in between.

The book's purpose is to share the movement combinations I have learned over 15 years of coaching golf using 3D motion measurement technologies. Each key point and movement I teach is backed up by graphs and data from 15 years of experience with 3D motion capture.

Once you understand how the Stock Tour Swing works and how to apply it to your game, you will never again look at the golf swing in the same way. You will have a roadmap to follow and real strategies that can be employed whenever you feel you are losing your game.

There isn't another book like this on the market. Golf instruction is currently flooded with wrong, misleading, and vague information. Many golf instructors don't care as long as some of their students improve. The common justification is, "who cares if it's wrong as long as the student improves?

I care. The golf science community cares. And the thousands of golfers who benefit from change to their golf game care.

My experience is that specific instruction, based on real science, explained in a practical way produces more consistent results than instruction based on feelings and pseudo-science.

It is my hope that this book is a step in the right direction not just for individuals, but for golf instruction as a whole.

Who this book is for

This book is for golfers who are willing to put in the time to improve, but fail to do so because they haven't yet found an improvement plan that truly helps balance their swing. It is also for:

Lifelong learners—golfers around the world who find joy in the journey while trying to troubleshoot their swing.

Competitive golfers—those trying to make a living by playing this great game. These golfers are most in need of clarity.

Coaches—those leading others in mastering the game. Clear, direct instruction is a reasonable goal for our industry. When a golf coach understands each moving piece of the game, simple instruction emerges.

Parents of junior players—juniors can make swing changes significantly faster than adults. But well-meaning adults can ruin a junior's chance with the wrong guidance.

What this program covers

Discover the secrets of the Stock Tour Swing. The Stock Tour Swing describes the movement combinations common to full swings made by the vast majority of elite golfers. We break down the shape of this elite swing throughout this program. As we decode the shape of the swing, you will notice which features of the swing are critical. I have simplified the swing's key movements into a series of guidelines and spectrums.

Learn what your swing is missing and how to balance any of its undesirable elements. Modern measurement technologies offer us an increasingly better idea of which movements make a golf swing work consistently well and which movements cause it to work consistently poorly. This book explores those distinctions. We also cover the tried-and-true solutions that have, in my experience, fixed students' common swing issues.

Establish a problem-solving framework to solve issues with your full swing. The problem-solving framework you will learn from this program considers:

What do you want the club to do?

How does the body best accomplish that?

What are the best ways to train the body to do this?

What you will learn from this program

Revolutionize how you see the golf swing. We will establish a common language for discussing the key aspects of the golf swing. Three golf swing objectives to consider are:

1. How do you control the path of the club head?
2. How do you organize the face-to-path relationship?
3. How do you create speed?

Promise yourself that every tip you try from this day forward will change either the face, the path, or both.

Learn to self-coach. If you are trying to learn the game on your own, I applaud you and want to do everything I can to help you. You will learn to self-coach by examining the practical application of contemporary ideas in golf science. You will become empowered to participate in the improvement and management of your game. You will learn to distinguish a good idea from a silly tip, which will save you months of wasted time and effort. By gaining true understanding, you will enable yourself to stick to a path that will produce long-term mastery if you put in the time.

Discover real strategies to employ whenever you lose your game. It is naive to think you will never struggle with your swing. Even the best players in the world experience lulls in their performance. The key to minimizing these is to know how to read the feedback hidden in each swing. This feedback will tell you exactly what you need to work on.

Learn how to save a round by reading objective feedback. The golf swing is fragile and requires precision. But if you understand what makes it work, you can realize why you are having a good or a bad day. This knowledge gives you a serious leg up on your competition. Most golfers have no idea why they hit good or bad shots, and when things go wrong they end up merely guessing what to correct.

Why I'm uniquely qualified to guide you

Over the last 20 years, modern measurement tools have powered the growth of a new field called golf science. Fifteen years of studying with the leaders in golf science have led me to the perspective that nearly all elite golfers share a common foundation—a combination of movements understood by them, but foreign to amateur golfers.

As a player, I reached a +2 handicap, thanks largely to my ball striking ability. My experience as an elite athlete offered me the ability to decode vague instruction. I could imagine what golf instruction tips would really *feel* like, and thus evaluate whether they would actually help me survive the stress of competition. This experience as a competitive golfer drove me to stay focused on finding impactful solutions.

As a coach, I started as a fitness trainer, which helped me develop a critical understanding of the body. I saw firsthand which physical changes resulted in changes to a swing and which ones helped golfers through the placebo effect. The second wave of my coaching career involved working with golfers on the range to change their swings. My knowledge of anatomy allowed me to take a very detailed approach, one I learned quickly that golfers appreciated.

Along the way I also learned there is a big difference between technical and detailed. I believe the swing should blend artistry and athleticism, but improving a swing always requires attention to detail.

Supplementary website

I am one of the cofounders of http://golfsmartacademy.com, where you can find many instructional videos. Many are free while others are exclusively available to site members.

At the end of 2014, I embarked on writing a step-by-step book that explains my problem-solving method for learning the golf swing. Once you have the framework (how the club works, how the body moves the club, and how to train the body), the videos will help you connect the dots as they relate to your game.

The videos most directly related to this program are at https://golfsmartacademy.com/stocktourswingbook.

CHAPTER 1

The Stock Tour Swing—Why Golf Is Harder than Any Other Sport

When I was a kid, I played sports any time I got a chance. Movement was a pure form of expression. I loved it. I worked hard to refine my skills in whatever I played, and training never seemed like work. This mindset helped me excel at almost everything I played. I also had the great fortune of having an older brother to chase and compete with. He was my model for diligent practice—a practice model I learned to love. I didn't just put up with practice; in many cases, I enjoyed it more than competing.

As a kid, my main sports were basketball and tennis. As I started competing in leagues and tournaments, I noticed that successful athletes all seemed to enjoy practicing. Even though I received technical coaching in basketball and tennis, I improved from hours and hours of practice. I spent long afternoons dribbling and shooting at the court to improve my basketball skills. My tennis skills were honed each night pounding balls against our garage. By the time I reached high school I was one of the school's more skilled athletes in both tennis and basketball. More importantly, I had a formula for learning movement skills—at least I thought I did.

The summer before I started high school, my grandfather took me to his country club's driving range. After one session hitting balls as hard as I could, I was hooked. I had been bitten by the famous golf bug. I thought about golf all the time. On beautiful days when I was outside on the basketball court, I would daydream about playing golf. In my mind, it was only a matter of time before I was a golf star, because I had the formula for improvement—put in hours of practice and it will happen.

I thought I could learn golf just like I did basketball and tennis. I had some clubs and a field behind my house. One kind neighbor put a flag in a makeshift green for me. For a summer I spent an hour or two every day in that field trying to build my skills, just like I had done for tennis and basketball.

When I started high school, I got a junior membership at the local golf club, and I played or practiced almost every single day. Though parts of my game improved a lot, I struggled with other parts regardless of how much work I put in. Frustrated, I solicited the help of one of the area's top coaches. With his input, I experienced big improvements in ball striking. However, just as I started to improve my full swing, my short game started to deteriorate. No matter how hard I worked, I couldn't figure out a way to do the basic chip and pitch shots consistently off of a tight lie. I was able to score pretty well thanks to my ball striking, but the short game was a huge burden.

I thought my short game would improve when I went to college, but it didn't. I played on a Division 1 college team, and during my collegiate career I had six double hit chips in tournament rounds...and many, many others when playing casually. The most frustrating thing wasn't the poor shots—it was the realization that my formula for success wasn't working. I had to keep looking for answers.

Coaches and teammates claimed I just didn't have very good touch, but internally I fought that opinion. I was a really good putter. I had a lot of touch out of the bunkers. I had great touch in basketball and tennis. I knew I had the potential to have great touch around the greens and it drove me crazy to not be able to do what seemed easy to others. I frequently asked myself, "How could a golfer have touch in every aspect of sports except this one?" It didn't make sense.

Though I struggled with chipping and pitching, I reached a handicap of two-better-than-par at my peak. When my ball striking was on and I missed greens in the right locations, I could easily shoot under par. But I knew deep down that I would never reach my true potential if I didn't improve my wedge play.

I kept working at my wedge game the way everyone said I should. I took lessons and put in hours upon hours of practice, but things still didn't click. Why could I drive it 325 yards off the tee and hit 70 percent of my fairways, but struggle with a basic 20-yard shot off the fairway? How is that even possible? Eventually, I decided the only way to find out was to study wedge play myself.

Luckily, I worked at a golf gym that pointed me toward the solution. This gym happened to be owned and operated by Dr. Greg Rose, the eventual cofounder of Titleist Performance Institute (TPI). He had one of the first real-time 3D measurement systems. He also connected me to a world of elite golf trainers and coaches. I had always had lots of questions; but now, when I had a question about a swing's movements, all I had to do was look at the data. However, there was a lot of data to look at with each swing!

Insight

By studying wedge data, talking with great coaches, and taking every seminar TPI had to offer, I came to the conclusion that there are different fundamentals for a driver swing than for a chip shot.

It wasn't just a simple, "Hands forward and play the ball back and make a mini swing" that I had tried for so many years. With the help of some elite coaches and by examining data from elite golfers, I was finally able to understand that my technique was great for the driver but *terrible* for chip shots. To borrow a tennis analogy, it was like I was using an overhead slam technique for a simple volley. I had no chance.

It wasn't that I lacked touch or that I was just "mental." When it came to wedge shots, I didn't understand the subtle technical keys to a finesse wedge shot. Those keys initially seemed unathletic to me, but when I started to coach amateur golfers, I realized that many of them also gravitated toward this method of swinging the club with the driver. While they struggled with the driver, many of them were skilled at hitting the basic chip shot. With my students' help, I gradually developed a clearer understanding of the golf swing.

The more I taught, the better I understood what made a golfer good at driving the ball, hitting irons, or having a solid wedge game. After a while, I could predict where a golfer would struggle by looking at just one or two swings. The golf swing was really starting to make sense! Students have been floored by my ability to accurately diagnose a problem via email or over the phone—but it all stems from my deep understanding of the swing, which you can learn, too.

Mission: *My hope is that by the end of this program, you too will have a solid understanding of what makes your swing work, why you struggle with certain areas, and how you can train for long-term improvement.*

What makes me different from other teachers?

I've used 3D systems to measure the golf swing since 2004.

Mission: *Using that platform, I have simplified the key movements of the swing into a series of guidelines and spectrums for you to learn in this program.*

I hope they are as helpful for you as they have been for me.

Two decades ago when I first started taking lessons, instruction was video based. In fact, I went to one instructor solely because I heard he had a great collection of Ben Hogan videos. Video is great for visualizing what you are currently doing and what you need to do differently—but you have to use it carefully.

In this program, you will learn to use video to recognize key movement patterns. But without an underlying understanding of the movements that build a good swing, it's common to focus on the wrong thing when analyzing video. It's easy to jump to the conclusion that everyone swings the club differently, or to chalk up Jim Furyk's and

Rickie Fowler's swings to the fact that they are just lucky, exceptional athletes. With 3D motion measurement, we can now scientifically investigate why Jim Furyk's swing works well, as well as precisely explain why golfers who look pretty struggle with certain areas of their game.

Mission: *This problem-solving approach to managing a golf swing is the backbone of the new wave of coaching based on golf science—a wave I am happy to call myself part of.*

The purpose of this book is to share the best movement combinations to swing a golf club. I have refined these combinations over 15 years of coaching golf using 3D motion measurement technologies.

Why this book now?

Until about 1995, after eyeballing a golf swing, the best that golf instructors hoped to offer their students were descriptions of athletic movements that sometimes worked. Suggestions like, "Swing more to right field," "Cover the ball," and "Use your legs."

Sometimes these worked well; other times they didn't work at all.

Over the last 20 years, the golf industry has shifted from observation to measurement. Force plates measure how the feet work with the ground. Launch monitors measure how the ball is actually flying and calculate how the club was able to make it do so. 3D systems and advanced computer modeling reveal how the body is swinging the club. I've studied the body, I've studied the swing, and I've studied the biomechanics. I initially studied these elements to understand my own game, but I have found great joy and satisfaction in watching my students improve thanks to the same clarity of concepts.

Mission: *My instruction method has been honed to the point where I am able to help golfers very quickly. My intent is that you will experience some real breakthroughs as you read this book.*

Most teaching professionals truly believe that if the situation had been right, they could have made it. For hardworking golfers on the rise, there is such a small difference between a +2 handicap and a +6.

Mission: *I hope this book will help influence golfers around the world who are simply trying to figure it all out. I want to share my understanding of the swing with as many of you as I can.*

Really, I want a time machine so I can share this information with my 19-year-old self who was trying to maximize his chances of playing in the big leagues. I know if 19-year-old Tyler had the information I share through the Golf Smart Academy, he could have had a real chance of making it prior to his injury.

Interestingly, my injury underlies the very motivation for this program. In 2008, I was a typical up-and-coming instructor, working as much as I could and taking every opportunity to read books, take classes, and shadow as many great instructors as I could access. Most of my trainings and certifications were in fitness or rehab. I started out designing exercise programs for golfers based on physical assessment and 3D data. I quickly realized it was incredibly difficult to get a person to change the way they moved, but I loved trying to figure it out.

One day, seemingly out of the blue, I started to experience some startling neurological and vascular symptoms. I saw a slew of doctors and tried a variety of techniques to understand and correct what was happening inside my neck. Some doctors helped a lot. Others not so much. As I pursued solutions, I increasingly came to understand the puzzle that was my neck injury. Similar to a golf swing, there were a number of factors at play, and no single piece was causing all my symptoms.

While I worked through rehab, I had time to reflect on my career and what I had learned so far. You see, for a couple years, I had issues working more than a couple hours a day without triggering debilitating symptoms. It was frustrating. I could no longer rely on youthful energy and work ethic to advance my career. I needed to learn how to leverage my time.

Once I figured it out, I had a lot that I wanted to share. With my exposure to 3D data, my access to elite golfers' swing files, my studies of the body, and my experiences as an elite athlete, I had information that was too valuable to keep to myself. I created some successful clinics and decided the best way to use my time was to organize what I had learned into programs for do-it-yourself golfers (the 80 percent to 90 percent of golfers who don't take regular lessons).

One of the suggested approaches for dealing with my neck instability was a series of injections called Platelet Rich Plasma (PRP). While the injections seemed very promising, they risked damaging the upper cervical region of my spine—or worse. Faced with the unimaginable, I came up with the idea to put all my thoughts about the golf swing down in video format.

I had become an expert in the 3D movement of the arms and hands and how those movements related to the rest of the body. I invested a lot of time taking classes on the body and learning how movement really works. I wanted to share this information as my potential legacy. It was weird to think about at 30 years old, but that's where I was. Just like hitting a great drive and ending up in a sand divot, I chose to attack my situation with the perspective, "What can I do from here?" instead of "Why me?"

A handful of different sport psychologists each shared the same key phrase with me: "Champions adapt." Instead of looking at my injury as a curse, I realized that in some ways it was a blessing. For almost a year, I taught the golf swing without the ability to demonstrate the movements. During that time, I learned to use my words and hands to get golfers to make changes. A hidden blessing of my injury became the gift of improved communication.

A second hidden blessing emerged over the next 2–3 years of teaching. By this point, I could once again demonstrate the movements, but I realized something amazing following a full day of lessons—I was looking at the swing without my own *personal feel* bias. During a lesson, a student asked, "What does it feel like when you do this movement?" And for a second I actually couldn't remember. I quoted some professional golfers describing the movement, but I truly couldn't recall what it felt like myself. I realized that when I looked at a golf swing, I was no longer able to see my swing in their movements—which was a good thing.

In my early teaching, I would frequently share with students what had worked for *me*. Sometimes it worked great for the student as well, but other times it didn't. I realized after a couple years of not playing golf that I was able to look at a student as a blank canvas. Looking at the swing without fresh memories of my own experiences forced me to focus on the key movements that had the biggest impact on the *student's* game. This blessing in disguise—looking at the swing and the student as a blank canvas—was the single greatest tool for helping me organize the sequence of issues to work on with each student.

When I created GolfSmartAcademy.com to host my videos, I initially expected my students and other coaches to enjoy them. But I was treated to an overwhelming sense of pride when golfers who I had never met sent emails reporting they had improved from watching the videos. Many ended their emails with a similar sentiment—"You really have something here, keep it up."

As the number of videos grew, I started to realize that new members probably found the site completely overwhelming. While the videos all relate to each other, promote common themes, and are organized into specific sections, they don't exactly flow in a sequential order.

Mission: *At the end of 2014, I decided to write a step-by-step book explaining my framework for problem solving the golf swing. Once you have the framework (how the club works, how the body moves the club, and how to train the body), the videos will be more helpful in connecting the dots as they relate to your game.*

I wanted the book to be thorough enough to stand on its own, but I also wanted it to complement the videos. It can be hard to learn movement from text and pictures, but watching the moves come to life can help it all click. I've seen it happen and I can't wait to hear more stories of it happening for golfers like you.

I'm a student of the game, and I relate to the golfer's mindset. Golfers are always looking for the new magic solution. I'm sure this won't be the last golf program you study. But I have two main goals for you while you're here:

> **Goal #1**—learn how to see the most critical parts of a swing. Obtaining this vision will lead you to the insight that all of the great golf swings share similarities.

> **Goal #2**—truly understand your own swing's strengths and weaknesses. This understanding will lead you to insights on how to balance your swing. Even better, knowing your strengths and weaknesses will help you prioritize what will improve your game the most effectively and dramatically.

Mission: *There is nothing that frustrates me more than watching golfers put in hours of practice but fail to improve because they waste their time on insignificant concepts.*

Golf is hard, but it is incredibly rewarding when it clicks. Nothing makes it click faster than having a clear understanding of what you're trying to do.

I hope you enjoy my first major attempt to communicate what I've learned over 15 years of following the field of golf science. After you experience breakthroughs from using this program, please send me a message on my site. It never gets old.

How this book is organized

This book is organized from most general to most detailed, because in my experience that is the curve people follow when they successfully learn movements. To learn to move you must first understand the big picture; in golf, the big picture is what the club and body do. Next, you'll want to experience the club swinging in the ideal pattern, and try to intuitively figure out how the body can do it. However, if you get stuck trying to figure out how the body does it, you'll want details about the key body movements that comprise the great swings.

Movement is hard to learn sequentially. Imagine if I described the sequence of events involved in walking. *Push off your big toe, then off your mid foot as it rolls inward. However, maintain the alignment of your knee over your foot as your pelvis rotates and your opposite arm swings behind you. Oh, and while you're doing this, your opposite arm should swing forward while the rib cage counter rotates the movement of the pelvis.* Now imagine getting into the muscles and decoding all the variables that could go wrong there. It's not a great way to learn to walk.

I'd rather start coaching with something along the lines of, *Here, watch this person walk. See their arms and legs work in harmony. Try that a few times.* After seeing what the student organizes in their brain, we can start to break the movement down into sections, phases, and specifics. This is possible because there is a framework in which to fit the new information.

Learning to golf works the same way. It's easier to start with the big picture and then delve into more specific details. Far too often, students come to me after playing the game for many years, yet they still lack a solid grasp of what both they and the club should be doing. Or, they may know what a textbook grip should look like, but they don't know *why* it is a textbook grip or how it relates to the other parts.

Mission: *You will learn to self-coach by examining the practical application of contemporary ideas in golf science. Through true understanding, you will enable yourself to stick to a path that will produce long-term mastery if you put in the time.*

In Part 1 of this book we explore our tool—the golf club—and what we want to make it do. Understanding this is non-negotiable. If you don't know what you want the club to do and how to read feedback, then all the tips in the world will be wasted.

Part 2 explores the big picture of the body, similar to describing the big picture of walking as swinging your arms in legs in rhythm. This will help you develop a personalized swing that makes the club do what you want.

But if you're like a lot of golfers and you've studied the swing, you'll need the information in Part 3. This is where we cover the body movements in each phase of the swing in detail. Expect to have a few Eureka! moments as you discover the combination of movements that works best for your swing.

In Part 4 you will learn to adjust your Stock Tour Swing specifically to hit the driver or the wedges, and to hit draws or fades. With all this technical understanding, Part 5 helps you understand the mental game and how to train the key movements.

Part 6 exposes the common swing patterns that prevent you from reaching your potential. Finally, Part 7 ties everything together and helps you create a plan for improvement.

Mission: *The three basic questions this book is designed to answer are:*

1. *What do you want the club to do?*
2. *How does the body best do that?*
3. *What are the best ways to train it?*

While this is probably not the last golf program you will ever try, I sincerely hope that the information it imparts will clarify whatever you have done before and whatever you will do after, and help take your game to the next level.

CHAPTER 2

Understanding the Stock Tour Swing
Program (Read This First!)

Before learning about the club, let me stress the importance of clearly understanding Part 1. You have a lifetime to master your own swing. Your understanding of the swing and how your own body produces it will grow with time. As you understand the key components of the Stock Tour Swing, you will waste less time on things related to your swing that are actually insignificant to your performance.

If you watch golf on TV, read golf magazines, or play with golfers who do so, you are likely bombarded with ideas, tips, and suggestions for improving your game. However, if you don't understand what the club must do, or fail to read the feedback hidden in each swing, you will easily be swayed by buzzwords that disguise misinformation as science. While some popular tips can help your game, others are disastrous.

Mission: *Part 1 is designed to give you a solid basis for understanding why any tip or program you have tried up to this point has helped you. More importantly, in the future, you will be able to explain why any tip might actually help. It's a bold task, but one I think you are up for. It's the only way I know to make any long-term difference in a golfer's game.*

Part 1 could easily be thought of as the program's absolutes. That is, without meaningfully understanding what you want the club head to do, all the swing thoughts in the world will be little more than Band-Aids.

Swings of elite golfers—more common ground than differences

How you swing the club is somewhat of a unique experience, full of your own blend of athleticism and artistry. Every golfer has a slightly different reference or feel for their own swing. However, the club swings and hits the ball universally, and independent of your personal feel. To master your game, you must recognize and interpret feedback. If you don't, you will likely never commit to working on any one thing long enough to truly change your game.

I like to think of golf as a sport that incorporates a tool to help you smack a ball around a field. The more traditional description of the goal of the golf swing is something like:

"To get the club to strike the ball in a way that moves the ball to a new, desired location. The method you use is of no importance as long as it is repeatable."

That sounds great, but in reality, some movement combinations are more repeatable than others. These combinations are what make up the Stock Tour Swing.

Mission: *The purpose of this book is to share the movement combinations that I have refined from 15 years of using 3D motion measurement technologies to coach golf.*

The way your body wants to swing the club depends somewhat on your movement background and how you visualize the ball's flight. We will cover these topics in later sections, but for now, know that the way the club swings and how the ball flies is due entirely to physics. We will begin this journey by looking at the physics of how to use a golf club.

Shot feedback—critical to solving problems in your golf game

Each golf club is a tool, and to understand how to play golf, you must know how to use the tool.

From a feedback perspective, the Stock Tour Swing can be summarized by the following formula:

Path of the club
+ Face angle at impact
+ Speed of the club
+ Contact location
= Quality of the golf shot

Let's break down this formula by its key pieces, starting with the path.

What does the path of the elite golf swing look like?

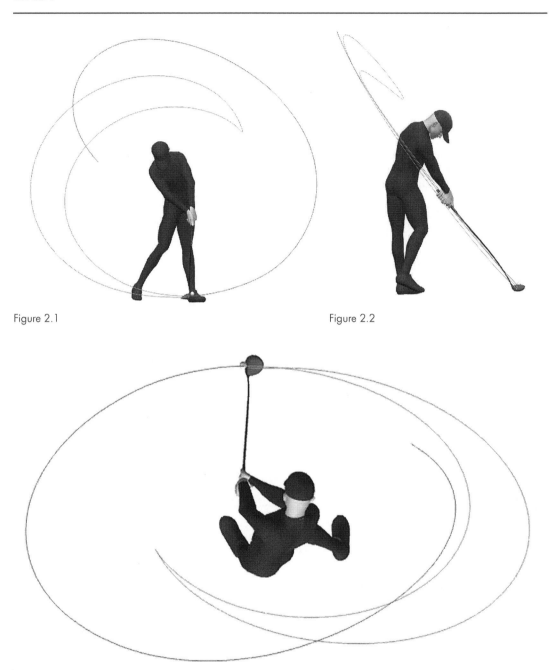

Figure 2.1

Figure 2.2

Figure 2.3

These three pictures give an overall sense of the swing. The golfer is shown at impact. The line shows the path of the middle of the club head. Notice how the overall shape of the swing is wide in the backswing, narrow in transition, then wide through the release.

Look closely at these pictures. What do you notice? This image, and all the others like it, are created using the GEARS 3D system. Of all the 3D systems on the market, GEARS creates some of the most impressive visuals. Unless otherwise stated, the images of elite golfers are generated from captures of tour pro swings.

Elite golfers have figured out a similar way to swing the club and make the ball fly. They swing the club around their body as their body stays mostly in the same place. They might have some funky body moves in the backswing, or a weird-looking strategy for bracing at impact. But in general, a good golf swing resembles the shape of a circle or ellipse around your body (as in Figures 2.1, 2.2, and 2.3).

Insight

Mission: *We will break down the shape of the elite swing throughout this program. As we decode that shape, you will notice which features of the swing are critical.*

For now, take some time to think about how the club head is swinging around the body and what the shape of that movement looks like. We will refer to the swing's general shape as the **circle** and to the specific path of the club head as the **path**.

The path is the first key variable in the formula for a quality golf shot, but it's not the only one. The direction of the club face is equally important. Swinging a golf club is not like a baseball bat, which has a uniform hitting surface in every orientation. The golf club has a rigid club face that points in a specific direction. To succeed at golf, your swing must control where the club face points at impact.

Figure 2.4

Figure 2.5

Pay attention to the details of different swings. These are two swings with a similar club path but different face-to-path relationships. One will work much better than the other because of this seemingly minor difference.

The club head's path and the orientation of its **face** are the two most important factors in a quality golf shot. Contact location consistency is very closely related to the path. If you get the path right, you will enjoy plenty of distance given whatever speed you create.

Evolve from "I'm trying a new golf tip" to "I'm building a concept to improve my game"

Mission: *Commit to yourself right now that every tip you try from this day forward will change the face, the path, or both.*

I'm not saying that everything you ever learned was wrong. Far from it. Together we will explore why many tips you have tried actually worked. Below are some common tips and what they actually affect:

1. Changing how you grip the club (changes face)
2. Swing easy and stay relaxed (changes path)
3. Finish in balance (changes path)
4. Keep your head down (changes path)
5. Keep your left arm straight (changes path)

All of the instruction throughout the history and future of this sport is designed to impact those two variables (club path and club face). Even the tips that we know to be wrong (for instance, keep your left arm straight and your head down) were intended to change the path of the club or where the face pointed. However, because when you tried them the tips weren't tied to what they actually did to the club face or path, your brain easily tossed them away as failed experiments.

The goal of this program is to solidify the key requirements of an elite golf swing. If you know these, you won't be able to give up on what your swing really needs. Instead of giving up on a concept, you should give up on a *feeling* of that concept and try an alternative feeling. You'll be less likely to try some random tip that is completely unrelated to what you know your swing needs. Most golfers treat their golf improvement like an Easter egg hunt, but by the end of Part 1, you will be able to see your improvement more as a map, one that can be tracked and followed.

Mission: *Modern measurement technologies offer an increasingly better idea of which movements make a golf swing work consistently well and which movements cause it to work consistently poorly. This book explores these distinctions.*

Solid shot, solid path

One of the best feelings in golf is hitting the ball in the middle of the club. A solid hit is a big reason we all play this great game. Hitting the ball solidly depends on the shape of your circle—specifically, your club head path. Solid shot, solid path.

When I refer to the club's path, all that really matters is the path on which the club is traveling for the .0045 seconds it is in contact with the ball. It's hard to have a good path at impact unless you have a good path from waist height on the downswing to waist height on the follow through. When it comes to solid contact, this parallel-to-parallel zone is where all the magic happens.

If you have a good path, all you need is a face orientation that works with your path to hit great shots.

The swings of elite golfers—common ground revisited

Hitting the ball solid and straight is great, but it is also important to hit the ball far. Doing so involves not just a good face and path, but speed as well. The good news is that once you learn to blend the movements like a tour pro, it is possible to have a good path, with a good face, and a lot of speed. The movements we will learn later in the book are designed to help produce a good face, a good path, and as much speed as your body is capable of producing.

Tour pros are the golfers who have figured out how to maximize the power-path-face equation. While we might be able to pick out differences in their swings, at their core are a lot of similarities. When you know what to look for, guys like Jim Furyk, Bubba Watson, or J.B. Holmes have more technique in common with each other than they do with a +15 handicap, and vice versa. This program will teach you how to spot these key similarities and figure out how to apply them to your own swing, without having to make yours look perfect. You never know—you might be the next Jim Furyk instead of Adam Scott.

Self-coaching

You might be thinking to yourself, "Why do I really need to know this stuff? Can't this guy just tell me how to grip the club and swing like Rory?"

No, I can't. At least, not if you want to self-coach like a tour pro. While almost every professional golfer has their own swing coach, tour pros frequently make tiny changes before a round or even on the course to right the ship when their swing is off. That ability to self-correct is part of what makes them great. I want you to be able to do that, too. This program will allow you to coach yourself with confidence, which comes from knowing how to read feedback and predicting how a change will actually affect your ball's flight.

It sounds complicated, but once you know 1) what to look for in a swing; 2) the body movements that make it look that way; and 3) how to read feedback, you will have a power over your game you never imagined possible.

Mission: *You will become empowered to improve and manage your golf improvement. You will learn to distinguish a good idea from a silly tip, which will save you months of wasted time and effort.*

From taking lessons and reading tips, most golfers end up with a piecemealed "Frankenswing." Such swings are put together in a fragile way and held intact by feelings of what the golfer thinks is correct. When these Frankenswings stop working, the golfer is usually left searching for a new technique to patch the swing back together. The search for the missing piece is a lot like hunting for an Easter egg, but your goal should be to follow a road map—and it's my mission to help you develop one.

To illustrate this point, consider a student of mine named Ron. When Ron first came to me, he was on the verge of giving up the game because he was frustrated with shooting in the mid 90s. He had been a good golfer many years earlier, but his game fell apart over time and now he was completely lost. He had so many swing thoughts going on in his head that he had no idea what to do or where to start. Was it his grip? His backswing? His tempo? Maybe his balance? He had no idea what to try next, since his golf lessons had all been built on memorizing tips rather than understanding concepts.

Ron and I worked on the swing's general concepts. We started by reading feedback from ball flight and making solid contact. Then we moved on to specific movements that were key to tweaking contact and ball flight. It took some time, but Ron worked hard (and smartly) on his golf game. After a year of regular lessons, he really started to get it. He would come to each lesson with an idea of what was wrong, and we worked together to find a solution. He was no longer completely lost or lacking any idea of what to do.

He would often know what he was doing just by looking at ball flight and contact. He would sometimes record his swing on video and could recognize a mistake almost instantly. When we first started working together, he was mostly concerned with his knee bend at set up, his funny pre-shot waggle, and his sway off the ball. After learning to read feedback he no longer worried about such moves, and focused instead on direct causes of ball flight. Not all the little non-critical moves, like his pre-shot dance over the ball or sway and arm bending at the top of the swing. He would know what to look at that would have a realistic chance of making a real change.

With this knowledge, he just needed help finding a way to tweak what he knew was wrong, rather than coming in to a lesson like a lost and desperate soul. Imagine going to a lesson and saying, "I'm having a little trouble with my transition. I'm getting steep and it's causing me to breakdown at impact and hit shots off the toe and to the right." It is remarkably empowering to diagnose problem areas in your own swing. This is what Ron was able to do—and with this book, I think you will too.

A lifelong program

This program is not designed to give you a swing that you will find and keep forever. Chasing such a belief is an enormous source of frustration for many golfers. As I said earlier, you will have great days as well as days where you feel totally lost. That is the nature of the game. Embrace that reality and use this program to quickly get your swing back each time you lose it.

Playing golf has ups and downs that are similar to going on vacation. Coping with bugs while camping is more frustrating if you thought you were staying at the Four Seasons. If you know you are going camping in a fairly buggy area, however, then the adventure is more enjoyable. Tour pros discuss the game in a similar way. The ones who succeed are committed to the process, and trust that progress will come as a result of a good process.

Mission: *The golf swing is fragile and requires precision. But if you understand what makes yours work, you can realize why you are having a good or bad day. This gives you a serious leg up on your competition. Most golfers have no idea why they hit good or bad shots, and when things go wrong they end up merely guessing what to correct.*

Back to Ron.

Once he knew how to read feedback, Ron was better able to correct things on his own. Other times, he would come in and I would ask him questions to lead him to the right conclusion. He would still get stumped, but because he knew there was a solution, he didn't feel lost anymore—he saw the road map for his success. He was able to ignore advice from other golfers unless he recognized it as a useful idea that was relevant to his particular issue at that time.

In the end, a game that almost drove him to quit is now a highlight of his week. Golf has become a fun challenge instead of a hopeless plight. Should Ron stumble and have a bad string of shots, he is able to troubleshoot the issue, regroup, and move on. By understanding what the club and body should do, you too will be able to self-coach your swing.

CHAPTER 3

How to Use This Book

Before you jump into the details of the club head in Part 1, let's address one big concept: How to use this book. We cover a lot of information in this program, so here's how I recommend you read it.

Golf instruction has always been too vague for my taste. For me and most successful golf students, the details have always been a fun way to free up a swing and bring out one's inner artistry and athleticism. That said, there is a big difference between being *specific* and being *overly technical*. As the saying goes, the devil is in the details. I cover many key details in this book. Once you understand the details of how and why the Stock Tour Swing works, you will never look at golf the same way again.

To fully benefit from the program, I recommend skimming it once to get an overview, reading it a second time to absorb the details, and then referring to it as needed after that.

When you first skim it, don't get overwhelmed. Look at the examples, peruse the diagrams, try the drills, and consider how all the key concepts fit together.

After you skim it, let it digest for a week or so before you dig in to the meat of the text. Go over Part 1 a couple of times, because it is the foundation for everything else in the program.

The second time you read it, try to grasp the details. Look for the subtleties and how they relate to your own game. It can be particularly useful to try and relate the program to all the golfers you know, the golf swings you see all the time. Why is Johnny great at driving the ball? Why does Sally have trouble with consistency? These mental exercises will initially challenge your thinking, but they will greatly accelerate your understanding of what makes the Stock Tour Swing work. Once you have a strong understanding of it, you can come up with a rational answer to almost every golf problem you can imagine.

Finally, keep the book nearby as a reference. If you pick up a new book that explains a hot new swing style, refer back to this book to evaluate why (or why not) this new swing might work. You may also recognize that a new method is just the same recycled information in a new package. But most importantly, if you get lost within your own game, use this book to help you zero in on why your swing is struggling and how to correct the problem.

The supporting website

It is difficult to communicate movement in words, which is why I am including as many pictures as I can. Even better for seeing the science come to life is the companion website, https://golfsmartacademy.com/stocktourswingbook. This site is designed to give you the full experience a tour pro would get from a lifetime of lessons with a skilled coach. The site provides free videos that support the concepts in this text. It also provides an easy platform for you to ask questions about concepts you don't yet understand. If you are confused about a topic, please don't hesitate to ask.

Golf is a challenging game, but it is the challenge that makes success so rewarding. It is a hard game to self-navigate, as I and countless others have learned.

Mission: *If you are trying to self-coach, I applaud you and want to do everything I can to help. One of my biggest pet peeves is when a golfer who has the desire to get better is unable to do so because he or she doesn't use practice time wisely.*

This program is designed to minimize your setbacks by adhering to the following logical progression:
1. What do we want to do with the club?
2. How do we want the body to do it?
3. What is the best way to train the body to do it?

If you feel ready to go down the rabbit hole and truly understand the golf swing, let's jump right in.

Part 1

What Should the Club Head Do in the Golf Swing?

If you've never thought about how the golf club swings, Part 1 will expose you to a new way to understand it. Many golfers want a feeling, or a thought, that will instantly improve their swing. These temporary fixes fail if they are not grounded in a clear focus on what the club needs to do. Layering technical thoughts on top of how the club truly swings will yield long-term improvement. The first step is to visualize the club's motion and how the golf ball and club interact.

CHAPTER 4

How the Golf Club Head Works—the Overall Shape of the Golf Swing

The first step to an elite golf swing is to visualize the shape the golf club's path should make. The goal is to make the path look like the images below.

Path of the club is circular

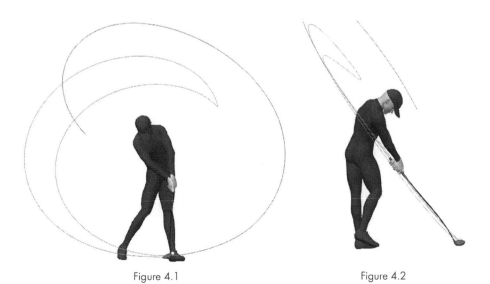

Figure 4.1   Figure 4.2

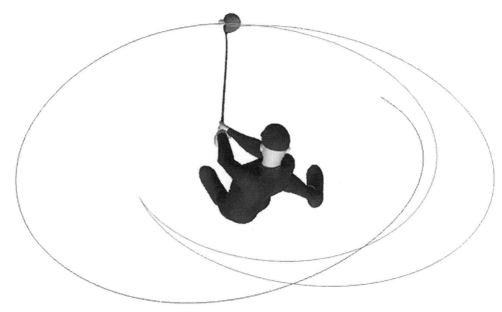

Figure 4.3

These three perspectives give an overall sense of the swing. The line shows the path of the middle of the club head. Notice how the overall shape of the swing is wide in the backswing, narrow in transition, then wide through the release.

The most important section of the circle is the bottom of the swing. That is where the club impacts the ball and frequently, the ground. With the driver, the club head floats through the air. But with an iron, the club head actually brushes the ground just after hitting the ball as the club continues moving along this circle.

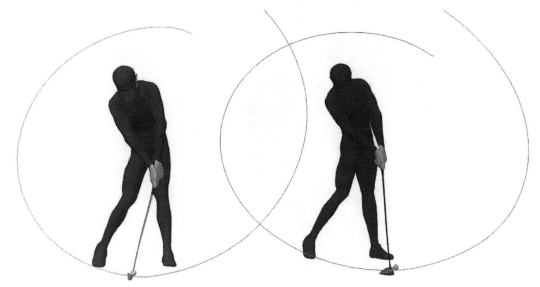

Figure 4.4

Notice the subtle differences between the body positions at impact and the overall shape of the circle when hitting an iron compared to a driver. The iron brushes the ground just after impact. Through impact, the driver is even more elliptical than the iron swing.

Is it really a circle?

As you look at the image below, you can study the path of the backswing and compare it to the path of the downswing. The backswing is the lighter color and the downswing is the slightly darker shade. Notice how the circle does not retrace the same path on the way back as it does on the way down. In the downswing, the circle will actually shift a little forward and squish vertically. Some say the shape is more like an ellipse than a circle. You can call it whatever you'd like; more important is that you start imprinting this image as the goal for your full swing.

Figure 4.5

The downswing path is narrower than the backswing. Then the path is wider again from impact through the end of the release.

From the down-the-line view, we can see that the circle is not straight up and down (like a Ferris wheel) or lying flat (like a helicopter); rather, it is tilted. We will refer to how vertical the circle is as **steep** and to how horizontal it is as **shallow**. Chapter 6, Steeps and Shallows, will further explore why the subtle tilts of the swing path are so critical.

Figure 4.6

The circle is tilted and the path of the club tracks along a fairly consistent plane. For now, it is good to visualize a tilted ellipse; we will clarify later in Chapter 6, Steeps and Shallows.

Also, it's not a true circle because the radius changes throughout the swing. For many, it is going to feel pretty much like the club head swings around you. Don't worry if you're not aware of the radius change. Many golfers aren't. However, since the shape of the circle is constantly changing, there are a couple of things that are really useful to monitor:

Where is the lowest point of the swing?

Where is the widest part of the circle?

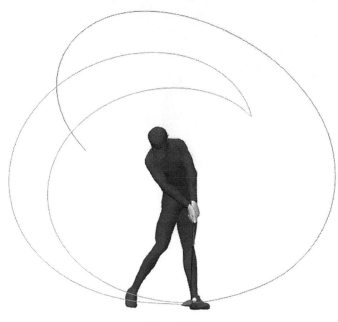

Figure 4.7

In a Stock Tour Swing, with an iron the wide point and the low point are both after the golf ball.

These two features of your swing can reveal a lot about your potential as a golfer, such as with which shots and clubs you will have the easiest time, and which parts of the game will drive you absolutely crazy.

> The best and most versatile golfers have the lowest point ahead of the golf ball with most clubs and the widest point well after the ball with every full swing.
>
> *Insight*

The low and wide points relate closely to a powerful phenomenon we refer to as the **Como Flat Spot**. Chris Como was the first golf instructor I came across who really highlighted this component with some measurable data. It appears that having this long flat spot at the bottom of the swing just after you strike the ball gives you a margin of error that helps with repeatability.

What part of a circle is flat? Exploring the Como Flat Spot

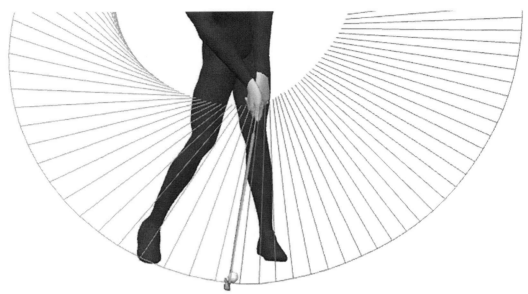

Figure 4.8

Each line represents the shaft at a moment in time during the downswing, impact, and follow through. Notice how the lowest point for the hands is before the ball, but the lowest point for the club is after it.

You may already be wondering how we will squish this circle down at the bottom. We will cover that in Part 3 when we get into every key body movement related to this critical piece of the swing.

In a general sense, the flat spot is created by bringing the handle of the club slightly up and in while the club head is going down and out. Going up creates a flat spot for the down part of the path; going in creates a flat spot in the club's in-to-out movement.

We will get into the details of how the body creates this motion, but right now, simply understand that it is a common component of all good golf swings for all stock shots. You do not want the handle moving down and out unless you are trying to hit a punch shot. All the golf ball really cares about is the little zone where the club is in contact with it. Whether your swing looks like Jim Furyk's or Rory McIlroy's, having a good impact zone and flat spot are common to all good ball strikers.

The geometry of the flat spot is reason enough to have the club leaning forward at impact. But there is another reason, one that is a little trickier to visualize. When the club approaches impact on a full swing, the shaft will kick the club head forward. To avoid hitting the ball really high from this shaft kick phenomenon, you will want the handle ahead of the golf ball. If the club was straight up and down, the shaft kicking forward like this would hit the ball very high in the air and cause you to hit it low on the face. Having the club leaning forward at impact helps get the center of the face on the ball and reduces the loft of the club.

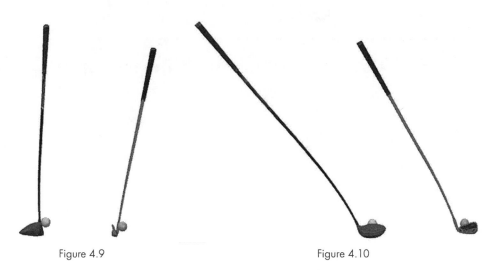

Figure 4.9   Figure 4.10

These two pictures demonstrate what the club will actually look like at impact on a full swing. The shaft will be bending down (droop) and away from the target (lead).

CHAPTER 5

Your Circle Has a Dent In It! The Flat Spot Explained

P roducing a good impact zone (including the flat spot, with well-placed low and wide points) is so important that we will explore it in detail.

Thinking about the Como Flat Spot reminded me of *The Impact Zone*, which I read many years ago. In that book, Bobby Clampet describes a low point spectrum, in which the best golfers had the club reach its lowest point the furthest forward. His data showed that tour players had the bottom of their swing about 4 inches in front of the ball, where high-handicap golfers typically had the lowest point of their swing behind the ball.

Many other instructors have described the low and wide point concept in their own way, and with good reason. Having the bottom of your swing in front of the ball may be the most important thing you can do to improve your game.

> **Insight**
>
> If you are able to train a low point ahead of the ball and a wide point well after impact by extending the handle away from you through impact, your ball-striking ability will improve dramatically. If you take nothing else from this book, let it be this.

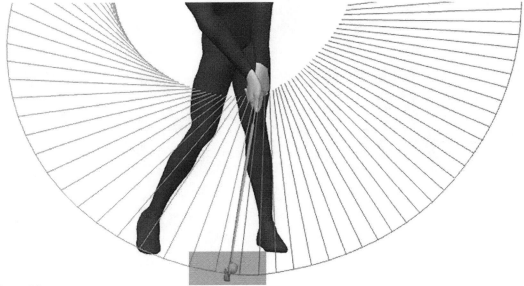

Figure 5.1

The lowest point will be somewhere in this shaded area. If it is behind the ball with an iron then you will have fat and thin contact misses. You'll increasingly understand this key area as you go through this program.

How the club strikes the ground produces a profound feeling. The ground can feel great to hit—or it can hurt! As the club head reaches its low point, it could brush the ground (which feels great), slam into the ground (which feels terrible), or never hit the ground and just pick the ball (which feels fine).

The only way to have the bottom of the swing 4 inches in front of the ball is to have a shallow angle of attack and an arc width that is widening at the same time. After my discussion with Chris Como, I explored the graphs of my AMM 3D system and found the arc width graph to be the measurement I was looking for. If I had to pick one graph to predict a golfer's skill level by just seeing one full swing, arc width would be it. By definition, arc width measures the distance between a point just behind the top of the sternum and the mid-hands point on the grip.

Golf science has revealed a common pattern among elite ball strikers, as well as one among amateurs. The relationship of arc width to ball striking exists even in funky-looking swings.

Don't worry if the graphs below are hard to follow—these are the only graphs I'll show in this program.

Mission: *Each key point and movement I teach can be backed up by graphs and data from 15 years of 3D motion capture.*

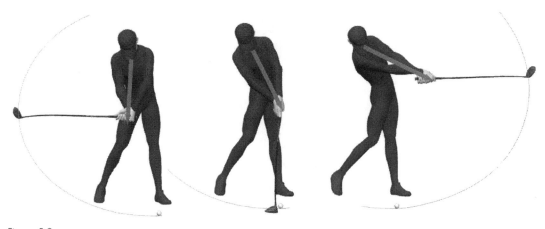

Figure 5.2

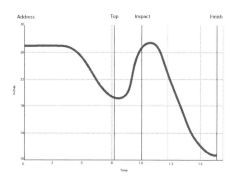

Figure 5.3

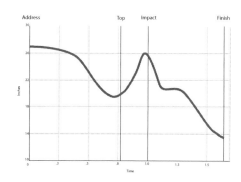

Figure 5.3

The top picture shows a representation of the arc width graph. Arc width is the distance between the mid-hands point on the grip and the thorax point (just behind the top of the sternum). This distance is affected by where the arms are positioned, how straight the elbows are, and how protracted the shoulder blades are. The first graph shows a representation of a PGA Tour winner. The overall pattern through the release is that the distance between the hands and thorax increases significantly and then remains wide after impact. The second graph shows a common amateur pattern. The golfer is widest before impact and the distance decreases significantly through the ball.

It is frequently emphasized that you need to hit down on the ball to hit good shots. Here is a chart of average angles of attack from Trackman for the PGA and LPGA Tour. With most irons, men are hitting 4 degrees down and women are hitting 2–3 degrees down. Many amateurs fall into the 6–10 degrees down range or more.

For amateurs, the key is not really to hit *down* but to hit *forward*. There are some technical aspects to doing this that we will cover in Part 3, but for right now just visualize this key concept.

PGA TOUR AVERAGES WWW.TRACKMANGOLF.COM

	Club Speed (mph)	Attack Angle (deg)	Ball Speed (mph)	Smash Factor	Launch Ang. (deg)	Spin Rate (rpm)	Max Height (yds)	Land Angle (deg)	Carry (yds)
Driver	113	-1.3°	167	1.48	10.9°	2686	32	38°	275
3-wood	107	-2.9°	158	1.48	9.2°	3655	30	43°	243
5-wood	103	-3.3°	152	1.47	9.4°	4350	31	47°	230
Hybrid 15-18°	100	-3.5°	146	1.46	10.2°	4437	29	47°	225
3 Iron	98	-3.1°	142	1.45	10.4°	4630	27	46°	212
4 Iron	96	-3.4°	137	1.43	11.0°	4836	28	48°	203
5 Iron	94	-3.7°	132	1.41	12.1°	5361	31	49°	194
6 Iron	92	-4.1°	127	1.38	14.1°	6231	30	50°	183
7 Iron	90	-4.3°	120	1.33	16.3°	7097	32	50°	172
8 Iron	87	-4.5°	115	1.32	18.1°	7998	31	50°	160
9 Iron	85	-4.7°	109	1.28	20.4°	8647	30	51°	148
PW	83	-5.0°	102	1.23	24.2°	9304	29	52°	136

Please be aware that the location (altitude) and weather conditions have not been taken into consideration for the above data. Besides these reservations, the data is based on a large sample size and gives a good indication of key numbers for tour professionals.

LPGA TOUR AVERAGES WWW.TRACKMANGOLF.COM

	Club Speed (mph)	Attack Angle (deg)	Ball Speed (mph)	Smash Factor	Launch Ang. (deg)	Spin Rate (rpm)	Max Height (yds)	Land Angle (deg)	Carry (yds)
Driver	94	3.0°	140	1.48	13.2°	2611	25	37°	218
3-wood	90	-0.9°	132	1.47	11.2°	2704	23	39°	195
5-wood	88	-1.8°	128	1.47	12.1°	4501	26	43°	185
7-wood	85	-3.0°	123	1.45	12.7°	4693	25	46°	174
4 Iron	80	-1.7°	116	1.45	14.3°	4801	24	43°	169
5 Iron	79	-1.9°	112	1.42	14.8°	5081	23	45°	161
6 Iron	79	-2.3°	109	1.39	17.1°	5943	25	46°	152
7 Iron	76	-2.3°	104	1.37	19.0°	6699	26	47°	141
8 Iron	74	-3.1°	100	1.35	20.8°	7494	25	47°	130
9 Iron	72	-3.1°	93	1.28	23.9°	7589	26	47°	119
PW	70	-2.8°	86	1.23	25.6°	8403	23	48°	107

Please be aware that the location (altitude) and weather conditions have not been taken into consideration for the above data. Besides these reservations, the data is based on a large sample size and gives a good indication of key numbers for tour professionals.

Figure 5.5

Tour pros demonstrate a subtle descending blow with all of their clubs (although some hit up on their driver to maximize distance).

Images provided by www.TrackManGolf.com 2017

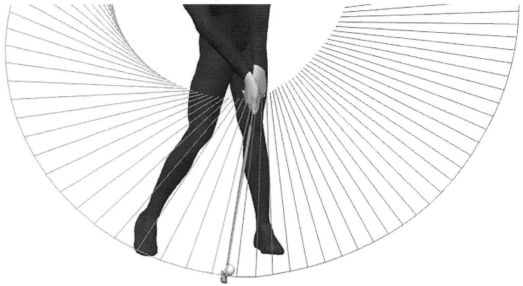

Figure 5.6

A higher-handicap golfer with a scoop will typically have the bottom of their swing behind the golf ball, even with an iron. They will have their wide point at impact instead of after, which gives them a much smaller flat spot. A narrow flat spot works well for wedges but terribly for the longer clubs.

Novice golfers typically swing a club in a shape that is wide in the downswing and then narrow in the follow through. The Stock Tour Swing does the opposite.

See the following images of a pro and an amateur golfer. The line around each body shows the path of the club head. Notice how the amateur golfer doesn't get nearly as wide after impact.

 Width in the follow through is what helps give the Stock Tour Swing the level of consistency and repeatability that you see on TV.

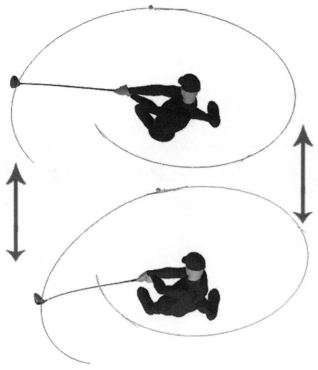

Figure 5.7

There are many differences between the typical over-the-top cast-and-scoop swing of an amateur versus the Stock Tour Swing, but from this overhead view, you can see the timing of the width as a clear pattern difference.

Width after the ball requires more than just extending the arms—body position plays a big role as well. We will cover this in Part 3, but in general, learning to get the club wide after impact with a gentle brush of the ground is the secret you have been searching for.

CHAPTER 6

Steeps and Shallows (These Two Words Will Change Your Life!)

As this program shows, the club head path is one of the most critical factors of good golf. It also tends to be the most consistent aspect of a golfer's swing. Let's face it—most golfers think they are very inconsistent. But from swing to swing, an amateur actually tends to have a pretty consistent path pattern.

Even though your swing tends to be consistent, some path patterns produce very inconsistent results. This leads golfers to think that they drastically change their swing each time they hit a ball. This is not the case.

Movement patterns are stored in the brain and are referred to as an engram or motor program. When you execute your swing, your brain will run your *golf swing engram.* Your golf swing is no different than tying your shoes, riding a bike, or signing your name. Just as your signature has a distinct recognizable pattern, so too does your golf swing. The most consistent piece of that pattern is the club head's overall path.

If you compare two of your swings, you might find you have a drastically different face or a slightly different low or wide point. The difference may result in a toe push-slice for one shot and a fat pull for another. But those two shots are part of the same path pattern.

It would be rare for your swing path to change very much from swing to swing—at least until you know how to deliberately change it. Since the path is so important and repeatable, we are left with two choices:

> Either learn to adjust your path for long-term improvement or learn to control the face and just play your path.

The choice is ultimately yours. But since the path is so important, let's investigate it further.

While the whole shape of the circle matters, the only part of the swing that affects the ball directly is the path of the club head through impact.

One metaphor to apply to the club head's path into the ball is an airplane landing. Jim Hardy is the first person I heard use describe it like this, and it's a great visual. If the airplane is coming down on a steep path, the pilot will have to pull up aggressively and have a small margin of error. If the airplane is coming in too shallow, it will have a shorter runway and the pilot will have to slam on the breaks aggressively. If the landing angle is correct (about 4 degrees for an iron), the airplane will land smoothly and the pilot has the whole runway to work with. It's a simple analogy that creates a powerful image.

> If your swing is too steep or too shallow, it requires perfect timing to create a solid shot.
>
> *Insight*

We all know what steep and shallow feel like. All of us have slammed a club into the ground and taken a swing that didn't even touch the grass.

> One of your first goals is to get the club to consistently brush the ground, preferably starting beneath the golf ball.
>
> *Insight*

In fact, if you are a beginning golfer or high-handicap player, getting the club to consistently brush the ground can dramatically improve your results in and of itself. I teach almost all of my students to **brush the grass**. It's one of the hallmarks of a good club head path and flat spot.

While Jim Hardy's airplane analogy is a great way to look at the path of the club head, I want to give full credit to James Sieckmann for the idea to balance steep and shallow influences. James said it so casually in a seminar I attended that I'm not sure the attendees realized how brilliant it was.

In a single moment, this concept changed how I saw the golf swing. If you remember my story of how I struggled with wedges, it was seeing that the balance of steeps and shallows worked differently on a full swing than on a chip shot. It still took me time to retrain it, but I really didn't have a chance to improve until I grasped the steep and shallow concept.

I finally understood that a solid strike was a balance of these two competing elements. It was not that the club was magically tracing a mysterious **swing plane**. In my experience, the easiest way to think about the club head path is in terms of steeps and shallows. You can know for sure that if you hit a solid shot, your swing had a good balance of steep and shallow moves that resulted in a strong club head path in the impact zone.

Steep and shallow formula

Steep elements + shallow elements = path direction and solidness of contact

If you incorrectly hit a shot, your swing did not have a good balance of steeps and shallows.

It takes time to learn to recognize whether a shot is too steep or too shallow. In Part 2 we will discuss how each part of your body can affect this balance. For now, just visualize the following:

- the club head coming into the ball on a path that blends down and out,
- with the club head brushing the ground underneath the ball,
- while the handle is moving up and in.

The following chart shows some of the common ideas and trends about steep and shallow. Again, recognizing steep and shallow takes skill, but thinking about it will keep you on the right track.

Figure 6.1

Shallow pattern
    Block/hook
    Heel hits
    Thin misses (picker with irons)
    More trail edge strike
    Good driver
    Poor wedges
    Overuse of the lower body/underuse of the upper body
    Early extension likely
    Prefers ball above the feet

Steep pattern
    Pull/slice pattern
    Toe hits likely
    Deep or no divots
    Leading edge strikes
    Poor driver
    Good wedges
    Overuse of the upper body/underuse of the lower body
    Cast/scoop/chicken wing likely
    Prefers ball below feet

As you look at this chart, you will likely identify more with either the shallow or steep traits. We'll explore these patterns when we expand the concepts of steep and shallow later in this program.

One last point about the circular club head path. I want to stress that I am talking about the path of the club head. *The path of the handle shouldn't follow the same exact path.* For instance, we've already covered the impact zone where the handle should move up and in while the club head moves down and out. We will clear up more differences in Part 2. For right now, get used to looking at the path of the club head in terms of steeps and shallows.

CHAPTER 7

Understanding How the Ball Flies

I'm confident that the shape of the swing makes a lot of sense to you, especially if you've watched golf on TV. I'm sure you have seen good golfers swing from different views, and it looks Figures 2.1, 2.2, and 2.3. Good players frequently have a good club head path, and poor players have a poor club head path. If you watch typical amateurs swing, you can see that they don't have a good low or wide point. You've probably never thought of it that way, but you can now start to see it in the swings you watch.

If you're like most people, at this point you have one key question floating around in your head: "How do I know if I'm doing it right?"

Most golfers answer, "If it feels right!" But your feelings change, so it's better to learn to read the objective feedback present in every full swing.

There are three types of objective feedback to help you decode each swing:

Club head contact with the ball

Club head contact with the ground

Ball flight

You already know that you want a brushing contact with the ground (brush starting beneath the ball) and you can probably imagine that you want center face contact. In this chapter, we will look at how the ball flies.

To get the ball to fly where we want it to, we must understand the subtle differences between our shots as well as the overall club head path pattern. Remember, our goal with each swing is to move the ball somewhere else with our tool, the club.

To understand ball flight, you need to know some simple physics about collisions, since the collision of the club head and the ball will dictate ball flight. Our goal with each swing is to put the center of the golf club's head on a path so it will collide with the ball. The club head path is a big contributor to the ball's flight, but the other key factor is face orientation. **Understanding this face-to-path relationship is critical for self-coaching**.

As far as feedback goes, there are two major questions to ask yourself after each shot:

1. Where did the ball start?
2. How did the ball curve?

Measuring devices exist to give you really detailed feedback, but I think with practice the naked eye is sufficient for monitoring your game. You might need to occasionally call in the experts, but for the most part you will be close enough if you learn to read visual feedback.

The easiest way to look at ball flight is to remove the target from the equation and observe how much the ball curved compared to where it started. Looking at ball flight in this simple way enables you to focus on the difference between the club face and the club head path.

For simple ball flight analysis, there are only three options. The ball will either

1. curve left;
2. curve right; or
3. have no curve.

The ball will roughly start where the face is pointing and curve based on the difference between the club head path and the club face angle. Looking at ball flight this way, you can reverse engineer where the face was pointed at the time of contact and what the club head path was compared to that.

The more the ball curves, the bigger the difference between the face and path. However, be careful comparing different clubs. The same face and path will curve more with a driver than with a wedge.

Figure 7.1

In this chapter's image, we are going to isolate the face angle and the path right around impact (shaded area) to learn how to read feedback from a shot.

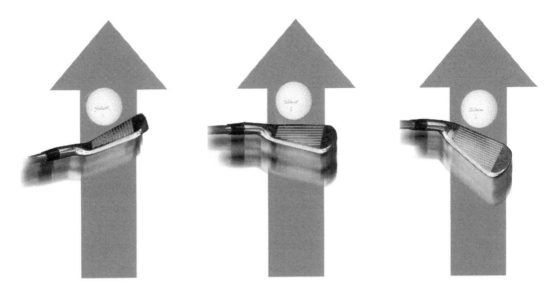

Figure 7.2

If you are just looking at face-to-path relationship, then reading feedback is easy—considering these images from left to right, the ball curved to the left, had no curve, or curved to the right as a result of the different relationships.

Using this method, you can look at where the ball started, which indicates the club face angle at impact. You can then deduce the path based on the ball's curve from where it started.

Figure 7.3

Figure 7.4

Figure 7.5

Regardless of where the ball starts, if the ball curves to the right there is an open face-to-path relationship.

If a right-handed golfer hits a ball that curves to the right (fade/slice or push fade/slice), then you know the club head path was more to the left of the face at impact. The amount of curve reveals whether the difference was large or small.

Figure 7.6

Figure 7.7

Regardless of where the ball starts, if the ball doesn't curve, you know your face-to-path relationship was square.

Figure 7.8

Figure 7.9

Regardless of where the ball starts, if the ball curves to the left there is a closed face-to-path relationship.

Mark this section and use it to reflect on every shot. Getting clear feedback is key to self-coaching your game. I find that my students often struggle with this at first, but with practice they start to trust the flight of the ball over what they feel.

Insight

Start to habitually read your ball flight and use the information to decode what you did in your swing. Only then should you worry about how the swing felt.

CHAPTER 8

Defining Ball Flight in Relation to the Target

ncluding the target into the feedback equation makes reading ball flight a little trickier. The physics remain the same, but the names for the different shots tend to change. Instructors and commentators more commonly use the target in their approach, so doing so is a good way to get on the same page with them.

Since we are getting down to details, let's clarify that the ball doesn't start *exactly* where the face is pointing; about 60 percent to 85 percent of it is controlled by the face position. The club head path controls the rest of the starting direction. You can still use the starting direction as a good indication of the face angle at impact, but know that it is not 100 percent accurate.

Example path/face start line for fade and draw.

Figure 8.1

Learning to decode your swing starts with correctly reading ball flight. The two important factors to notice are: Where did the ball start? How did the ball curve?

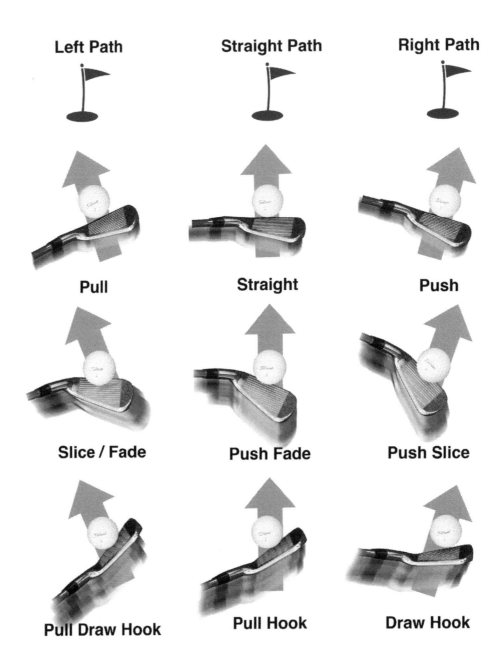

Figure 8.2

For a right-handed golfer: Left path—Pull starts left of target with no curve. Slice/fade starts left of or at target and curves right. Pull draw/hook starts left of target and curves left. Straight path— Straight flies to the target with no curve. Push fade starts right of target and curves right. Pull hook starts left of target and curves left. Right path—Push starts right of target with no curve. Push slice starts right of target and curves to the right. Draw/hook starts right of or at target and curves left.

Early in the learning process, you can chart shots to identify the club head path pattern. It is rare that a golfer would swing 10 degrees outside-in on one swing and 10 degrees inside-out on the next. It very well might feel that way, but the truth is that the club head path just doesn't change that drastically without major intervention.

In fact, from a practical standpoint, **golfers have a fairly consistent club head path (within a few degrees), and the face can be variable (5–10 degrees or more).** This changing face and slightly differing low points, combined with a consistent path, produces a predictable set of misses that you need to recognize. With practice you will be able to see the fat pull hook and the thin slice as a result of the same path (outside-in), but with different face orientations and low points.

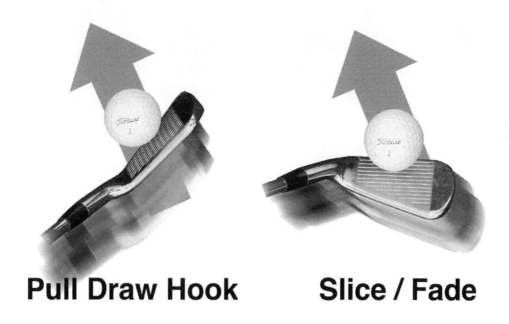

Pull Draw Hook   Slice / Fade

Figure 8.3

Here, a golfer has a very similar path but different face alignments. These two swings resulted in drastically different-looking shots, but the swings had a similar overall pattern.

One of the most common amateur patterns is an outside-in club head path with a low point at the ball and a wide point just after it. A golfer with this pattern may hit a slice off the tee with a driver and then a fairly straight wedge, and believe the swings were drastically different because the wedge swing felt smoother. In reality, this golfer made practically the same swing, but the pattern exaggerated the problem of path and wide point for the driver.

I don't want you to get bogged down in numbers and start pulling out your calculator on the range. That said, it can be helpful to be aware of the playable range. How much the ball curves reveals the difference between your face and path. Speed is a big factor as well, but that's more of an issue when comparing two different golfers. If you hit 10 shots with your six iron, the ones that curved the most had the biggest difference between face and path.

According to an article by golf engineer Dave Tutelman, a 5-degree difference in face and path would produce a big slice; a 1-degree difference would produce a small fade; and a 3-degree difference would result in a significant curve.

These numbers confirm what researchers Alastair Cochran and John Stobbs discovered. In their revolutionary book, *The Search for the Perfect Swing*, they report that on a 200-yard shot, a 1-degree difference produced 7 yards of curve. You don't really need to know exactly how many degrees different your face and path are, but this formula is a handy rule of thumb.

Insight

It would be difficult to get to a scratch golf level if you consistently have a face-to-path difference of 10 degrees. Getting in the ballpark of a few degrees makes for a fairly repeatable shot pattern.

One word of caution. Just as having too much face-to-path difference is tough to play, having a face-to-path relationship that is too straight can cause problems as well. It makes it so that your misses are hard to predict. Don't get overly concerned with the math, but it helps to see that a small fade with a short iron traveling 150 yards could produce a big slice if you have the same face-to-path relationship on a 250-yard drive.

This is part of the reason why golfers have a hard time decoding feedback and think they hit "everywhere" or "all over the place." To break from the herd and become a smart golfer, you must learn to decode your swing pattern. However, you'd be surprised at how good you are at it without trying. In fact, take a second and try it now. Think of your typical ball flight and try to identify your path pattern from the six likely options:

Outside-in—slightly, moderately, severely

Inside-out—slightly, moderately, severely

Knowing this is key to understanding your swing.

It sounds daunting at first, but learning to objectively read feedback is one of the greatest skills you can develop. You will be able to use the ball flight to confirm whether you made a specific movement. This helps you calibrate your feels and develop a high level of touch with your game.

For example, imagine you are working on twisting the club shaft to close the face (a move called the **motorcycle** that you will learn later in this program). You hit a shot and think you did the motorcycle. But if the ball curves to the right of where it started, then you know you didn't close the face to the path.

Many students have sworn to me that they did a movement regardless of how the ball flew. In such cases, I will show them on video that they did not. Eventually, they start to believe the flight of the ball more than their feel for what happened. This is a critical paradigm shift to accelerate your evolution as a golfer following a long-term plan for success. Your feels will change from round to round, but the physics of how the ball flies will always remain the same.

With feedback telling you exactly what the impact conditions were like, you can decide (based on your feels or on video evidence) if you did the motorcycle move but undid it before impact, or if you need to do it more, or earlier, or later. Ball flight helps you see the net result of your swing, and you must use it to your advantage if you want to become self-reliant.

> Failing to take advantage of shot feedback is especially common on misses (which are the best opportunity to learn).
>
> *Insight*

Most golfers are already thinking about the next swing, and fail to take advantage of all the information. The skill of reading ball flight takes time and practice, so be patient as you work through it.

Let me stress how beneficial it is to accurately read ball flight. In this department, you want to develop the decoding skills of Sherlock Holmes. Only then will you be able to read your swing pattern. The better you get at reading ball flight, the more you will be able to self-correct on the course, which is how you make bad days more bearable and turn good days into great ones.

CHAPTER 9

The Two Ball Flights That Will Trick You The Most

To illustrate how ball flight can be misleading and confusing, let's discuss the two shots that will trick you the most. Recognize that any shot can fool you if you're not paying attention, but the two ball flights covered in this chapter are the most common ones that I see with students on the lesson tee.

It's easy to see the difference between a slice and a hook, but let's learn from a couple scenarios that are sometimes tough to distinguish.

Weak Right

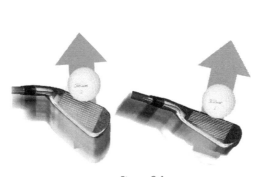

Figure 9.1

Figure 9.2

These two face-to-path alignments produce similar-looking right shots but require different solutions.

These two flights look almost identical, but typically require different fixes. Pay attention to height and amount of curve.

A block (inside-out path with a square/open face) and a push fade (straight or leftward path with an open face) can look very similar, but they require different fixes. If this ball flight occurs with a short iron, sometimes it is due to an open club face; sometimes it is due to a path that is *slightly* left and an open face; and sometimes it is due to a path to the right with a square face.

Snap hook

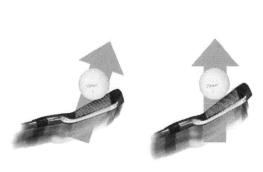

Figure 9.3

These two face-to-path alignments produce similar-looking hard left shots but require different solutions.

Figure 9.4

These two flights also look almost identical, but typically require different fixes. Pay attention to the start line and amount of curve in the air.

Good players sometimes battle the hooks, and the worst of all of them is the ball that starts straight or just left and immediately dives hard left. This could be from an overly right path and closed face, or a slightly left path (steep angle of attack) and a slightly closed face. To determine which **snap hook** you have, try hitting a few seven irons. If you are hitting more pulls, it is likely the path left snap hook. If you are hitting more fat shots or big draws, it is usually the path right version. Just like the high right, getting the details correct is the difference between having the unplayable ball flight lasting the whole round or limiting it to one bad swing.

These examples show how details are critical for identifying your swing path pattern. Knowing them helps you make smart decisions about how to practice so you can stop hoping the stars will magically align for your game.

Chapter 10

Angle of Attack—How Hitting Down or Up Changes the Path

I f only understanding club head path was as easy as taking a video and looking at it from the right perspective. Club head path is influenced by two variables:

1. Horizontal swing plane (swing direction)
2. Angle of attack

When we discuss path, it is useful to know that the true path through impact is affected by these two components. First, let's define **horizontal swing plane**. This is the swing direction relative to the target line at impact.

Looking at the following three images, you can identify a neutral horizontal swing plane, a leftward horizontal swing plane, and a rightward horizontal swing plane. Very likely, the path for these swings will be close to the horizontal swing plane, but it won't be exactly where the red arrow is pointing. The reason is because of the angle of attack.

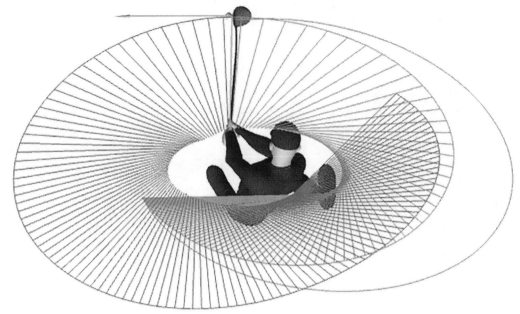

Figure 10.1

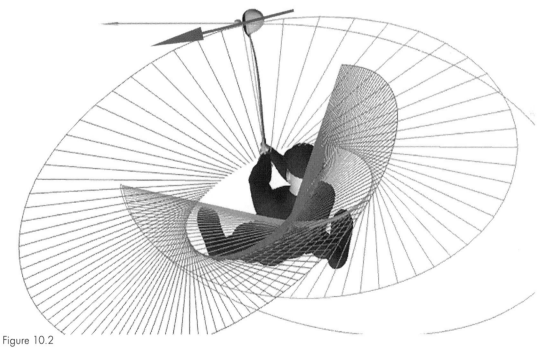

Figure 10.2

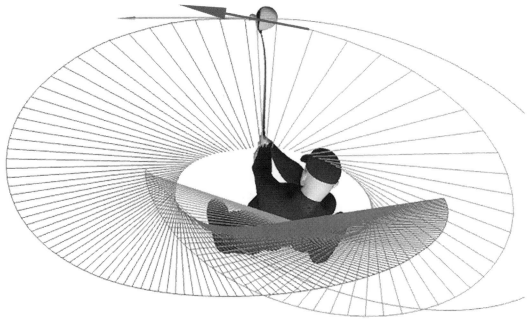

Figure 10.3

Do you notice the overall shape and direction of each swing? The large arrow gives a rough approximation of the horizontal swing plane, or swing direction. On top, the connected frames form a plane that points relatively close to the target line at the bottom. The slicer has a plane that is shifted well to the left, and the hooker has a plane that is shifted slightly to the right.

The **angle of attack** is how much the club is traveling down or up as it strikes the ball. When the club is traveling downward, it is also traveling in-to-out more than it looks like based on the swing direction. When the club is traveling upward, it is also traveling out-to-in more than it looks like based on the swing direction.

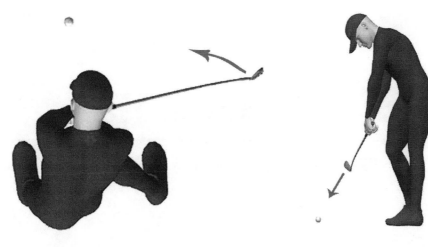

Figure 10.4 Figure 10.5

Notice how the club is not only moving down but also more in-to-out. Hitting more down on an iron than a driver is part of the reason why irons don't slice as much as woods for amateurs. The opposite is true for why amateurs slice their driver. If you hit more up on the ball, the path will be more to the left, which is part of the reason golfers with an already left path slice it more with the longer clubs.

When you hit down on the ball before the club reaches the bottom of its arc, it also moves slightly more out than it looks. How much? It depends a bit on the club. With the driver, it's about 1 degree more in-to-out for every degree you hit down on the ball. With an iron it's a little less than that. The tour average of around 4 degrees down will change the path a few degrees compared to the general shape. But if a 5-degree difference in path can create a big slice, then a few degrees is very meaningful.

From a practical standpoint, consider two golfers who have identical swing directions. Suppose one hits down on the ball and makes a divot, while the other picks the ball cleanly. If the face is pointing in the same direction, then the one who hit down will have the ball draw more (or fade less) than the golfer who didn't take a divot.

> The change in flight from hitting up or down can significantly tweak ball flight. The fact that hitting down moves the path to the right is the reason why it is typically easier to draw your irons than your driver—or why they slice less than your woods. The opposite is also true: hitting up on the ball moves the path more out-to-in. This path change is a major reason why longer clubs slice more for an amateur golfer.
>
> *Insight*

CHAPTER 11

The Club Face—Where Is It Pointing?

Hopefully the club head path is starting to take shape in your mind. Knowing your club head path tendency is truly the foundation of understanding your own swing. In addition to knowing your path, understanding how the face is oriented to that path is critical for understanding your pattern. For the most part, the curve of the ball will reveal the face-to-path relationship at impact.

As you can see, there are two key references for the face:

1. Face orientation to target—controls majority of start direction
2. Face-to-path relationship—controls amount of curve

Of the two, identifying the face orientation is harder than identifying the face-to-path relationship.

As you learned in Chapter 8, the ball starts mostly where the club face is pointing (60 percent to 85 percent) at impact. This is absolutely true, but it is much harder to identify *why* the face is pointing in a given direction in golf than in other club sports. In most sports, the face is controlled by changing the alignment. But in golf, there are three ways to change the face—moving the handle up/down, forward/backward, or rotating it closed/open.

To avoid getting overwhelmed, categorize how you control the face in one of two ways—either with shaft rotation or with shaft movement in the plane of motion.

Ask yourself whether you twist the shaft closed or just tilt it forward and backward to square the face. These are the two biggest movements that change the true location of the face at impact.

> **Insight**
>
> Better players control the face more with early shaft rotation than they do with late in-plane shaft movement.

Visualizing how the face changes

Shaft rotation: Left = closed, Right = open
In-plane shaft movement (shaft tilt): Back = closed, Forward = open
Off-plane sh

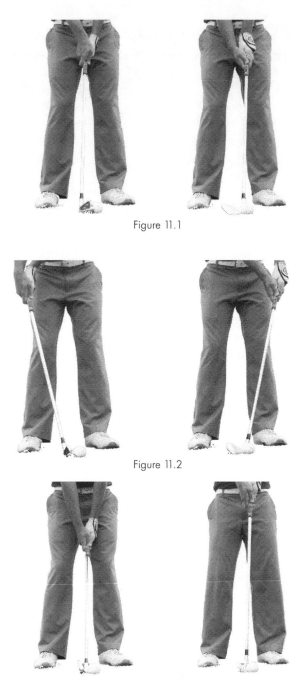

Figure 11.1

Figure 11.2

Figure 11.3

I'm demonstrating these moves at set up or impact, but this can be observed at any point in the swing.

It can be tricky to identify your club face control method. Ask yourself the following simple question: "Is the shaft fairly vertical at impact or do you have shaft lean?" If you have shaft lean, then you had to rotate the shaft to avoid hitting it right. If you have very little shaft lean, then you almost certainly squared the face with in-plane shaft movement.

Discussing a square club face

There is one more component to understanding the club face. You will frequently hear the term **square**, and understanding it will prevent a lot of confusion.

You have three options in the impact zone:

1. If the club face is pointed in the same direction as the club head path, the ball will fly straight.
2. If the club face is angled right of the club head path, the ball will curve to the right.
3. If the club face is angled left of the club head path, the ball will curve to the left.

Golfers constantly refer to achieving a square club face. But what does square mean? In reality, the reference for square constantly changes throughout the swing.

Three common positions in which square is discussed are:

1. the top of the backswing;
2. shaft parallel in the backswing and the downswing; and
3. impact.

Observing the swing from down the line, these are typically good clear angles for roughly identifying where the face is pointing. But the common references don't really make sense.

Top of swing

Figure 11.4

The club is considered open, square, and closed (as seen from left to right), compared to the forearm at the top of the swing.

At the top of the backswing, conventional wisdom says the face is considered square if it is parallel to the lead forearm, as seen in the center image.

Shaft parallel

Figure 11.5

The club is considered open, square, and closed (as seen from left to right), compared to either the spine or vertical at shaft parallel.

At shaft parallel, conventional wisdom says the club face is square if parallel to the spine. Others say the club face is square if it is straight up and down, or just turned down past vertical. (However, in contrast with the top of the swing, no one says square is parallel to the forearm at this location.)

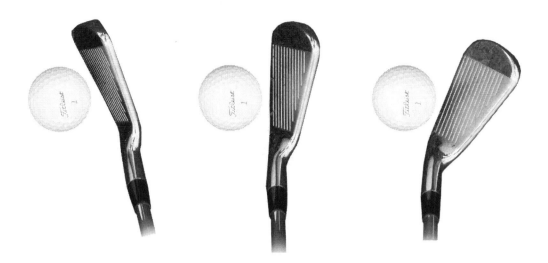

Figure 11.6

The club face is considered closed, square, or open compared to the target at impact.

At impact, the club face is considered square if pointed at the target.

Since the references change, the term *square* almost seems like an arbitrary distinction. But because each of these three locations is easy to see on video, there is something to be learned from each.

Changing references—what we can learn from square references

Using the top of the swing as the reference, if we kept using the lead forearm as the square reference, then the club would be closed at shaft parallel and even more closed at impact. In sum, the club face is closing to the shaft the whole downswing in this method.

Using the shaft parallel as the square reference, the club face would be more open to the path at the top and more closed to the path at impact. In sum, the face is closing to the shaft the whole downswing in this method.

Using impact as the square reference, the club face would be open at the top, less so at shaft parallel, and square at impact. In sum, the face is closing to the shaft the entire downswing in this method.

If we try to hold the same club face and arm position throughout the swing, we can only use in-plane shaft movement to square the face. If we do so we can't have shaft lean, *which means we can't have a good brush location.*

This is simpler to visually demonstrate.

Figure 11.7

Figure 11.8

From an overhead perspective you can see the changes from set up to impact. A good impact position requires both a square club face and shaft lean. From left to right—set up, set up with shaft rotation, impact—set up with shaft rotation and shaft lean.

While the majority of tour golfers gradually twist the club face closed the entire downswing, some open the face-to-path during transition and then close it faster later. The second method may create more speed when you close it, but this technique frequently results in golfers who complain about inconsistency, even at the tour level. As a result, there are far fewer pros who use this second method.

I'm sure some of you instinctually want to keep the club face the same the entire swing, but this is not a recommended technique. The downswing pattern used by the majority of tour golfers involves gradually twisting the club face closed to the shaft. One key feature of this pattern is that at impact, the club is more closed to the shaft than it was at set up. The only way to hit the ball straight with a club that has shaft lean is to close the face to the shaft. It's actually quite simple:

1. Shaft lean at impact requires the club face to be rotated closed to the shaft.
2. No shaft lean at impact requires the club face to be perpendicular to the shaft.

Because the circle is shifted forward on the downswing, and impact happens before the bottom of the swing, the club face must slightly close to the shaft for the ball to go straight.

If the face is square to the swing path and you have shaft lean at impact, you will hit it way off to the right if you hit down on the ball.

Figure 11.9

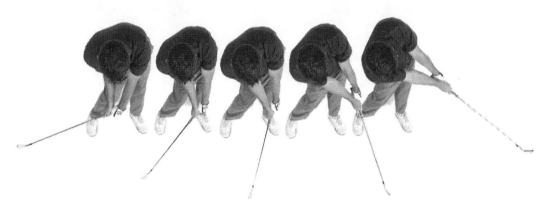

Figure 11.10

These two overhead sequences show how the club face and club head path can line up differently. In the first sequence, I use more of a scoop and the shaft is vertical at impact. In the second I use more shaft rotation and the shaft has lean at impact.

Here's a practical scenario of how it works. From a similar shaft parallel spot, there are two possible impact positions that would start the ball at the target. The first used in-plane shaft movement (I scooped it), so the shaft is vertical and the path of the club is to the left. This ball will slice. The second method used shaft rotation and had shaft lean. This ball will draw. You may be more used to seeing this pattern from down the line, as shown below.

Both of these methods produce a similar face orientation at impact, but very different face-to-path relationships. Hopefully you see why it's so important to monitor both of those key factors.

Figure 11.11

Figure 11.12

Here is the same sequence from the down-the-line view. Notice how the top sequence (scoop) has far less body rotation and side bend and the golfer had to stand up to point the club face at the target.

CHAPTER 12

Why Wood Feedback Is Trickier than Iron Feedback

Quick summary of how to use ball flight to identify your pattern

Four useful factors for determining your pattern are:

1. Club head path pattern
2. Angle of attack influence on path
3. Club face orientation to target
4. Club head face-to-path relationship

Identifying those four factors—either with ball flight, video, or help from a coach—puts you in a great position to design an improvement plan.

Now that you are clear on these key swing components, let's discuss the two reasons why feedback is more challenging with the woods than it is with the irons.

(NERD WARNING: If you are trying to be a scratch (or tour) golfer, then understanding gear effect can help decode your swing pattern. If you just want to break 90, I'd skip this chapter and just go with the feedback model, in which the ball starts where the club face is pointing and curves based on the face-to-path relationship.)

What do you need to know about the woods to accurately read the feedback? There are two major physical differences when you compare a wood to an iron:

1. The face on a wood is curved instead of flat.
2. The center of the club head's mass is significantly behind the face.

The curved face makes it harder to identify the face-to-path orientation. The curved face makes the exact face point in different directions depending on contact location. The difference in exact face direction changes about 2.5 degrees for every half inch across the face. That means if you hit it 1 inch out on the toe, the center of the face was pointed 5 degrees more to the left than where you hit it.

Think about it this way. Imagine you hit two balls with the exact same swing, but one was a maximum toe strike and the other was a maximum heel strike. The difference in contact between them would be about 3 inches. Using the above formula, the exact face angle for each shot was really 15 degrees different.

Recall from Chapter 8 that a 5-degree face-to-path difference produces a massive curve with the driver. If you are not making contact with the center face, then factor that into your interpretation of where the club face was at impact.

The second challenge in reading feedback from a wood comes from the center of the club head's mass, which is significantly behind the face.

The center of the club head's mass behind the face changes the way the ball spins in mishit shots due to a phenomenon called gear effect. Gear effect makes it more challenging to identify the face-to-path orientation for woods.

When the club head's center is farther behind the face, the ball's spin will change when hit away from the sweet spot. When you make contact on the toe, the club face will open and produce more draw spin. When you make contact on the heel, the club face will close and produce more fade spin.

The change in curve can make you think the face and path are more different than they really are.

Figure 12.1

The more the ball is hit on the toe side, the more it will start to the right (curved face); however, it will have more draw spin (gear effect). The more the ball is hit on the heel side, the more it will start to the left (curved face) and have more fade spin (gear effect).

When hitting woods, the most common way the feedback will trick you is with the outside-in toe hit and the inside-out heel hit.

Look at your driver. If most of the impact marks on the club are on the toe, and you hit little draws, then your face is more closed and the path is more left than you think. This situation is common for golfers who hit a pull every time they hit it on the actual sweet spot.

The other scenario is the golfer who swings too much in-to-out, but hits it on the heel with the driver to negate some of the possible hook spin. This golfer typically hits a big block, when they hit it solid.

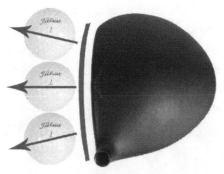

Figure 12.2

Reading feedback from the woods is more challenging than from the irons because of the woods' slightly curved face. This means that the face orientation is dynamic depending on how far from the center you make contact with the club.

Figure 12.3

An outside-in swing frequently hits a straight shot with contact on the toe. If this swing hits the center, it will typically result in a pull.

Figure 12.4

An inside-out swing frequently hits a straight shot with contact on the heel. If this swing hits the center, it will typically result in a push.

For the very low handicap golfer

Be aware that there is also a vertical gear effect. Hitting it low on the face causes more spin and a low launch. This can trick you into thinking you had more lean than you really did. If you hit the ball high on the face, it will launch higher and have less spin. It can help on the drive to hit slightly above the middle of the club. The driver typically has a similar amount of curve from top to bottom as from heel to toe, so for every half inch you hit above or below the sweet spot, it will change the loft by about 2.5 degrees.

Higher contact on the face results in less spin and higher launch. Lower contact on the face results in more spin and lower launch.

The moral of this story is to monitor the exact location of contact when hitting woods. If you consistently make contact on the toe or heel, factor the different face and spin readings into your pattern.

Insight

A simple way to gauge the location of impact is to put Dr. Scholl's foot spray on the club face before hitting a ball. The mark it leaves will tell you where the ball was hit, but the spray won't change the way the ball flies the way impact tape will.

CHAPTER 13

Reading a Divot—Shaft Lean and Compression

Always remember the three types of objective feedback for decoding each swing:

    1. Club face contact with the ball

    2. Club head contact with the ground

    3. Ball flight

To hit the club's sweet spot with shots from the fairway, you need a bit of shaft lean. (A driver study showed 12 degrees of lean with the grip; a wedge study showed 14 degrees). I like to ballpark it as 10–15 degrees of shaft lean at impact. Typically, that shaft lean will cause you to take a small divot. The divot gives us additional feedback, so let's investigate what we can learn from it.

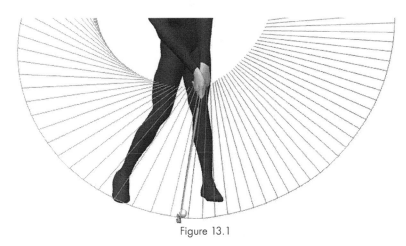

Figure 13.1

About 10–15 degrees of shaft lean will help you hit the ball in the sweet spot and provide more consistency.

A divot offers a decent representation of the swing direction at impact (see the section on horizontal swing plane in Chapter 10). I say decent because the angle of attack is slightly down, so the club head's true path at impact was probably a little right of where the divot is pointing unless you hit the ball fat. Very straight iron shots are typically hit with a slightly left divot. The reason is because of the path change from hitting down.

If the divot is deep, you are probably steep; but if you don't take a divot, that doesn't mean you *aren't* steep. If you take a long skinny divot that is about the width of your club and it's pointed at, or slightly to the left, of the target and leaves the roots, then you probably have a good shallow swing path.

Remember how we want the club to look when swinging an iron (the airplane landing analogy)? We want a club that is gently moving down, which will just skim the ground instead of gouging it like a shovel.

> **Insight**
>
> At the driving range, when hitting an iron, strive for a long skinny divot pointed at, or slightly to the left, of the target.

Shaft lean is important for having a flat spot, and for hitting the ball with the sweet spot.

> **Insight**
>
> The sweet spot is in the middle of the club; if you have the shaft vertical, your face contact will be lower on the club than on the sweet spot. The two ways to hit the sweet spot are shaft lean or to tee the ball up. If you like the first cut of rough more than the fairway for hitting irons, then you probably have too little shaft lean (since the first cut of rough tees up the ball a little bit).

Many golfers struggle with getting shaft lean without steepening the angle of attack. We'll talk about how to get shaft lean and all the other key looks of a good swing in Part 3.

CHAPTER 14

Using Images to Recap What We Want the Club to Do

You may have experienced information overload while reading Part 1, but a summary of what we've learned so far shows that it's actually quite manageable. If you still feel overwhelmed, watch the related videos at https://golfsmartacademy.com/stocktourswingbook. Sometimes seeing the images and words together provides clarity.

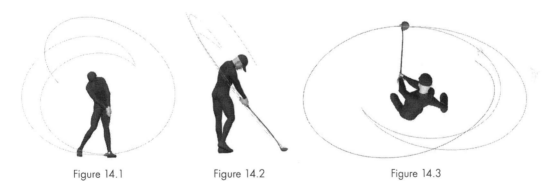

Figure 14.1   Figure 14.2   Figure 14.3

- Club head path—tilted circle with you at the center

- Circle doesn't exactly retrace; it moves forward on the downswing

- It's not a true circle; it changes radius throughout and has an important **flat spot** at the bottom

- Be aware of the low point (club head vs. ground) and the wide point (club head vs. you)

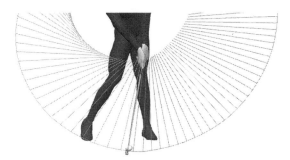

Figure 14.4

- Club head path—the low and wide points offer good reference for your flat spot
- Details of flat spot
- Brush vs. slam vs. pick—different low point results
- Balance of steeps and shallows produces solid contact

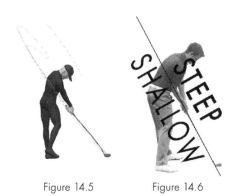

Figure 14.5   Figure 14.6

- Read feedback from each shot—club head on the circle hits ball to make it fly
- Three ball flight options

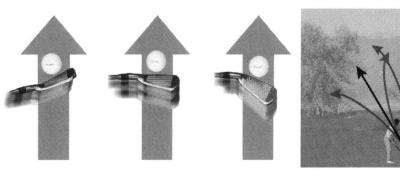

Figure 14.7   Figure 14.8

- Ball flight starts close to where the face is pointing at impact (60 percent to 85 percent)

- Curves based on difference in face-to-path; greater difference = more curve

- Unfortunately, using club head path isn't as easy as using video; you can get an idea of horizontal swing plane but can't see angle of attack

- Read feedback from club head path—how angle of attack affects path

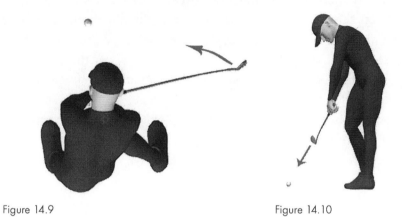

Figure 14.9   Figure 14.10

- Down is more in-to-out

- Up is more out-to-in

- Tour iron is about 4 degrees down; amateurs—really steep is over 10 degrees down, pickers are around 1 degree down or even up

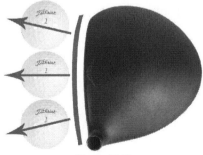

Figure 14.11

- Read feedback from woods—curved face impacts start line and curve for woods

- Gear effect—exact impact location on the face affects the curve of the ball for woods/hybrids, but it's hard to see

- Read feedback from divots—shaft lean helps to hit the sweet spot, but don't lose your shallow path

Recap: Linking the Secrets of the Stock Tour Swing

We've covered a lot thus far, and before we move on to looking at how the body makes a golf swing, let's recap what we've learned.

The club head swings in a somewhat circular shape around your body. It's not exactly a true circle, since the radius between your hands and your body changes. It looks more like an ellipse, shifted slightly toward the target. This shape also includes a flat spot down near impact where the club head will brush the ground.

Two important characteristics of this flat spot are the low point (where the club hits the ground) and the wide point (where the club is farthest from your body). With an iron, both of these should be after the ball; with a driver, only the wide point should be.

The ball will fly based on the shape of the club head path and face-to-path relationship. Impact is the only time the ball is in contact with the club, but the club path influences the impact zone during the rest of the swing. To know how you are swinging the club, monitor the three sources of objective feedback:

1. Where did I contact the ball on the club?
2. Where and how did the club contact the ground?
3. What was the ball flight?

Contact between the club and the ground is a direct result of how steep or shallow the club path is. A good way to envision the proper angle of attack is to think of a plane landing. Following that image will produce a brush of the ground. You should also strive to have a wide point after the ball; keep your hands away from your body after impact. The ball flight curve will result from the relationship between the face and the path.

When reading ball flight, know that the ball will start roughly where the club face is pointing and will curve based on the club face-to-path relationship. The greater the difference between the club face and the path, the greater the magnitude of the curve.

The path is influenced not just by the shape of the swing, but also the angle of attack. A divot can give you a good representation of the swing direction (horizontal swing plane), but the true path is adjusted by how down or up you hit. Hitting more down makes the path more in-to-out, and hitting more up makes the path more out-to-in.

Woods' feedback is a bit trickier to read because of the slightly curved face. Balls hit more on the toe will start more to the right and have more draw spin. Balls hit more on the heel will start left and have more fade spin.

Learning to interpret shot feedback will help you make educated guesses when balancing your golf swing.

CHAPTER 15

Putting Part 1 Principles into Practice The Stock Tour Swing Decoder

"Swing the club around your body and be aware of the club head working away from your body through the release."

I know it sounds simple, but there are a few ways to lose that shape. Since you are now aware of the ideal club head path based on contact and flight, you are ready to use our golf swing decoder. It's simple and looks like:

Name: _____ Handicap: _____ Age: _____ Right or Left Handed: _____

Driver: Average Distance of 10 shots

Shot	Contact		Starting Direction	Curve
1	Solid / Toe / Heel	Solid / Thin / Heavy	Left / Center / Right	Draw / Straight / Fade
2	Solid / Toe / Heel	Solid / Thin / Heavy	Left / Center / Right	Draw / Straight / Fade
3	Solid / Toe / Heel	Solid / Thin / Heavy	Left / Center / Right	Draw / Straight / Fade
4	Solid / Toe / Heel	Solid / Thin / Heavy	Left / Center / Right	Draw / Straight / Fade
5	Solid / Toe / Heel	Solid / Thin / Heavy	Left / Center / Right	Draw / Straight / Fade
6	Solid / Toe / Heel	Solid / Thin / Heavy	Left / Center / Right	Draw / Straight / Fade
7	Solid / Toe / Heel	Solid / Thin / Heavy	Left / Center / Right	Draw / Straight / Fade
8	Solid / Toe / Heel	Solid / Thin / Heavy	Left / Center / Right	Draw / Straight / Fade
9	Solid / Toe / Heel	Solid / Thin / Heavy	Left / Center / Right	Draw / Straight / Fade
10	Solid / Toe / Heel	Solid / Thin / Heavy	Left / Center / Right	Draw / Straight / Fade

Iron: Average Distance of 10 shots

Shot	Contact		Starting Direction	Curve
1	Solid / Toe / Heel	Solid / Thin / Heavy	Left / Center / Right	Draw / Straight / Fade
2	Solid / Toe / Heel	Solid / Thin / Heavy	Left / Center / Right	Draw / Straight / Fade
3	Solid / Toe / Heel	Solid / Thin / Heavy	Left / Center / Right	Draw / Straight / Fade
4	Solid / Toe / Heel	Solid / Thin / Heavy	Left / Center / Right	Draw / Straight / Fade
5	Solid / Toe / Heel	Solid / Thin / Heavy	Left / Center / Right	Draw / Straight / Fade
6	Solid / Toe / Heel	Solid / Thin / Heavy	Left / Center / Right	Draw / Straight / Fade
7	Solid / Toe / Heel	Solid / Thin / Heavy	Left / Center / Right	Draw / Straight / Fade
8	Solid / Toe / Heel	Solid / Thin / Heavy	Left / Center / Right	Draw / Straight / Fade
9	Solid / Toe / Heel	Solid / Thin / Heavy	Left / Center / Right	Draw / Straight / Fade
10	Solid / Toe / Heel	Solid / Thin / Heavy	Left / Center / Right	Draw / Straight / Fade

Sand Wedge: Average Distance FROM PIN of 10 shots

Shot	Contact		Starting Direction	Curve
1	Solid / Toe / Heel	Solid / Thin / Heavy	Left / Center / Right	Draw / Straight / Fade
2	Solid / Toe / Heel	Solid / Thin / Heavy	Left / Center / Right	Draw / Straight / Fade
3	Solid / Toe / Heel	Solid / Thin / Heavy	Left / Center / Right	Draw / Straight / Fade
4	Solid / Toe / Heel	Solid / Thin / Heavy	Left / Center / Right	Draw / Straight / Fade
5	Solid / Toe / Heel	Solid / Thin / Heavy	Left / Center / Right	Draw / Straight / Fade
6	Solid / Toe / Heel	Solid / Thin / Heavy	Left / Center / Right	Draw / Straight / Fade
7	Solid / Toe / Heel	Solid / Thin / Heavy	Left / Center / Right	Draw / Straight / Fade
8	Solid / Toe / Heel	Solid / Thin / Heavy	Left / Center / Right	Draw / Straight / Fade
9	Solid / Toe / Heel	Solid / Thin / Heavy	Left / Center / Right	Draw / Straight / Fade
10	Solid / Toe / Heel	Solid / Thin / Heavy	Left / Center / Right	Draw / Straight / Fade

You can find them to print here on our site http://golfsmartacademy.com/stocktourswingbook.

Use the decoder to identify your club head path and club face tendencies. **Remember, the club head path tends to be consistent in direction. It changes slightly in magnitude but the face alignment varies a lot more than the path.** Using this decoder will help you identify your pattern, which will make it easier to pinpoint what to work on regarding your swing.

In Part 2, we will break down how body movements make the golf swing work. You will get much more out of Part 2 after you begin monitoring the feedback from each full shot and better understand your general path and face pattern. Once your pattern becomes clear, Part 2 will be much more relatable; you will be able to see why you have misses and good shots and why you love or hate certain shots.

Before you get into the body movements in Part 2, complete the decoder at least once. Try the brush-the-ground drill to experience how the club works. For a lot of golfers, this drill is more useful than the detailed body drills, at least at first.

Insight

DRILL: BRUSH THE GROUND DRILL

Figure 15.1   Figure 15.2   Figure 15.3

Set up

Without a golf ball, take your normal address posture.

Execution

Make a swing either parallel-to-parallel (9–3) or full swing. Attempt to get the club to brush the ground in the direction of the target for as long as possible, starting ahead of the middle of your stance. Just slightly to the left of the target is ideal.

Focus and questions

Is your upper body staying centered? Make sure it does, and focus on the sound the club makes when it contacts the ground. You want a soft and gentle brush, not a loud thud. A thud indicates a steep angle of attack.

Part 2

Big Picture How the Body Swings the Club

You now know what you want the club head and face to do in the golf swing. The next step is to understand how to get the body to do it. As we explore how the body swings the club, your understanding of Part 1 will become clearer. In Part 2, approach the body movements from a general perspective; taking a bird's-eye view of how the body works will prepare you for the detailed phases covered in Part 3.

Part 2 covers three critical concepts:
- The body swings the arms for power.
- The arms and body both influence the path of the club head.
- The arms have the greatest influence on the club face orientation.

CHAPTER 16

The Body Swings the Arms

R emember the general shape of the club head circle?

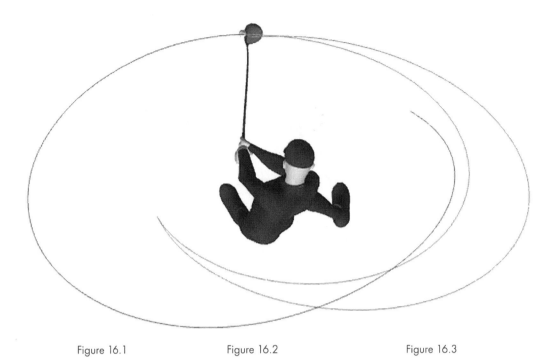

These three images provide the platform for studying the full swing. In Part 2, we break down the general ideas about what the body does during the swing.

Remember, there is a human body at the center that makes the swing work. Do you recall the description for learning to walk? How you just swing your arms and legs as you shift from one foot to the other? We start with this style for describing the general concepts of how the body swings the club in the shape of a squished circle.

As you can see, the swing's overall shape is somewhat circular, and you have to find the center of the circle to understand why. While the center of the swing technically shifts, a good reference for it is around the T11 vertebra—between your belly button and the bottom of your sternum (chest bone).

You might think the circle's center is up in your neck where your arms connect, but it's not. When the club is moving fast near impact, the momentum of the club wants to pull you into a straight line, almost like playing tug of war. Imagine it: If you were to position yourself to aggressively pull on a rope, where would you put your arms? Most people would put their hands a little above their belly button height, which happens to be roughly where the center of your circle is.

Compare the elite golf swing to a sports car. Your big muscles function like the engine of movement. Your arms act more like a steering wheel and work by directing the speed the body creates toward the ball. At the same time, the arms also control the face-to-path relationship.

The arms lack the ability to generate significant speed on their own—the big muscle groups in the legs and core are better at this. Relaxing your arms as you swing them gives you the best chance for creating a swing shape like the pictures above. Relaxing your arms and powering the swing with your body is the only way to achieve the squished circle shape with the low and wide points after the golf ball.

Figure 16.4   Figure 16.5   Figure 16.6   Figure 16.7

Here are two different ways to start the downswing from the same top of backswing position. One requires pulling on the club with your arms. The other requires pulling on the club with your body, through your arms.

Many high-handicap golfers do the opposite, however—they use their arms for power and their body for control. If you power the swing with your arms and control the swing with your body, you will likely struggle to achieve the low and wide points after the ball.

When arms are used to create the speed, they tend to straighten. If the arms are straight before impact, it is very difficult for them to lengthen more through impact.

Straightening the arms later is key to creating the desired flat spot. Typically, if you power the swing with your arms, you will struggle with the driver and long irons more than golfers who power their swing with their body.

Insight

To produce a good path, you need to have your arms pretty relaxed. You don't want them so loose that they just flop around, but just loose enough so they follow the bigger muscles without resisting or inhibiting the body's other movements.

To clarify, the arms are not completely passive, but relaxed enough to make the body the primary engine of movement during the backswing and transition.

Relaxing the arms during transition allows them to narrow a bit. This is critical for widening through the impact zone. If the arms are active and straighten in transition, they will become too straight too soon and will bend during the impact zone. If you have ever been told you have a "chicken wing," then you are very familiar with this pattern. Arms straightened too soon in transition typically limits body rotation at impact. This combination makes it hard to create the flat spot or be consistent with the longer clubs.

Middle-out versus ground-up—which powers the swing?

You may have questions about whether to use your legs or your core (that is, swinging from the middle of the body or swinging from the ground up) to create speed. There is currently debate over this very issue. My take is that these are two different perspectives of the body and how it works. It is very likely that the two sides are describing the same thing in two different ways—one mechanical and one neurological.

To illustrate the debate, consider the "dead bug" exercise, a common rehab movement for back pain. To set it up, you lay on the ground with a towel or blood pressure cuff under your back. Then, you have to activate your core to keep your spine from moving. You challenge your core when you move your leg in different directions.

Neurologically, any movement should originate in the core. If you push your leg against the ground, your brain should activate your core a split second before you activate any leg muscles. From the neurological perspective, the middle acts first.

But from the mechanical perspective, if you measure (or observe) the timing of the body's different segments, the trail foot pushes into the ground before the hips and pelvis change direction. From the mechanical perspective, the foot moves before the core does.

If you think about it from the brain's sequencing (neurological), it's middle-out. If you think about it from the first measurable forces (mechanical), it's ground-up.

It doesn't matter which perspective you personally take as long as you correctly use your legs and core together to initiate the downswing. The argument of middle-out or ground-up is more over comparing neurological feels and looks to mechanical measurements.

On the importance of "feels"—what you feel is happening may not actually be reality.

Don't get too caught up trying to find the "perfect feel." Rather, understand the big picture (that you want the body to power the swing) and use drills to reinforce proper technique. After you have good technique, you won't need the perfect feel to play well.

Ultimately, I want you to swing the club with your body and let your arms transfer that speed to the club head. Doing so determines whether your swing will produce the narrow part of the circle in transition and the flat part of the circle through impact.

When it comes to powering the swing with your body, some golfers feel their feet interacting with the ground. Others feel their middle controlling the movement. It's a different sensation for almost everyone. If you use your middle and the ground, it will look like the images below.

Figure 16.8   Figure 16.9

If you lead the downswing with a slight bump (see the Jackson 5 move in Chapter 36 in Part 3) and regain the flex of your spine, you will almost certainly be using both the ground and your core properly.

The importance of using drills to master checkpoints

From years of working with golfers, I want to stress an important point about feels—relying on checkpoints to improve swing quality and consistency is better than relying on feels.

Our goal is to shape your swing using drills and concepts rather than *feels*. Feelings vary from golfer to golfer, and within a golfer from day to day. Although you may have drastically different swing thoughts round to round or week to week, your swing typically changes gradually. The change in feel doesn't reflect the extent to which your swing has actually changed. Changing feels is why it's important to have reliable checkpoints for your swing and drills to train those checkpoints.

Learning reliable checkpoints allows you to gauge whether you are actually creating the change you desire. Without checkpoints, you are stuck relying on how the swing feels.

Feels are unreliable until they are well calibrated. Until then, your progression will be steadier if you consistently read feedback from each shot and practice drills that let you monitor key checkpoints. Putting in the reps until using feedback is second nature helps you build your own checkpoints and develop feel.

Pay close attention to the details of the drills—they are critical for getting the most out of each rep. Most of the drills I discuss in this book (as well as hundreds I don't discuss) can be found on the companion website http://golfsmartacademy.com. The body drills are designed to get you to feel your feet and middle working together, but where you feel it is less important than the changes you experience in your movement pattern.

Let's take a second to reinforce how important it is to power the swing from the body. To do this, we must start the downswing sequence with the big muscles in the legs and trunk. Doing so not only helps create a lot of force on the club handle, but swinging the club from the body is key to producing the overall shape of the circle. Swinging with the arms can feel powerful, but it's hard to produce the good flat spot that improves consistency.

CHAPTER 17

Steeps and Shallows, Part 1—Breaking Down the Path

can't emphasize enough how important the path is to understanding your personal swing pattern. When discussing the path, we will frequently use the terms steep and shallow. These terms are clearer than high/low and right/left. But as a quick refresher:

- steep is high to low, and usually outside-in;
- shallow is less high to low, and usually inside-out.

Once you're accustomed to using steep and shallow, it is unlikely you will want to go back to any other naming convention. You'll realize that steep and shallow movements are critical to decoding your path. That said, let's investigate how the body actually controls the path of the club.

Most golfers agree: The greatest feeling is hitting a solid shot in the middle of the club face. The ball launches off the face like a rocket; the club brushes the ground like a hot knife through butter; and the overall experience is that of blissful power.

Solid contact takes place when the path of the club head is just right.

Insight

When the club head path is right, the center of the club strikes the ball in such a way that it transfers maximum energy.

In the past, instructors tried to force the club on some ideal swing plane, but this is a poor approach. Forcing the club to be **on plane** is a guiding motion rather than a swinging one. A swinging motion allows the club to travel on a circular path, but a guiding movement is less likely to do so. The trick is to find a swinging motion that moves the club head into the ball on a usable plane and path but also has an adequate face to create good ball flight.

Figure 17.1

To get a general sense of the club swinging, try this experiment. Hold the club like a walking stick and keep your hand in the same place. Take the club up to parallel, then just let it drop. Guide the club head by rotating your wrist. Next, try the same experiment, but deliberately try to change the path on which the club head is swinging. If you try to guide it, you will feel the path wobble. The second half of the downswing should be similar to the first version of this experiment. Just let the club swing and it will produce a planar path.

As Part 1 discussed, a solid strike is the result of a balance of steep and shallow movements in your swing. You want to swing the club in a way that naturally produces an on-plane swing, rather than trying to force the club to be on plane.

Insight

If I had to pick one of the two, swinging the club is more important than being on plane (within reason). A swing that is slightly out-to-in or in-to-out can be successful. Most important is knowing what movements might push it onto a path that's too steep or too shallow.

As you work on the technical movements in Part 3, keep in mind that the overall goal of this exercise is to achieve a free swinging motion.

Figure 17.2

Figure 17.3   Figure 17.4   Figure 17.5

Two great checkpoints for your balance of steep and shallow are shaft parallel before and after impact. Before impact, if the club head is inside the hands, the path is shallow. After impact, it switches—if the club head is outside the hands, the club path is shallow.

Defining steep and shallow

Shallow means there is too much **under plane**, or in-to-out. Steep means there is too much **over plane**, or out-to-in.

Mathematically, given any height of the club head, the amount of steep and shallow can be seen as the distance from the club head to the ball. On plane is the standard. If the club head is outside the line, there will typically be less distance to cover, so it's steep. Inside the line there will be more distance to cover, so it's shallow.

You probably thought you'd never use algebra for anything useful, but it now becomes useful to remember that slope equals rise over run. In the impact zone, we're looking for an angle of attack of around 4 degrees down with the irons, pretty flat with the fairway woods, and slightly up with the driver.

Ideally, we want a balanced blend of movements that make the club steep and ones that make it shallow. If a swing favors either type of movement too heavily, the circle will tilt too much and you will have contact problems. Remember the airplane landing? The Stock Tour Swing should result in the club head gliding into a smooth landing in order to produce the flat spot.

So, this raises the question—how do you swing the club with a good plane or club head path?

| Figure 17.6 | Figure 17.7 | Figure 17.8 | Figure 17.9 |

If you are too shallow (left images), you lack enough steep moves. If you are too steep (right images), you don't have enough shallow moves.

CHAPTER 18

Steeps and Shallows, Part 2—Body Movements

Body movements balance the path of the club head when you hit a good shot. The problem with using a good shot to monitor club path is that you have to wait until impact to do so. But how can you know if you are at risk of hitting a bad shot before impact? Every segment of your body influences the club path at each point in the swing.

Note that like the rest of the program, these movements are considered steep or shallow from the perspective of a right-handed golfer.

Steep and shallow influences for the big movements of the body.

Steep—flexion, left rotation, left side bend, left sway, negative thrust, negative lift
Shallow—extension, right rotation, right side bend, right sway, thrust, lift

Steep Shallow   Steep Shallow

Figure 18.1

These major body moves will have a big impact on the club head path.

The arms also significantly influence the path of the club. At this point, let's just group them into categories:

Steep—chop, left rotation, narrow, left of body (arms leading)

Shallow—lift, right rotation, wide, right of body (arms trailing)

Steep   Shallow

Figure 18.2

The arm movements have a significant impact on the club head path, but the body has a greater influence.

In general, we want the body and arm movements to be gradually blended. This helps balance the steeps and shallows and tilts the circle the right amount. To do this, you will see common combinations during the downswing.

The backswing is significant because it primes the body for the movements that create the steep and shallow movements of the downswing. But for our discussion, since it is the downswing that hits the ball, the downswing is the primary part of the swing to examine steeps and shallows.

As we talk about movement combinations, it helps to break the downswing into two phases: transition and release.

The transition is the part in which you build speed in the grip. The release is the second part in which you transfer speed from the grip to the club head. We will explore this in more detail in Part 5, but for now know that the shift from building to transferring is roughly the body position in the next image. Transition is before that point and release is after it.

Figure 18.3

This is roughly the point at which the swing goes from building to transferring. If you get steep or shallow before this point, it is probably the result of how you create power. If it is after this point, it is likely due to how you control the path or face.

Keep in mind that it is easier to train the swing than to talk about it (just like how it is easier to learn to walk by doing rather than discussing it). You just need a good idea of what you want to do; put in the reps with good feedback and you will be able to build your swing. To create a good image to model, we have to discuss concepts in a technical way. But once you experience a position, movement, or concept for the first time, your brain can translate it into something that is more specific to your swing.

Next let's explore how the path of the club head is created during the two key phases of the downswing.

CHAPTER 19

Steeps and Shallows, Part 3—Elite Golfer Steeps and Shallows in Transition and Release

Remember from Figures 2.1, 2.2, and 2.3 in Part 1 that the circle doesn't exactly retrace itself. During transition we want the club path to narrow a bit as it also shallows. Using the body to power the swing enables these two trademarks of the Stock Tour Swing. The narrowing results from the body leading the arms and from the arms staying relaxed during the change in direction. The shallowing results from the weight of the club and the arms staying relaxed during the change in direction.

 Insight   If the arms are tense in transition, neither the narrow nor the shallow are likely to happen.

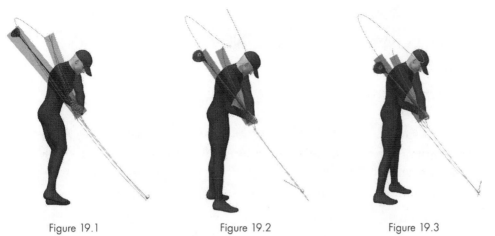

| Figure 19.1 | Figure 19.2 | Figure 19.3 |

Powering the transition with the body and having the arms lag causes the club to naturally follow a shallower path during transition. Both the classic slice (middle image) and hook (right image) will come with a hand path and a club path that are more parallel than the Stock Tour Swing.

Steeps and shallows in transition

Tour pro body movements (mostly steep):

- Shifts to the left (steep)
- Flexes forward (steep)
- Rotates to the left (steep)

Tour pro arm movements (mostly shallow):

- Rotates to the right of the body (shallow)
- Falls to the right of the body (shallow)
- Lifts slightly (shallow)

When these body and arm movements balance each other, the club head path will naturally create the **swing plane**.

Steeps and shallows in release

The release is an even gentler blend of steep and shallow movements. This helps achieve the right path and angle of attack to produce a long flat spot.

Tour pro body movements (blended):

- Side bends away from the target (shallow)

- Extends (shallow)

- Continues to rotate to the left (steep)

It sounds like a lot, but it will feel like one athletic movement when you try it. We will cover it in more detail in Part 3 (Chapter 36) as **bracing**. In addition to bracing, other movements are simultaneously occurring:

Tour pro arm movements (mostly shallow):

- Works across the body to the left (steep)

- Arms extend away from the body (shallow)

- Left forearm rotates leftward (steep)

This combination produces a great path that is repeatable in the best way possible. Your own personal style will dictate how much of each movement you will perform, but the best ball strikers adopt a pattern that is fairly similar to this blend of motion.

What goes wrong for novice golfers during transition

The most common problem novice golfers have during transition is that they tend to make **steep arm movements**. Steep arm movements combined with shallow body movements can create a swing plane that looks similar to the Stock Tour Swing. However, it won't work as well because the club handle will be higher off the ground. There are very few tour pros who have steep arm movements in transition.

On the other hand, some tour pros have shallow arm movements but are still steep because of their body movements. The overall look of the club is steep despite the fact that they are shallow with their arms. This is very different than when a golfer swings with steep arms.

Figure 19.4

A big problem for many novice golfers is that their arms rotate left, move to the left of the body, or chop down too soon in the downswing. These steep arm movements require a shallow body move, which prevents body rotation.

Novice body (blended, but mostly steep):

- Either rotates or restricts rotation (steep or shallow)

- Extension (shallow)

- Upper body shifts toward the target (very steep)

- Very little right side bend or excessive side bend (steep or shallow)

Novice arms (very steep):

- Extends earlier (shallow)

- Left rotation (very steep)

- Chops down vertically (very steep)

Being steep with the arms is usually a leftward arm rotation or a chop movement. Overly steep arms can produce either big hooks or big slices, depending on the sequence of body rotation.

With steep arms, if the upper body rotates too much, the club head path will be over-the-top and steep. However, if the body doesn't rotate enough, the golfer will usually stand up to avoid hitting it fat, and shallow out the path of the club head even more. This golfer will struggle with an overly in-to-out swing.

What goes wrong for novice golfers during the release

"Every golf swing is different." How many times have you heard that on the course? Technically it's true. Similarly, everyone's walking pattern is different. Despite this, I have yet to hear someone at the golf course mention that everyone walks a little differently. It's easier to see the patterns in walking than it is in golf, but if you know what to look for you can see them there too.

During the release, many amateurs balance in a less repeatable way than tour pros. Novice golfers tend toward the following:

Novice body (blended, but very restricted, unathletic):

- Limited body rotation (very shallow)

- Extension (shallow)

- Upper body shifts excessively toward the target (very steep)

- Very little side bend (steep)

Novice arms (shallow):

- Extends earlier (shallow)

- don't rotate left as much (shallow)

- they flip their wrists (shallow).

Compared to the tour pro who has a good gradual balance of steeps and shallows during the release, novice golfers tend to have a steep body position and very shallow arm movements. However, for most novice golfers, the steep body position trumps the arm movements and creates a steep angle of attack and a leftward path. With such a steep body position, the arm movements have to be shallow in transition—they have no other choice.

The best way for amateurs to improve these release problems is to practice the single-arm release drills from Chapter 36 in Part 3.

Two common struggles—overly steep (the "slicer") and overly shallow (the "hooker")

Golfers typically experience two common struggles—being overly steep or overly shallow. The steep golfer is frequently called a slicer or caster. The overly shallow golfer is usually called a hooker or early extender. Part 6 further details the common faults most golfers face, but for now let's discuss the big picture of these two problematic path patterns.

Slicer (caster)

Figure 19.6

The big steep moves for the caster are a spin of the upper body, a lunge of the upper body, and a left rotation of the arms.

For a slicer (caster), the big body movements are a spin of the upper body and a flex forward of the spine during transition. A slicer will not have nearly enough right side bend during the release. These factors create a steep and leftward path. A slicer typically needs more right side bend and/or spine extension to balance out the steep elements.

The slicer typically rotates the arms left (steep) and pulls down too much (steep), but also straightens them (shallow).

Hooker (early extender)

Figure 19.7

The big shallow moves for the early extender are a thrust of the hips toward the ball, an upper-body move away from the ball, a right side bend too early, and, usually, a straightening of the arms too soon.

For a hooker, the big movements in the body are right side bend and extension of the spine. The hooker typically needs more steep elements—more flexion during transition and/or body rotation during the release to balance out their big shallow movements.

With an overly shallow body move, most hookers will be steep with their arms in transition.

How steeps and shallows fit into your personal roadmap for success

I should stress that we are not trying to have a perfectly neutral ("zeroed out") swing. That said, we want to recognize our path pattern so we can keep it in check. It's common for problems in the path to become exaggerated under pressure. In other words, if you are shallow on the range, you will typically battle getting too shallow under pressure. Knowing why your swing tends to be shallow (or steep) will help you train and make progress on your personal roadmap.

A good balance of steeps and shallows helps achieve the ultimate goal of the swing—to produce a forward club brush location and a late wide point.

CHAPTER 20

Club Brush Location and Its Relationship to Steeps and Shallows

Where the club head brushes the ground is a result of your blend of steeps and shallows. Remember, all this body movement stuff is designed to create the shape of the swing you learned in Part 1. One of the big keys to consistency is to have the club head low to the ground for a long time after impact.

Details of brush location (the practical application of the Como Flat Spot)

The exact location of the bottom of your swing directly affects the quality and repeatability of your shots. Ultimately, the movement combinations are what really matter, but positions can be useful checkpoints for identifying movement combinations.

There two major factors that control the location of the swing's low and wide points:

    1. Where is the sternum at impact?

    2. What are the arms doing in the impact zone?

It sounds simple but can be tricky, so let's examine each piece in detail.

Figure 20.1

While these two impact positions might produce equally good shots, the one on the right will have a longer flat spot, resulting in more consistency.

Anatomically, the sternum is the vertical bone in the middle of your chest. Technically, the sternum is where your arm bones actually connect to your body. This connection is what makes it so pivotal to the brush location.

When it comes to the sternum, it is not just the spatial location, but also the orientation, or angle, that influences where the club head swings. The arms have nearly unlimited movement combinations, but they are limited in strength. When the club head has a lot of speed, the arms have fewer options.

At the bottom of the swing, the club swings more than 100 mph, and the arms extend (more or less) out in front of your sternum. Comparing the impact position of professional golfers reveals that their chests are generally in the same spatial position and point at the same angle.

> The pros point their chests out in front of the ball, a few feet along the target line. If your sternum is not in a similar position and orientation before impact, it is almost impossible to have the arms extend through the ball, which in turn makes it very challenging to develop a good flat spot and club brush location.
>
> *Insight*

The arms influence the location of the sternum, and vice versa. The arms affect the club brush location based on a few parameters:

1. Straightness of the elbows
2. Protraction of the shoulders
3. Angle of the wrists

Figure 20.2   Figure 20.3

Example 1—The classic tour brush pattern. The sternum is pointed out in front of the golf ball, but has a fair amount of right tilt. The elbows are both straighter in Figure 20.3 than Figure 20.2, but the right arm more so. The lead wrist is in flexion and the trail wrist is in extension, but they are both working toward neutral.

Figure 20.4   Figure 20.5

Example 2—A golfer who battles snap hooks. In this example, the brush location will be shorter than the tour model. The sternum is higher and is pointing more at the ball than out in front of it. At impact, the trail arm is straighter and the trail wrist is already fairly straight. The lead wrist is already extended and the club will start working up away from the ground quicker than in Example 1.

Figure 20.6   Figure 20.7

Example 3—An upper-body lunger who struggles with the driver. This golfer has a slightly shorter flat spot than the one in Example 2. The arms are very similar, but in this case, the sternum is less side bent so the arms will work more down and up instead of out toward the target.

Figure 20.8   Figure 20.9

Example 4—High-handicap golfer; this swing only works with short irons. This golfer will have an even shorter flat spot because the sternum is pointing more at the golf ball than at the target.

Figure 20.10   Figure 20.11

Example 5—Big slices and pulls. Of all the examples, this golfer will have the shortest flat spot because the arms are bending through the ball. This helps account for the fact that the sternum angle points more at the ground, because of the lack of the Jackson 5 move (a move you will learn in Chapter 36 in Part 3).

With a good golf grip, you can only have one wrist flat at a time. We want the left wrist to be pretty flat at impact, which means the right wrist will be somewhat bent. **This doesn't mean you should hold the right wrist back.** It just means that it will not have fully straightened at impact.

Another benefit of delaying the trail wrist flex is the influence on the wide point. The right hand is lower on the club for right-handed golfers when the right wrist is straight; that's as far as you can have your arms away from you (wide point).

The more that the body is rotated and side bent at impact, the more the wrists will delay straightening, and the more you will have a flat spot after impact. The straighter the arms, the less rotation and side bend you can have at impact and the less likely you are to have a good flat spot after the ball.

A good body position at impact is the result of the body powering the downswing. It also results from a good blend of the rotation/side bend/extension during release. This impact position is key for producing a good flat spot/club brush location and reveals a good balance of steep and shallow movements during the downswing.

CHAPTER 21

The Centered Pivot—Using the Ground to Create Power

To control the club brush location, most pros keep their upper body in a relatively small bubble. Their torso doesn't move much laterally or vertically. The body rotates and changes angles, but laterally, the upper body moves very little (1–2 inches in backswing and a couple inches in downswing). Vertically, it moves down a little bit in transition and up a little bit during release (this helps get the hands moving up and in). But when we are looking at a scale of less than 2 inches, it's easy to see why a lot of good ball strikers develop a feeling of staying centered.

This does not mean you should try to be a statue over the ball. In reality, you shouldn't hold still, but rather use your full body in a way that your upper body stays relatively centered.

Your upper body is not still just for the sake of being so. Actually, stillness results from good body mechanics and from how the body pushes against the ground to create speed.

Everything is connected in the swing, so how a golfer generates speed helps create the club brush location, and vice versa. The centered pivot idea also helps the golfer use the ground to create speed.

The body creates speed by pushing against the ground in different amounts and directions. To jump off the ground, you push down to create the force that helps to propel you up. To run forward, you push backward. Pushing backward propels you forward. To rotate to the left, you have to twist your feet against the ground to the right.

All land-based sports use the ground for power. Golf is no different. Swinging powerfully requires you to use your body against the ground. It's not just about how hard you push the ground, but rather certain biomechanical relationships.

One way to classify the ground interaction is to pinpoint where the pressure from the feet is compared to the mass of the body. The bigger the difference between the two locations, the easier it is to use the ground for speed.

Think of two soccer players making a cut. Which one looks like they will be able to change direction more powerfully?

Figure 21.1

Which of these two athletes looks like they could change direction more explosively? If you shift your upper body off the ball, you have to wait for it to get back into position before you can use your lower body. Golfers who shift off the ball in the backswing usually use an arm pull as their dominant power source.

The left image shows more power potential because there is a bigger difference in where their feet are pushing and their body (mass).

You're probably wondering—how does this concept apply to the golf swing?

To push with the right foot and build speed, you can't allow your upper body to shift too much off the ball (only 1–2 inches horizontally). During the downswing, to push the left foot and transfer speed, you can't shift too much toward the target.

However, staying centered reflects *how you use the ground*. It is not just some arbitrary goal. When you make a full turn in the backswing, you are doing so to push the ground away from the target with the legs (which you loaded during the backswing). Next, when you unload in the downswing, your upper body stays behind the ball. This gives more power to push against the ground with the front foot to transfer the speed to the club head.

These images of the runner changing direction should help you envision the relationship you want as you start the downswing. These images should also influence your goal for the backswing.

Figure 21.2   Figure 21.3   Figure 21.4

Figure 21.2: Top of backswing likely has a good relationship of mass to pressure, but still stays mostly centered. This enables proper pressure direction in the downswing. Figure 21.3: Top of backswing doesn't shift mass enough away from the target to allow for a powerful shift in the downswing. Figure 21.4: Top of backswing has too much lateral upper-body shift to produce lateral force from the lower body.

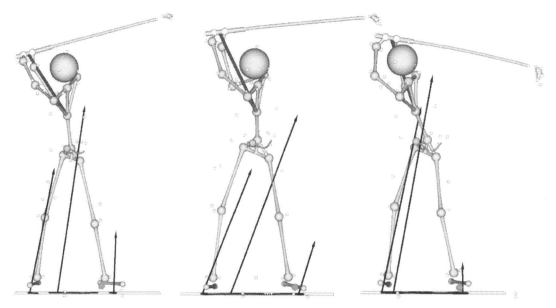

Figure 21.5

Here are force diagrams of three tour-caliber golfers with different top-of-backswing positions (provided by researcher Dr. Young-Hoo Kwon of Texas Woman's University). You can see that different body positions and ground interactions can yield different force vectors. This is the way to measure the phenomena described above. The arrows can help you visualize how different body positions interact with the feet.

The other key time to monitor this foot-pressure-to-body-relationship is during the release.

CHAPTER 22

How the Hands and Arms Influence the Club Face

At this point, you know how you want the club head path to look when you swing, and you have a pretty good idea of which big body movements create the ideal club head path. In this chapter, let's revisit what we learned in the first section—the club face movements and how the body achieves specific alignments of the club face for dependable impact.

As we said in Part 1, there are three key factors to producing a desired ball flight:

1. The path of the club
2. The face relationship to that path
3. The face relationship to the target

Put simply, if the club face is square to the club head path, the ball has little curve. If the club face is open to the club head path, the ball will curve to the right. If the club face is closed to the club head path, the ball curves to the left.

Let's go over the key factors that control the orientation of the club face to the club head path.

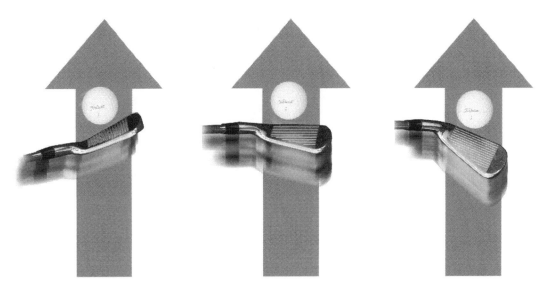

Figure 22.1

Learning to recognize the face-to-path relationship is key for accurately reading ball flight. The face can either be closed, square, or open to the path. When you read shot feedback, the extent to which the face is open or closed is identified by the amount of curve.

Square club face

Remember from Chapter 11 that the club face direction can be changed by moving the club handle in one of three ways:

1. Handle up opens; handle down closes
2. Shaft rotation left closes; shaft rotation right opens
3. Forward in plane shaft movement closes; backward in plane shaft movement opens

To create a good flat spot, the club face needs to be more closed to the shaft at impact than it was at address, so let's discuss the ways to do that with the body.

What movements influence face orientation?

The three ways to move the face orientation are shaft rotation; moving the shaft forward/backward; and moving the handle up/down. Simply put, any body movements that move the club in those three ways open or close the face to the shaft and to the path.

Rotation: left = closed, right = open

Shaft back = closed, forward = open

Shaft up = open, down = closed (more so with more loft)

While the body has the biggest influence on the club head path, the arms and hands have the biggest influence on the club face. We can look at what the arms and hands do at two different places: set up and during the swing. At set up, the grip has the primary influence on the club face. Aside from the grip at set up, during the swing the movements you make with your shoulders, arms, and wrists equally influence the club face orientation.

Club face variables

The major club face influencers are the grip at set up and the forearm movements during the swing.

Grip

The grip is a key building block of any swing. Depending on how you start the club in your hands, it will end up in a directly related way when you come into impact.

Golf grips are traditionally categorized by strength. They fall along a spectrum from strong to weak, with neutral in the middle. There is a tendency in sports to assume that strong means better, but that convention doesn't really apply here. Tour pros use a wide range of grip strengths, and most use a grip on the strong side of neutral.

Typically, grip strength is identified by the number of visible knuckles or where the Vs are pointing (the V is formed between the thumb and index finger).

Figure 22.2

Everyone's grip is slightly different, but the general ranges are strong (V pointing outside of trail shoulder) to weak (V pointing at nose). How you position your hands on the club and the movements of the arms during the swing are the only two factors that influence the face-to-path relationship.

Trail Hand

A strong trail hand grip is when the V of your trail hand is pointed away from the target, or when you look down you see fewer knuckles on your right hand than your left. All else being equal, a stronger grip closes the face to the shaft by means of rotation.

Lead Hand

A strong lead hand grip is when the V of your lead hand is pointed more away from the target, or you can see more knuckles on your left hand than your right. All else being equal, a strong grip also closes the face to the shaft by means of rotation.

Compared to a weaker grip, a stronger grip turns the club face more closed compared to the hands. So if you make the exact same swing with two different grips, the one in which the grip is stronger will result in less loft and a face that is more closed to the shaft.

If the face-to-path relationship is not what you want (that is, the ball curves more than you want), your two options are to change your grip at set up or change your arm movements in the swing.

Insight

Making arm movement changes in the swing can be tricky, so most golfers who aren't satisfied with their ball flight curve (face-to-path relationship) should try changing their grip before they experiment with their arm movements.

Changing your grip is the easiest way to change the face-to-path relationship and ball flight. The more the hands are rotated to the side of the grip, away from the target at set up, the stronger the grip is and the face will be closed more to the shaft at impact. Alternatively, the more the hands are positioned on top of the grip or even toward the target at set up, the more the club face will be open to the shaft.

Movements of the wrists/forearms

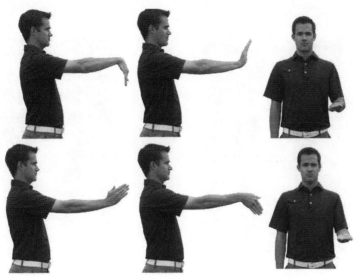

Figure 22.3

There are three basic movements of the wrists/forearms. How they affect the face-to-path relationship depends on when the movement takes place.

Along with grip orientation at set up, there are also forearm and wrist movements that alter the face orientation in the swing. While the grip may result in a more immediate change, altering your arm movements can yield more significant long-term gains because of the way it promotes a good club path and brush pattern.

The basic movements your wrist can make are flexion/extension and ulnar/radial deviation. The forearm can rotate, which is called pronation/supination. These three movements can change the club head path, but they also have a big effect on the orientation of the face to the path.

Rotating the face closed to the shaft

Figure 22.4

Figure 22.5

When the wrist is bent 90 degrees to the shaft, club face rotation is controlled by flexion/extension.
When the club is in line with the forearms, the club face rotation is controlled by pronation/supination.

Like a screwdriver, or a barber pole, rotating the grip changes the face significantly. In the downswing we need to rotate the face more closed by rotating the face toward the target.

The two movements that have the biggest influence in closing the face are flexion of the lead wrist and supination of the lead forearm. The trail arm would be the opposite (extension of the wrist and pronation of the forearm). Typically, flexion and the supination of the lead arm take place in different phases of the swing. When the club is 90 degrees to the forearm, closing the face is flexion/extension (we call this the motorcycle movement). When the club is in line with the forearm, closing the face is pronation/supination. In between, it is a little of both.

Shoulder movements

Shoulder rotation can either supplement how the forearms rotate the shaft or neutralize shaft rotation.

If the club is out in front of me, I can adjust the orientation of the face to path by rotating either my shoulders or my forearms. If they rotate in the same direction, the movement is amplified. If they rotate in the opposite direction, the movement is neutralized.

Ideal combination of set up and movements

Most professional golfers close the face partly with their grip (set up), and partly with their wrist movements during the swing.

> It is a mistake to think that the downswing goal is to get the hands and club to impact in the same position as where you started. It's important to understand that the hands are in a completely different position at impact than they were at set up (we will cover the exact changes in the Impact chapter (Chapter 33) of Part 3).
>
> *Insight*

Simply put, the club head circle has shifted forward. Therefore, if you don't change anything about the wrists between set up and impact, the club face will be wide open to the target at impact and you will hit a ball that starts off way right of the target.

Grip orientation—combined with gradual closing movements in the downswing—enables rotation/side bend of the body. The combination of rotation and side bend helps create that ideal long forward brush location and late wide spot. How the pieces fit together will make even more sense when you start using the drills to train movements.

> The more you use your arms and hands to close the face to the shaft, the more your body can rotate open at impact (and create a flat spot). The less you close the face to the shaft with your arms and hands, the less your body can rotate open at impact (hurting your chances for a good flat spot).
>
> *Insight*

CHAPTER 23

Body Movement Influences on the Club Face

'm going to deal with the body as a whole while discussing how body movements affect the openness of the face. The more shaft lean and club head lag you have compared to your body, the more you delay closing the face; the less shaft lean, the sooner you close the face. Good shaft lean happens naturally in an impact position, in which your body is sufficiently rotated and side bent at impact. Inadequate shaft lean comes from an impact position that relies on standing up instead of rotating or side bending.

Body movements—shaft lean

Shaft lean = open face
Less shaft lean = closed face

Remember from Figure 5.7 that the shaft should have some lean (10–15 degrees) in order to contact the ball with the sweet spot (if there is no shaft lean, you will contact the ball lower on the face, below the sweet spot). The fact that the club is leaned more toward the target at impact will require you to have the club face more closed than it was at set up if you want to hit the ball anywhere but right of the target.

Adding face to the discussion of steeps and shallows

Let's revisit how to balance steep and shallow movements and add in discussion of how the face works. Recall in transition that the arms are mostly shallow—they will rotate right, lift slightly, and fall to the body's right. The rotation of the arms to the right opens the club face, as does rotating the body.

Those two features of an elite swing open the face. They need to be balanced by some closing elements if the face is to point at the target. Most tour golfers close the face using shaft rotation, which is the only option for closing the face while retaining shaft lean. Tour pros rotate the shaft early in transition (the motorcycle move you will learn in Part 3). In the release, tour pros gradually rotate the shaft with their lead arm.

> When you combine the key movements—having flatter arms, shaft rotation from the wrists, and shaft lean from body rotation—you get a very powerful and consistent pattern. Good golfers tend to use this gradual club rotation to close the face. In contrast, poor golfers flip the club and take away shaft lean instead of rotating the club to close the face.
>
> *Insight*

Figure 23.1

The earlier you close the face to the path (with flexion of the lead wrist/extension of the trail wrist), the more you can power the swing with your body and have your body open at impact.

The major face problem to avoid

Opening in transition and closing late or never

A common problem in transition is to rotate the face open. The face already opens from the arm shallow movements, so if the shaft also rotates open, you have a lot of closing to do later in the swing. With the club face open in transition, it's almost impossible for the body to power the swing.

Most golfers almost always close the face late by stalling their body's rotation and flipping their hands. This combination usually causes the sternum to point at the ball at impact. However, remember that it is critical for the sternum to point ahead of the ball at impact, a few feet down the target line, if you want to produce a good brush location and wide point.

Instead of rotating the face closed to the shaft, a lot of golfers use in-plane shaft movement to point the face at the target. This pattern looks like a scoop move. The stall and scoop does close the face at impact, but with a lot of loft and a limited flat spot.

Regarding the face-to-path relationship, the face orientation is equally influenced by the grip at set up and by the arm movements. Most tour golfers employ a neutral grip and close the face to the shaft 30 degrees or so from set up to impact. You'll learn more about this in Part 3 when we break down the phases of the swing.

Figure 23.2

To achieve an impact position that looks similar to the Stock Tour Swing model, start with a neutral set up. Then perform the next two moves in transition (motorcycle and let the arms fall to the right). Perform the third during the release. How much you do of each move and the timing of each will change the way it looks, but the pattern is pretty consistent.

Every good golfer closes the club face during the downswing. Some employ a weak grip and then significantly bow the wrists during the swing; others employ a strong grip and only flex the lead wrist slightly. No matter how they do it, every good golfer closes the face a good amount during the downswing. But how much do they close it?

> At impact, there is an intimate relationship between where the sternum is pointing and the amount of club face closure needed. The more open the body (sternum), the more the face will need to be closed. The more closed the body, the more the face will need to be less closed.
>
> *Insight*

If you have a curve you don't like, you now have options for how to change it. For example, suppose you slice the ball and the face is open to the path. You can either close the face with your grip or close the face by rotating the face to the shaft. Either approach can match the face to the path, and the ball will fly in the direction of the path. Then, if you add a move or two from Chapters 17–20, you can move the path more toward the target.

Mission: *This is the power of the Stock Tour Swing program. Ball flight is no longer a mystery.*

Don't worry if you feel overwhelmed by what we've covered—you have a lifetime to perfect these techniques. If you're feeling mentally fatigued, take a break and watch some of the related videos at http://golfsmartacademy.com. It's easier to learn new concepts when you can experience them in different formats. And frankly, many of the concepts in this program are easier to demonstrate than to explain. Also, feel free to send us a message if any concepts aren't coming through clearly for you.

Knowing what your club face is doing is one of the most significant benefits you get from reading feedback. Remember, reading feedback is what prevents you from feeling lost out there. Every golfer hits bad shots, but in the heat of a round, good golfers learn from bad shots and move on. Bad golfers panic and try something random, praying that it might help.

This program will help you understand your swing so you can become the golfer who learns and moves on.

CHAPTER 24

Creating Power

The foundation for identifying your swing pattern is reading feedback. With accurate feedback, you can answer the key question:

What is my swing pattern?

As you work through this program, you have the option to dig deeper. Digging deeper enables you to answer a more challenging question:

Why do I have this swing pattern?

Identifying your main power source is critical for answering the second question.

As we have established, the face and path dictate how well the ball was struck and the direction in which it flies. But to really enjoy the game, you have to hit the ball a reasonable distance. Interestingly, how you create speed is directly related to how you organize the face and path.

Often times, your club head path is off the ideal shape because of how you create speed. In Chapters 17–20, you saw how each body movement changed the club head path. If you create speed in one area of your body, you can expect your path to shift too much in the way that movement changes the club head path. For instance, if you spin your upper body to create speed, you will always struggle with a path that is too steep.

In this chapter, we break down how a golfer uses the body to create speed. As you read, keep in mind that a solid path and good face orientation are more conducive to good shots than creating maximum speed.

Build versus transfer

Figure 24.1

This image shows the common point of maximum speed of the handle. The early part of the downswing is for building speed, but most of the downswing is spent transferring speed to the club head. The entire blue section is used to speed up the club head, while the handle slows it down.

The downswing can be broken down into two phases:

1. Building speed—speeding up the handle as much as you can; and
2. Transferring speed—transferring the handle speed to the club head.

I call the building phase the "transition" and the transferring phase the "release."

The overall pattern is similar to throwing a baseball or hitting a tennis ball. The general procedure is to step (shift weight/pressure); turn the body (build rotational speed); and use the arm (to transfer that speed to the ball).

The sequence is pretty much the same in golf, but most golfers are shocked by how soon the body starts to transfer the speed. With a golf club, you start transferring earlier than if you were throwing a ball or swinging a light object like a tennis racquet.

During the building speed phase, all of the big muscle groups smoothly apply force to the grip. During this phase, the biggest muscles in the body pull on the club all at once before each segment peels off during the downswing. Use your body's big muscles for power. To understand how, let's compare a squat to a bicep curl.

Squat versus bicep curl

Many amateurs (and some pros) tend to use their arms for power and their body for control. Consider a squat versus a bicep curl. Even if you are bad at squatting, you are more likely to be able to squat more weight than someone doing a curl because you use your whole body. **Similarly, you are more likely to hit the ball far if you use your whole body, so long as you don't compromise the shape of your circle too much.** In Part 3 we will look more closely at how the whole body works to create the swing shape.

Using the body to start the downswing causes the arms to shallow. Just like a baseball pitcher who steps with the legs and causes the arm to lag behind, moving the lower body creates the look of lag. The weight of the club lagging behind also causes the club to start shallowing into the proper path.

> **Insight**
>
> Using the body to start the downswing is much better than using the arms. When the arms get active too soon in transition, it causes the club to go steep (because of chopping and left rotation). If the arms are to do the right things in transition (be shallow and narrow), they need some fluidity. So relax those arms during transition.

The release is then triggered when the lead leg pushes against the ground and causes the upper body to switch from moving toward the target to away from it. I call this bracing. When the body braces, it triggers the arms to extend as you begin the release. When the arms extend later in the swing, it will help you create the nice flat spot after the ball.

> **Insight**
>
> If thinking about bracing invokes fears of hitting it fat, you probably have a cast pattern. We will address that in the faults and fixes section (Chapters 45–49). You can still play great golf with a cast pattern, but because the flat spot is not as good as a body swing, you will likely struggle with consistency, especially with the longer clubs.

Overhand versus underhand—which is more powerful?

Another way to think about how the body powers the swing is to consider the difference between an overhand throw and an underhand toss. In an underhand toss, everything moves together, and most of the power comes from swinging the shoulder. In an overhand throw, the body moves in sequence to build maximal speed.

The sequence is key. First the body steps. Then it twists. Then the arms propel the ball. Compared to hitting a golf ball, the full swing is more like an overhand throw than an underhand toss. The sequence of shift/turn/extend the arms helps create the swing's look. If you are curious about the underhand toss idea for the short game, check out this book's companion website, http://golfsmartacademy.com.

Along with power, using the body's big muscle groups for speed can improve the path. Using your legs and core for speed helps narrow the path of the club head during transition and gets your body in position to generate a swing with a later low and wide point.

> A swing powered by the arms might have a good direction, but it is not ideal for producing the good wide point and flat spot after the ball. Golfers who use their arms as their engine tend to have consistency problems with the long irons and the driver.
>
> *Insight*

Identifying your pattern (with either ball flight feedback or video) is key for long-term improvement. Video can help identify big-picture things to work on as well as critical small-picture things, like figuring out the precise point at which the swing path gets off track. Part 3 will help you see why your swing may be getting off track, and how to train it.

CHAPTER 25

The Body's Different Power Movements

L et's discuss options for using your whole body to create speed. As I've cautioned, you don't need to feel all these movements; you just have to monitor your major ones. You can create power using different parts of your body. The ideal swing uses a blend of power sources, as opposed to using just one power source at its maximum capability. The most common power sources are:

Leg

| Jump | Lunge | Twist |

Figure 25.1   Figure 25.2   Figure 25.3

Core

Stand up (spine extension)

Figure 25.4

Spine twist

Figure 25.5

Side bend (side crunch)

Figure 25.6

Crunch

Figure 25.7

Shoulder/arm

Chop

Figure 25.7

Lift

Figure 25.8

Left rotation of the arms

Figure 25.9

Shoulder abduction/ adduction

Figure 25.10

Triceps straightening

Figure 25.11

Forearm/Wrist

Flexing and extending the wrists   **Forearm rotation**   **Unhinging**

Figure 25.12   Figure 25.13   Figure 25.14

There are plenty of options, but just one or two major power sources define your swing. Each option has a different influence on your face and path, so it's important to know your pattern.

For example, growing up I played basketball and tennis, and so I learned to power my swing with a hip rotation (from my tennis forehand) and spine extension (from my jump shot). I was capable of using most of the options, but I gravitated toward those two. That combination works great on the driver, but causes major contact issues with a wedge since both options make the path shallower.

Use the following descriptions to identify your major power sources. Keep in mind how each power source will likely change the path of the club. The path changes use a right-handed golfer as the reference.

Leg options

Figure 25.15

Jump

Any good jump begins with a squat. Load the jump by hinging the hips and knees. The jump itself is a firing of the loaded knees, hips, and ankles. Jumping is a common power source in golf and many other sports. Because the lower body is a bit in front of the upper body when the jump powers the downswing, it tends to shift the club head path to the right and shallow out the angle of attack.

Figure 25.16

Lunge

A long forward step or a step up onto an object is an example of a lunge. One can lunge in any direction, but in golf it is more common to laterally lunge, whereby you shift toward the target. A lateral lunge (or hip slide) shifts the club head path to the right and shallows the angle of attack unless the upper body goes with it. If the upper body goes with the hip slide, the combination does the opposite—it steepens the angle of attack and moves the club head path left. We typically call the upper body going with the hip slide a forward lunge.

Figure 25.17

Hip rotation

This is a powerful movement sourced from your glutes and thigh muscles. It makes your full body rotate like a top. Hip rotation is one of the foundations of power in most throwing and striking sports. Rotating the hips shifts the club head path to the left and steepens the swing.

Core options

Figure 25.18

Spine/hip extension—standup

Like a jump, a standup is also a hinge of the hips, but doesn't involve the knees as much. When this is done improperly, most of the standup move comes from the lower back instead of the hips. When done properly, most of the power comes from the glutes. An example of this movement is a deadlift. The standup movement shifts the club head path to the right, shallows out the angle of attack, and causes the club face to close faster near the ball.

Figure 25.19

Spine twist

Spine twisting is found in many sports that involve body control and spatial awareness, such as gymnastics, figure skating, and most martial arts. It is also a key power source in throwing or hitting. Twisting the spine shifts the club head path to the left and steepens the angle of attack.

Figure 25.20

Crunch

A common spine movement is a crunch. This is a powerful move from the abs but tends to pull the upper body toward the lower body. This steepens the angle of attack and slightly shifts the path to the left.

Figure 25.21

Side bend—side crunch

Side bending to the right uses the right-side obliques and lower back muscles. It will shift the club head path to the right and shallows out the angle of attack. This can be a great power source option, but becomes a problem when combined with strong hip extension. Golfers who do both of these moves in excess will almost always battle big hooks and blocks.

Shoulder and arm options

Figure 25.22

Chop

A chop is one of the most powerful movements of the shoulders and involves the lat muscles as a primary engine. The chop involves pulling down the arms, as seen in splitting wood with an axe. It moves the club head path left and steepens the angle of attack.

Figure 25.23

Lift

A lift is the opposite of a chop. It involves raising the arms and uses the shoulders as a primary engine. The lift can be seen in the underhand toss featured in softball, horseshoes, or bowling. It shallows the angle of attack and shifts the club head path to the right.

Trail shoulder internal rotation (left rotation)

Figure 25.24

This is loaded by external rotation in the backswing and powered by the pecs and lats. Trail shoulder internal rotation is a common power source of all throwing activities. It shifts the club head path to the left and steepens the angle of attack.

Lead shoulder abduction

Figure 25.25

This is the arm working across your body, as seen in a backhand shot in tennis or a backhand throw with a Frisbee. It shifts the path to the left and steepens the angle of attack.

Elbow extension

Figure 25.26

This is an extension of the elbow and is frequently seen as a jab in boxing or as part of a throw in most other sports. In golf, this movement is usually seen in the right arm and combines with right wrist flexion. This movement combination shallows out the club head path and moves it to the right.

Forearm options

Figure 25.27

Forearm rotation

Forearm rotation (pronation/supination) is used with arm extension in good throwing mechanics or in racquet sports. In golf, this movement moves the club head path to the left and steepens the angle of attack.

Figure 25.28

Flexion of trail wrist (scoop or flick)

This is a simple wrist flexion movement and is frequently seen in racquet sports and the end of a forehand Frisbee throw. It is one of the key movers of a scoop and shallows out the club head path while moving it to the left.

Figure 25.29

Unhinge

This is often seen in the wrist movement that accompanies using a hammer. It moves the club head path left and shallows it out.

Identifying your power source

The power sources show up during transition. Look at your swing on video and identify what is moving aggressively during the early part of the downswing. Are you twisting your shoulders? Are you pulling with your arms? Do you look like you're jumping? Identifying your main power source is a key step in identifying your pattern.

Despite the variety of power source options, we typically only use a couple. For instance, an upper body–dominant swing could emphasize more of the forward lunge or the upper-body twist. It doesn't need to use both of them consciously to fit in that category. Below are the common combinations.

Common combinations

Upper body–dominant swing

Legs—minimal, if any
Core—forward lunge, twist, crunch
Shoulders and arm—chop, internal rotation
Forearms—left forearm rotation, flick/flexion of trail wrist

Lower body–dominant swing

Legs—lower-body lunge, twist, jump
Core—spine extension, right side bend
Shoulders and arm—lift
Forearms—unhinge, flick

Stock Tour Swing model

Legs—jump, lunge, twist
Core—spine twist, side bend
Shoulders and arm—rotation, lift, or chop
Forearms—unhinge, left forearm rotation

Because it uses the whole body to generate power, the Stock Tour Swing puts less demand on any one particular area. As a result, the swing path is more resilient to large path changes that come from overusing any one power source.

After you identify your main power sources, you can predict what will happen to your path if you swing harder than normal. You'll also know how to try and gain extra distance.

> Instead of turbocharging your normal power source, try gaining distance by engaging a source you weren't previously using.
>
> *Insight*

I learned that if I wanted to max out my distance, I couldn't swing any harder from my preferred power source (jump/squat). But I could use more trunk rotation and trail shoulder adduction to create more speed. This gave me another 20 yards when I really wanted it, but was harder for me to time than my normal lower-body swing. I used it when I had good timing on the range before a round, or on a hole when I really needed the extra distance.

If you are unable to identify your major power source by looking at video, notice **where you experience soreness after a long practice session or after repeatedly swinging hard**. This gives you a good idea of which power movements you are using.

CHAPTER 26

Loading Up for the Building Phase— Displacement and Time

Two things must be present in the backswing to apply force to the club head on the downswing: distance (displacement) and time. Ideally, the backswing provides maximum time and displacement to apply force on the downswing with as many power sources as possible. You can see this on TV or when playing with your golf buddies—the longest hitters tend to have full backswing movements, while shorter hitters do not.

If you are lacking in distance off the tee and are sure you make a full backswing (and power it with your whole body), gym training is your best hope for increased distance.

Insight

If you hit the ball farther from a shorter swing, it is usually due to better contact or better path shape rather than a "tighter coil" with more speed. If you do actually pick up speed with a shorter swing, it means that when you swing full, you get yourself out of position to use the bigger power sources. For example, many golfers who try to make a full turn do so by overextending their lower back. This prevents them from recruiting some of their core muscles on the downswing. So even though they create greater displacement, they actually lose distance by taking away big power source options.

The shape of the circle contributes more to hitting it far than producing slightly more speed. If you swing harder, or make a bigger swing, and you lose that circle shape, you will probably hit it shorter due to poorer impact alignments.

This program offers you options to make smart decisions. If you want to hit the ball farther and you already have good launch conditions, then greater club head speed is your only option. Some of the movements that create more speed might temporarily upset your impact alignments. Now you can decide if short-term struggles from losing your impact conditions are worth the long-term gain of greater distance—assuming you can regain the same launch conditions after training a fuller backswing.

Try making a full backswing while maintaining a relatively centered pivot, and powering the downswing with the big muscle groups. Doing so gives you the best chance of hitting far. Part 3 covers all the key movements of the backswing.

CHAPTER 27

The Hand Path Versus the Club Head Circle

Our next task is to compare the path of the hands to the path of the club head. This is key for understanding the downswing. Specifically, it is key to conceptualizing how the Stock Tour Swing looks effortless but still produces satisfying power and consistency.

It is critical to note that the path of the hands and the path of the club head are not identical. Let's investigate the two key swing phases where the path of the hands and the path of the club head are different—impact and transition.

Impact—handle up and in, club head down and out

Even though we want the club head working down (unless you're hitting a driver) in the impact zone, during impact the handle (and thus the hands) should move slightly up and slightly in. This helps achieve the two major swing goals—a later arc width (wide point) and a good, late flat spot.

Looking at the whole body reveals a few factors that influence the handle movement, such as the timing and direction of the arm movements. To get the handle working up and in, the arms should work across your body. During release they should eventually extend out ahead of the ball (instead of traveling straight at the golf ball).

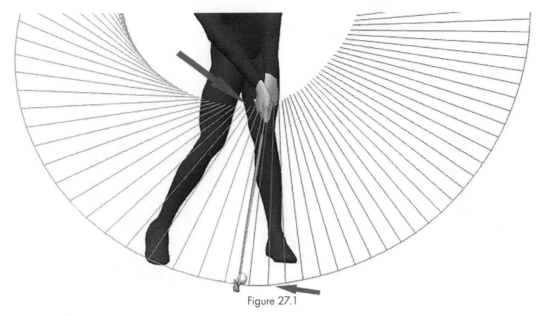

Figure 27.1

The tip of the arrows shows the two key low points. The low point of the hands is slightly before impact, whereas the low point of the club is a few inches after impact. This is largely achieved by the body's bracing movement more than by an active upward pull from the arms.

> Bringing the handle up and in primarily results from body movements, not arm movements. The body's right side tilt raises the left shoulder through impact. The combination of right side bend and rotation helps produce the correct path and angle of attack.
>
> *Insight*

The hands should be moved up and in fairly subtly. This is because even though your shoulder is moving up and in, your arms are extending away from your body. You may *feel* like your hands are moving more down and out; use video to confirm if they actually are. It should be a subtle up-and-in. If the handle is coming too up-and-in, you will be bending your elbows instead of just using the tilt of your body (bracing it).

Shallow move in transition

Transition—Sasho – Club path under hand path

| Figure 27.2 | Figure 27.3 | Figure 27.4 |

The pro golfer (left image) has his club head path working on a flatter plane than his hands are moving, while the amateurs both have their hands working on a similar path to the club.

Transition is the other key time when the hands and club head move along different paths. During transition, the club head path should follow a flatter path than that of the hands. I call this move the *shallow arm movement* in transition. It is critical if your hands are to work properly during release. The arm shallowing drill in Part 3 is the best way to practice it.

> *In golf science forums, the shallow arm movement is often referred to in combination with the name Sasho. Dr. Sasho Mackenzie was the first researcher I saw discuss this swing characteristic in detail (although it was described in golf speak by a lot of great instructors prior to Dr. Mackenzie).*

To produce the shallowing arm movement in transition, the arms need to be soft and relaxed. If your arms (especially your forearms) are tense, the club head path will be closer to the hand path. If your arms are relaxed and you shallow correctly, the club head will drop. This helps the club to square when you execute the release (which we will cover in Part 3).

While this move is critical to the Stock Tour Swing, it poses two challenges to amateurs.

Insight

Power

The shallowing arm movement allows you to power the transition with the large muscles of the legs and core without causing the overall path of the club to steepen too much. Since many amateur golfers pull with their arms for power, this shallowing movement can feel very odd and weak at first.

Face

Another reason why amateurs tend to not do this shallowing movement is because it opens up the club face. Tour pros achieve club face balance with a twist of the shaft (the motorcycle movement discussed in Part 3), but amateurs are not as familiar with gradual club face rotation. Instead of using the motorcycle, amateurs stand up or swing left as a way to close the face to the target. Having a club face that is overly open in transition should be avoided. Since the shallowing arm move opens the face, many amateurs avoid it completely. Once a golfer commits to steep arms in transition, he/she also commits to compensating with an undesirable shallowing move during the release.

Hopefully you're starting to see how these building blocks and concepts all relate to each other. You can't just turn your body and not stand up unless you also apply the arm shallowing and club face squaring techniques. Remember also that everything doesn't need to be perfect to improve your swing shape—you just need to execute a few key movements well.

CHAPTER 28

Tempo—Move the Body to Your Inner Beat

We've all seen a swing that looks smooth and effortless, and ones that look fast and jerky. Smooth swings have good tempo. Jerky swings don't. There is some golf science regarding tempo that can help produce a smooth and effortless swing.

Tempo's measurable components include sequencing, duration of movement, and rate of acceleration. If your body moves in the right sequence with the right rate of acceleration, your swing will look smooth and effortless. If your body moves out of sequence, your swing will look jerky. Part 3 examines the details of each phase—details you have probably never considered before.

Preparing to learn movement—from Bambi's first steps to a metal rollercoaster

Before we discuss tempo, we should talk a little bit about learning new movements. Sometimes learning new movements can cause golfers to become stiff and robotic. This is temporary—stick with what you learn and try to make the moves smooth and rhythmical.

I often joke with my students that when they try something for the first time, I expect to see something akin to Bambi's first steps. After trying the movements a few dozen times, your brain will smooth out their pieces.

> **Insight**
>
> Training rhythm is great for short-term performance but rarely causes long-term path changes. With practice, you'll find that there is a time and place for training moves and a different time and place for training rhythm.

A new movement will likely feel awkward the first few times you train it. As a dance instructor once told me, "You have the moves right. Now we want the feeling of a metal roller coaster, not a wooden one." Going from a rickety wooden roller coaster to a modern, smooth one is a good way to think about your golf swing. First you lay the tracks (positions), then you feel like a wooden roller coaster (awkwardly working through the positions). Finally, you learn to glide smoothly through the positions like a modern metal rollercoaster (smooth and with no wasted effort).

If you only improve the positions of your swing, you will hit better good shots but your swing won't always feel great. When you develop a rhythm, your swing will become increasingly consistent, resulting in more frequent high-quality shots.

To play at the highest level, dependable tempo goes hand-in-hand with high-quality shots. In fact, tour golfers have such consistently timed movements that there was a book written on the subject (*Tour Tempo* by John Novosel).

3:1 tempo

The tour sequence model is roughly a 3:1 ratio of backswing to downswing. That means that a backswing takes roughly three times as long to complete as a downswing.

> To gauge your own tempo ratio, it's easier to investigate with video than a stop watch. Start from the downswing. Use video and count the number of frames between the top of the swing and impact. Then go back and count frames in the backswing. I would be hesitant to change the natural timing of the downswing, so use the downswing to adjust your backswing. For example, if a solid downswing lasts for 20 frames, accept 20 frames as a good duration. If you need to tweak something with your tempo, try to speed up (or slow down) your backswing so that it takes 60 frames. If you are like most people, you will see that you tend to have a slower-than-normal backswing.
>
> A slower backswing usually results from guiding the club instead of swinging it. Guiding the club prevents you from loading your hips/glutes in the backswing. To involve your lower body more in transition, speed up your backswing.

Insight

This ratio of 3:1 occurs naturally when the body moves athletically instead of forcing the club into perfect positions. It is important to find a swinging rhythm as you learn movements.

Always keep in mind that we want the body to move athletically and freely. There are many more bad swings that are saved with good tempo than there are good swings ruined by bad tempo.

Figure 28.1

Remember the exercise to feel the swinging of the club head (see Figure 17.1)? This is a great way to adopt a natural tempo. It should be similar to the smooth acceleration of the club head you will feel during the release.

The Navy SEALS have an expression: "Slow is smooth, smooth is fast." This idea applies really well to golf and relates to tempo.

> **Insight**
>
> There appears to be a relationship between body tension, level of focus, and smoothness of your tempo.

It can be hard to recognize slight differences in tempo, but you can feel tension levels throughout your body (especially under pressure). Keeping your body relaxed tends to give you more consistent and smooth tempo. Extra tension can be anywhere, but students and other golfers typically store tension in the following places:

- Eyes
- Jaw
- Shoulders
- Belly

- Lower Back

- Forearms

- Feet/ankles

A swing looks smooth when these areas are soft and relaxed. As you improve your sequencing and learn to power the swing from your body, your swing will typically look smoother and have a natural rhythm to it.

CHAPTER 29

Summary of Part 2—Big Picture

How the Body Swings the Club
  Recap of images of the big picture of the body
  Club head path

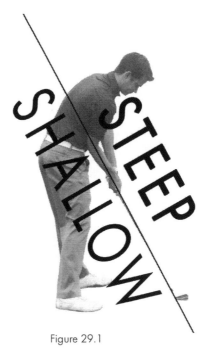

Figure 29.1

Steeps and shallows—check with video; compare to Stock Tour Swing blend
  Before impact—under is shallow, over is steep
  After impact—over is shallow, under is steep
  Want a blend of steeps and shallows throughout

a)   Transition—tour pro blend of steeps and shallows
 b)   Tour pro body movements (mostly steep):
  (1)   Shifts to the left (steep)
  (2)   Flexes forward (steep)
  (3)   Rotates to the left (steep)
 c)   Tour pro arm movements (mostly shallow):
  (1)   Rotates to the right of the body (shallow)
  (2)   Falls to the right of the body (shallow)
  (3)   Lifts slightly (shallow)
d)   Release
 e)   Tour pro body movements (blended):
  (1)   Side bend away from the target (shallow)
  (2)   Extends (shallow)
  (3)   Continues to rotate to the left (steep)
 f)   Tour pro arm movements (mostly shallow):
  (1)   Work across the body to the left (steep)
  (2)   Arms extend away from the body (shallow)
  (3)   Left forearm rotates leftward (steep)
The hand path and club head path are not always the same

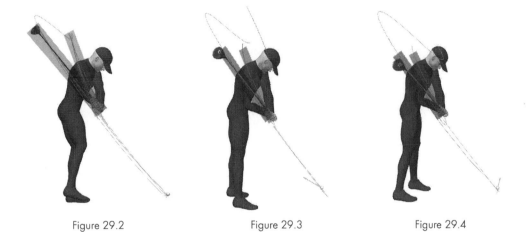

Figure 29.2   Figure 29.3   Figure 29.4

Figure 29.5   Figure 29.6

Impact zone—brush location controlled by
  The sternum's orientation
  What the arms are doing

Figure 29.7

Centered pivot with upper body (less movement than you think)
  Backswing—minimal shift—1–2 inches
  Downswing finishes with upper body going back as lower goes forward—1–2
  inches total difference from set up to impact
  Natural result from how we use the ground, not from trying to stay centered
  Club face movements

Figure 29.8

Figure 29.9

Factors

Grip strength right hand

Grip strength left hand

Movements

a) Wrists

b) Shoulders

c) Body

Ideal combo—grip orientation + gradual closing movements on downswing allow for spine rotation/side bend to produce a long forward brush location and late wide spot

Hand path
    Transition—club head weight under the hand path
    Release—handle up and in as the club head travels down and out
    a)   Ideally from body bracing movement
Overall swing
    Power
    Build phase (before arm parallel)
    Transfer phase (after arm parallel)
    Squat vs. bicep curl
    Backswing for loading total body and club head displacement
    Overhand vs. underhand
Tempo

Figure 29.10

Sequence of movements makes a swing look effortless
Learning movements—want a metal roller coaster, not wooden
Smoothness of about 3:1 ratio

Recap: Linking the Secrets of the Stock Tour Swing

The club head swings around you like an ellipse. Your body is at the center of the swing.
The goal is to produce a swing where the club head gently brushes the ground—a sign

of a good low and wide point. Shot feedback from contact and from ball flight helps you understand the club head and club face at impact. But what about the rest of the swing?

A good way to monitor the club path is to distinguish which movements make it steeper and which ones make it shallower.

Before impact, shallow

- is horizontal

- has a wider radius

- is more in-to-out

- moves the low point back, before the ball

Before impact, steep

- is more vertical

- has a narrower radius

- is more out-to-in

- moves the low point forward, after the ball

Overall, a blend of steeps and shallows throughout the swing will help the club head produce a good brush location and a good flat spot.

To create a good path balance in transition, your arms must be shallow so your body can be slightly steep. Steep body moves in transition create more speed than shallow ones, but they need to be balanced by the arms.

During the release, you want a blend of steeps and shallows from both the body and the arms. Part 3 covers movement combinations in more detail.

The downswing can be broken into two phases. First is the transition, where you build speed in the handle. Next is the release, where you transfer that speed to the club head. To create speed in a dependable golf swing, it is best to use your body's large muscles. During the release, use your body to transfer speed to the club head and use your arms to control the club head path and the club face-to-path relationship.

The all-important brush location (low and wide points) is controlled by a few factors in the impact zone. These include sternum location, elbow straightness, wrist position, and shoulder blade protraction. The impact position can be analyzed by checking how the sternum is oriented and assessing what the arms are doing.

In general, the Stock Tour Swing has a relatively centered pivot. The center of the upper body only moves 1–2 inches away from the target in the backswing. A centered pivot is essential for a swing that properly uses the ground to create speed in transition.

Producing a good path helps you hit the sweet spot and create maximum speed, but to hit straight shots you must also control the face-to-path relationship. Since we want shaft lean at impact, the club face will be more closed to the shaft than it was at set up. The overall pattern is that the club face closes gradually to the shaft during the entire downswing—the shaft rotation balances the club face opening created by shaft lean at impact.

When it comes to creating power, think of a squat versus a bicep curl. A squat uses the whole body and creates more force than if you were to just use your arms. When swinging, use your whole body to create power instead of just your arms and upper body. To produce distance, good impact alignments are more important than absolute speed, since hitting too far off the sweet spot costs major distance. A good training drill is to try using your whole body to swing the club (but make sure you keep a good brush location).

You can produce the Stock Tour Swing by using the whole body to generate speed, a good blend of steeps and shallows, and good club face control. To really dial in your swing, make sure you produce the model swing with fluid tempo. A good way to think about fluid tempo is to consider the difference between riding a metal rollercoaster and a wooden one.

When each body movement is sequenced correctly, your swing should have smooth transition of movement from the ground to the club head. Correct sequencing is critical in the power creation and delivery phases, from the top of the swing to impact.

CHAPTER 30

Putting Part 2 Principles into Practice

The Stock Tour Swing Philosophy

Many golfers want to see overnight improvement. That's possible if you have just one major issue (such as club face or one big path change) and experience a Eureka! moment in which you figure out exactly how to correct it. It's fun when that happens, but more often, the journey to success is a steady climb characterized by big leaps forward and setbacks. Having and sticking to a road map can help you keep climbing the mountain with confidence. Without a road map, it's tempting to return to the bottom and try something new.

I sometimes ask my older golfers, "At what point would you switch to lottery tickets as your retirement strategy?" Most of them give me a puzzled look, then laugh and say, "Never!" They have a road map for their retirement, and it's clear that haphazard strategies like playing the lottery have no place. While winning the lottery will no doubt advance somebody's financial situation, it is unlikely to help the majority of those who play.

However, most golfers jump from idea to idea because they don't REALLY understand the connection each piece has to each other piece, or how the pieces fit into a long-term plan. In Part 3, we cover the details of the swing, but applying this guidance will only result in long-term improvements if you mentally connect Part 3 to the book's first two parts.

I don't let my students focus on things that don't make sense for their swing unless they can argue how it will change the answer to one of these key questions:

How will the idea change how their swing creates or transfers speed?

How will the idea change the path of the club head?

How will the idea change the way the student controls the club face?

Picking random tips because they sound good is like buying a lottery ticket. Choosing tips that sound good in the context of a solid plan is like smart, long-term investing. If you get overwhelmed in Part 3, take a second to step back and think about how a given detail relates to the overall goals of the swing.

Before diving into Part 3, revisit the brush-the-ground drill in Chapter 15. This time, see if you can focus on how the body changes the brush location of the club head. You may find that your hands control the club head for you. Or the location of your sternum may seem more important. You may find that if you produce a good brush, you also lose the club face. Any relationship you can identify is a clue to ultimately understanding your own pattern. Pay attention to the clues and see what you can decode about your golf swing from this simple drill.

When you're ready, move on to Part 3, where we explore the details of the key movements of each phase of the swing.

Part 3

Details of the Swing's Phases

In Part 3, we investigate how to execute each phase of the Stock Tour Swing. As you read, keep in mind the overall shape of the circle and how each phase fits within that model. You may learn about some small key movements—like "bracing" or "the wipe"—that you never even considered. You will be able to discern which movements are critical if you keep in mind the overall swing's shape.

If you have read a lot of golf books, at some point in Part 3 you might find yourself thinking, "So *that's* what that other coach meant when he talked about this." There is a good chance that some movements in each phase will remind you of other descriptions. Perhaps the details and the drills, as well connecting each phase to the overall goal will help you experience a leap with your game.

CHAPTER 31

Why Dissecting the Phases of the Swing Accelerates Learning

Part 3 covers in detail techniques for swinging a club with power, a good flat spot, and a late wide point. It may take a few reads to digest all the details, but be patient. Part 3 is also intended to be a helpful reference you can return to whenever you are working on a specific phase of the swing.

> All the great golfers have developed their own version of the same swing. The indispensable components are all there when you study the swings of elite golfers. As you explore the key movements of each swing phase, you will further understand this point.
>
> *Insight*

When a tour golfer discusses his or her swing, they are often describing their own version of each key movement.

Framework of swing phases

Breaking the swing into rough phases enables:

- Deeper learning of the elite swing
- Stronger breakthroughs in your game
- More efficient problem solving
- A solid foundation for long-term improvement

Your goal in executing a swing is to generate one fluid movement that satisfies all the objectives we discussed in Part 1 and Part 2. However, learning that fluidity involves temporarily dissecting those movements into phases (or chunks). The phases are best learned in isolation, using isolation drills. They can then be put together into a whole, fluid movement, using tempo drills.

Learning to swing a golf club is like learning to play the piano. First you practice what one hand does; then the other hand. Finally, you put both hands together. Think of each phase of the swing as a different hand playing the piano. When you know the goal of each phase, you can recognize which phase needs troubleshooting.

Enjoy the process – learn to focus your training

Remember Ron from Chapter 2? When he understood the swing's different phases, he could identify which was giving him trouble and focus his energy on solving the problem there. Because he knew the objective of each phase, he could focus his efforts. Sometimes problems resolve quickly, but others require more trial and error to negotiate. Enjoy the discovery process.

If you don't know how a drill will serve your swing, you are guessing more than you are problem solving. Truly understanding each phase of the swing lets you adopt a focused framework for troubleshooting it.

> **Insight**
>
> The most important question I ask a golfer when focusing on a certain phase is, "What is the likely miss pattern while you focus on this move?" If your answer is, "I don't know, I should just hit 'em all good. Right?" you need to delve deeper into your understanding of club face, club path, and the club head face-to-path relationship.

When I want to test a student's understanding of a drill, I'll ask, "How close was it to working?" This requires the golfer to identify what worked as well as what didn't work. Their answer reveals how well the golfer read the feedback from the practice session.

Most golfers want just one thing to focus on—one magic swing thought that makes everything click. And in fact, that's the end goal to which most students should aspire. Golf is a lot of fun when you only have one or two things to keep track of to make your swing work. However, to get to that stage, you have to know everything about how your swing works *right now*. Otherwise, when it stops working (and every swing thought will at some point) you will have no clue how to recapture the magic. Getting that one magic swing thought is the whole reason we are learning to be a diagnostician of swing mechanics.

For example, take my swing.

I have the tendency to dominate my swing with my lower body. This tends to create a swing that is too shallow. On the long clubs I can save it by rotating hard and having a stronger release. But that compensation causes me to become too steep with the short clubs, and I can struggle with wedge contact.

The solution for my tendency is a clear feeling of a good transition. Over the years I have learned that if I have a good backswing position to hit, my transition is usually solid. If my swing gets off, those are usually the two areas on which I need to focus to reclaim control of my swing.

Eventually, you can learn your swing and develop one or two thoughts that work for you every time. The only way to get there, though, is to explore each phase during some segment of your training.

Prepare yourself mentally to learn a craft—the craft of the elite golf swing

Golf is a precision game, and developing precision takes time. I think of the process like wine tasting. When you first start tasting wine, you have no idea how others taste oak or cherry—it's just wine! But if you train your palate, you too can detect the subtleties in each glass. It takes patience and discipline to train precision. Mastering a precise activity takes repetition with clear feedback.

Once you have practiced each phase for a month or so (longer for the release and transition), you will be able to adjust more than one phase at a time and enjoy really big performance leaps.

For example, a student I was recently working with was very close to having it all click. He was working on shallowing his path a bit and started to hit some well-struck balls, but they were just a little high and right. That is a likely miss when working on arm shallowing because it opens the club face.

I asked him to try and make the same body move, but to add a little more motorcycle. Because he had worked on the motorcycle move earlier in the year, he recalled that movement to close the face slightly with shaft rotation. Changing two complementary phases at the same time pulled everything together, and he hit some of the best looking shots of his life!

He was unable to have that breakthrough the first time we talked about the motorcycle because it was too much to focus on at one time. As you work through Part 3, you too will likely feel overwhelmed by the details, but with time and practice, you will see how each key phase fits. Eventually you will grasp the simplicity of the Stock Tour Swing, just like all the great golfers have.

Rough phases (movements) and checkpoints (positions)

Set up (position)	Backswing (movement)	Transition (movement)	Impact (position)

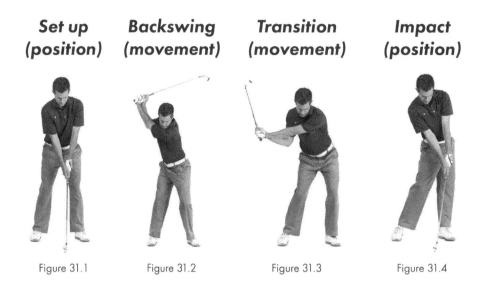

| Figure 31.1 | Figure 31.2 | Figure 31.3 | Figure 31.4 |

Release (movement) leads to follow through (position)

Figure 31.5

If it is hard to visualize something in this section, see it come to life in our videos at http://golfsmartacademy.com/stocktourswingbook.

CHAPTER 32

The Set Up

The set up prepares the body for the swing. There is no magical set up that guarantees a good golf swing. There are, however, set up characteristics that encourage or discourage certain movements.

Let's recap the critical goal of the golf swing:

- To swing your club head in a circle/ellipse around your body on a path angled at the ball, with a good club head flat spot in the impact zone.

- To swing the club that way, your body needs to create a somewhat centered pivot and a swing that is powered from the legs and core.

Using the Stock Tour Swing problem-solving approach, set up should give you the best opportunity to use your legs and core to power your swing, and to position your body in a way that promotes a shallow delivery path. Set up is not just about the body. It also includes your grip and arm position. A good set up includes a grip that matches your swing and an arm position that lets you easily control the club face and club path.

Set up has a few key goals. As with everything in this program, we start with some images and then dive into the finer details.

Set up images:

Figure 32.1   Figure 32.2   Figure 32.3

Three different perspectives of the same set up. Your goal is not to recreate the exact same look, but to satisfy the set up objectives in a way that works with your body.

Set up objectives:
Bend from the hips (not the lower spine)
Establish consistent alignment to encourage your body to rotate
Establish proper lead foot turnout
Let the arms hang
Use a grip that supports free wrist movements and desireable club face alignments

Bending from the hips

Bending from the hips tilts the circle at the ball without over-bending the spine. Bending the spine too much challenges its ability to rotate, while bending from the hips prepares those muscles, and those of the core, to pivot. In the backswing, we want to rotate into the trail hip as we rotate, extend, and side bend our spine. To make this combined spine movement easier, we want set up to include a neutral spine. There are some common ways that golfers create set up challenges.

| Figure 32.4 | Figure 32.5 | Figure 32.6 | Figure 32.7 |

- S posture—excessive anterior tilt of the pelvis, excessive extension of the lumber spine, excessive kyphosis in the upper back

- C posture—posterior tilt of the pelvis, flexed lumbar spine, excessive kyphosis in the upper back

- N posture—relatively neutral pelvis and lumbar spine, slight rounding of the upper back

- Excessive knee bend—nearly vertical pelvic angle

> Achieving a neutral posture is not just for appearance. It's to set up the right muscles. Set up posture—along with a good hip hinge—should primarily engage the glutes and abs, and should secondarily engage the quads. Using the hips to bend and the abs to stabilize creates a strong platform to load in the backswing and fire in the downswing.
>
> *Insight*

Body alignment

Figure 32.8

Amateur golfers often think they must be perfectly aligned to hit a good shot. While perfect alignment is impossible, there is one key alignment of which to be aware. Excessive spine twist can limit a rotational sport like golf. If the shoulders and pelvis are pointing in drastically different directions, the swing is in trouble. A common amateur error is to have the shoulders significantly more open than the pelvis.

Lead foot turnout

Figure 32.9   Figure 32.10   Figure 32.11

The lead foot position can impede a good impact position. If your lead foot is perpendicular to the target line, you need a lot of hip rotation to achieve a finish position. It's important to pick a foot position that better supports your swing. Setting up with the lead foot square to the target line makes sense visually, but limits lower-body rotation.

To identify the lead foot position for your swing, try an experiment. Assume your set up posture, but place your hands on your hips instead of the club. Next, without standing up out of your posture, turn your belt buckle to point at the target. If you can't point your belt buckle at the target, stop and restart the experiment. On a second attempt, turn out your lead foot more and repeat the drill. Repeat until you find a lead foot position that allows you to reach a full finish.

This new foot position may change your backswing a bit, but building a swing around solid impact makes more sense than building a swing around a good backswing.

Arm hang

Figure 32.12   Figure 32.13   Figure 32.14   Figure 32.15

It doesn't really matter where your arms are at set up; what matters is where your arms are at impact. That being said, if your arms don't hang at set up, or if they are too far from or close to the body, it can be challenging to maintain good balance throughout the swing.

If at set up, your arms are tense or your shoulder blades are shrugged forward, you will likely initiate your takeaway with the muscles of your shoulders and arms instead of the hips and spine. To avoid an arm-dominated takeaway, your arms should hang roughly from the shoulder socket. The exact position depends on which club you are using.

Try another experiment. Start in your set up posture and take your trail hand off the club. Let the arm hang with no muscular effort, and notice its location compared to the lead hand.

With the driver, the right hand should swing evenly with the pinky side of the left hand. With an iron, the right hand should swing even more to the index finger side of the left hand.

Grip

A good grip enables the wrists and arms to move freely. The contact points between the hands and club are the most important part of the grip.

Time for another experiment. Assume your normal grip, and then remove one hand at a time to see how each hand contacts the grip. A good reference is to compare the grip contact to the knuckles. Is the grip above or below the knuckle (distal metacarpal)? If it's on the fingertip side or below the knuckle, the grip is "in the fingers." If it's on the palm side of the knuckle, it's in the palm.

Gripping below (toward the finger side of those bones) is like gripping a suitcase, or a ball. Gripping above (toward the palm side of those bones) is like gripping a baseball bat or tennis racquet. In golf we do a little of each.

For the lead hand, you want the index finger knuckle below and the pinky finger knuckle above, so it works diagonally into the palm. With the trail hand, you want to grip it more in the fingers. Look at the contact points anatomically, then see how it looks in practice.

Images of keys to good grip—it's all about the knuckles

Lead Hand—locations of contact

1—Palm side of pinky metacarpal, finger side of index finger metacarpal

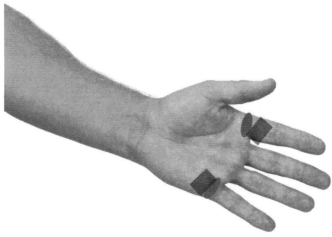

Figure 32.16

For the left hand, the pressure will be at the round spots in this image, on the palm side of the last knuckle and the finger side of the first knuckle.

2—Trail Hand

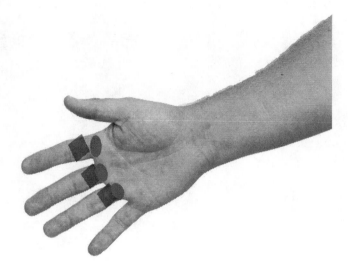

Figure 32.17

For the right hand, the pressure will be at the round spots in this image, on the finger side of the first, second, and third knuckles.

Grip strength

How the hands are placed on the club is typically referred to as grip strength. For this section, I'll use a right-handed golfer as the example instead of saying lead and trail.

When swinging the club, the arms create a certain alignment at impact. The club face can be rotated right (open) or left (closed) compared to that alignment. The more the club face is turned to the left (closed), the more it delofts the club and is a "strong" grip. The more the club is turned to the right (open), the more it is a "weak" grip.

Each hand has an influence on how open or closed the club face is at impact, but in my experience, the left hand has a greater influence.

The range of grip strength is fairly small. A common grip strength reference is the line from your thumb and index finger. The V formed by the thumb and index finger will point between your chin and your trail shoulder. This range creates a "grip strength window." If the Vs points more toward the chin, the grip is weak. If the Vs point more toward the shoulder, the grip is strong.

Figure 32.18

Figure 32.19

The more the thumbs are pointed toward the right shoulder, the more the grip is considered strong. The more they are pointed toward the chin, the more the grip is considered weak. Here, from left to right, we see different combinations of strong, neutral, or weak. Note that the reference lines from each hand don't have to match each other, but they often do.

The more the Vs point toward your nose at set up, the more they add loft, open the face, and require the wrists to change between address and impact. You are also more likely to fade/slice and will need to bow (motorcycle) to hit straight shots.

The more the Vs point toward your trail shoulder, the more they decrease loft, close the face, and require body rotation and side bend between address and impact. It doesn't necessarily make you more likely to hit a hook, but you will be more likely to hit it low.

Danger position—weak trail hand

A potentially dangerous grip set up is a weak trail hand. While most tour pros have a stronger grip than most amateurs, there are a number of great ball strikers who have a weak lead hand. This means they simply flex the wrist more to compensate.

But in my experience, if you position your right hand in an overly weak position, it is physically impossible to extend the wrist enough to square the face. As a result, you will have trouble getting sufficient shaft lean and chest rotation at impact.

> If you set up with a weak trail hand, at impact your torso will be more square to compensate. This can work for short irons but can be a major barrier to creating the flat spot with the driver.
>
> *Insight*

Grip pressure

Grip pressure is frequently discussed (you may have been told to hold the club like a baby bird or a tube of toothpaste), but hard to measure. Sensors can be placed in the grip, but since the hands overlap, it's hard to know exactly which hand is pushing. Also, since the club has a lot of momentum in the swing, at certain times it's hard to tell if the golfer is pushing on the club or if the club is pushing on the golfer. The sensor reads each scenario exactly the same.

The data presented in grip studies suggests that amateur golfers have more grip pressure than professionals at a couple key points in the swing.

- Set up—professionals tend to have softer grip pressure at set up, especially with the trail hand.

- Top of the swing/transition—professionals tend to decrease grip pressure of the trail hand during transition, while amateurs tend to increase it during the same time. **Too much grip pressure in the trail hand prevents the club from shallowing during transition.**

- Impact—professionals have very little grip pressure at impact with either hand, but the trail hand is usually less than the lead. Amateurs tend to still have a fair amount of grip pressure at impact, especially with the trail hand.

Insight

The old adage of keeping your arms relaxed during the swing appears to be supported by research. If you use your body as the engine, your arms will be fairly relaxed and you will benefit from the decreased grip pressure.

Useful set up parameters

Every chapter in Part 3 offers ranges for each part of your body at set up. The numbers are intended to serve as a guide. You should not obsess over them or use them to achieve perfection.

Remember, the movements of the swing are designed to work together in a harmonious swing that produces the shape of the club head path and club face control you learned in Part 1.

Knowing the ranges can help you identify checkpoints for when you get lost. You might be excited or intimidated by the level of detail, but don't worry. In addition to the detailed breakdown, I also provide ways to simplify each checkpoint to one or two drills in this book. Additional drills can be found on my website.

Useful set up parameters

Figure 32.20   Figure 32.21   Figure 32.32

Body parameters

- Thorax bent forward (about 40 degrees)
- Pelvis bent forward (about 20 degrees)
- Thorax side bend (about 10 degrees)
- Minimal spine rotation

Arm parameters

- Lead arm elbow bent (about 20 degrees)
- Trail arm elbow bent (about 35 degrees)

Wrist Parameters

- Lead wrist extended (about 25 degrees)
- Trail wrist only slightly extended or slightly flexed

Even if you are not a very technical person, set up drills can be trained with precision because they take place before the actual swing. Once you have a solid set up, the next checkpoint to explore is impact.

Recap: Linking the Secrets of the Stock Tour Swing

A good set up does not guarantee a good swing, but it can reveal whether a golfer intends to create speed with the arms or the body. Poor posture at set up can promote poor movements during the downswing. Good spine alignment is key. You don't need to have a perfectly parallel set up to the target line. However, making a solid pivot can be difficult if you have the upper body and pelvis rotated in different directions. In addition to spine alignment, having the front foot too square to the target line can make it more challenging to reach a good finish position.

Set up includes more than just body position—it also includes the grip. Having a grip in the fingers at set up is important to have free movement of the wrists.

Another important alignment is that of the hands to the shoulders. Check your set up distance by relaxing your right hand completely and see where it is in relationship to the left hand. It should be close to the same place whether on the grip or hanging down.

CHAPTER 33

Impact! (The Moment of Truth)

t may seem odd to discuss impact right after set up. Shouldn't we discuss the backswing next?

If you think about it, in most sports it is typical to learn set up first and then contact. In golf, your goal at impact is to transfer as much energy as possible into the ball. To transfer maximum energy, there are a few desired positions to achieve. These positions are proof of quality movements, which we will discuss in the "Release" section in Chapter 36.

Impact—How has the body changed from set up.

| Figure 33.1 | Figure 33.2 | Figure 33.3 | Figure 33.4 |

As you can see, the body position is completely different at impact then at set up. We will break the swing movements down into trainable chunks, but for now, just notice this difference.

A common misconception among novice golfers is to think that impact position is identical to set up. This is not the case, not at all. Every part of the body changes from set up to impact.

The body

How has the body changed position compared to set up?

- The upper body is slightly closer to the ground.
- The upper body is side bent away from the target.
- Both the upper and lower body are rotated toward the target.
- The pelvis is shifted laterally toward the target, more so than the upper body.
- The lead wrist is flexed, and the trail wrist is more extended.
- The elbows are more bent (but extending); the trail arm more so.

One drill unifies all those changes into one checkpoint—the merry-go-round drill in this chapter. In the release section (Chapter 36), we will learn about the movements that create this impact position. But training impact as a reference is helpful for many golfers. You can even train the position at home or the office!

The club

One of the biggest changes from set up to impact is that the club handle is closer to the target than where it started. The key is to shift the handle closer without steepening the club head angle of attack. To avoid becoming steep, a balanced mix of steeps and shallows need to create the handle forward result.

Figure 33.5   Figure 33.6

The club handle is closer to the target at impact. This creates the shaft lean we want. Shaft lean is critical for transferring energy to the golf ball and for building the flat spot.

The body parameters

Figure 33.7

Observe the changes between set up and impact. A good reference for unifying the changes is the sternum. Notice how much the sternum has changed position from set up to impact.

Rotational changes

1. The lower body is rotated significantly (40 degrees).
2. The sternum is also rotated significantly (30 degrees).
3. The upper body is side bent (25–35 degrees).
4. The pelvis is side bent (10 degrees).
5. The pelvis is flexed (15 degrees or more).
6. The chest is flexed about the same as it was at set up.

Linear changes

1. The lower body is closer to the target (3–6 inches).
2. Driver—the upper body is farther from the target (1–2 inches).
3. Irons—the upper body is closer to the target (1–2 inches).
4. The lower body is barely closer to the golf ball.
5. The upper body is barely moved away from the ball (about 1.5 inchs).
6. The lower body is lifted (1–2 inches).
7. The upper body is about the same height.
8. The upper body is barely moved away from the ball (less than 1 inch).

| Figure 33.8 | Figure 33.9 | Figure 33.10 |

Set up

Get in your golf posture with your arms crossed. Hold a club across your shoulders so that it sticks out past your trail shoulder.

Execution

Bump your hips and then rotate your upper body so the golf club points in the general direction of the ball—usually about a foot or two behind the ball, but on the target line.

Focus and questions

Did you stand up? Are your hips closer to the target than your sternum?

The body is rotated, side bent, and bracing away from the target (see Chapter 36 for more on the bracing movement). The extent to which the body is rotated and side bent depends on the club. There is more bracing with the driver, and less with the wedges. We will cover the differences between the driver and iron swings in the shot shaping section (see Part 4, Chapter 38), but establish a baseline impact position before you make those adjustments.

To feel the overall impact body position, try the merry–go-round drill. It gets you close to where your body wants to be and combines all the different parameters into one feel.

This body position is a key reference to train because it sets up the flat spot. Remember that wherever the sternum is pointed at impact is roughly where the arms will extend. It is easier to achieve the desired flat and wide spot with a lot of body rotation and side bend at impact.

To better understand the arms, let's explore how they've changed from set up to impact.

Arms

Right elbow bent but extending (about 40 degrees).

1. Right shoulder adducting (working across the body).
2. Left wrist flat or bowed (20–40 degrees more flexed).
3. Right wrist cupped (20–30 degrees more extended).
4. Left forearm more pronated (about 30 degrees more pronated).
5. Right forearm supinating.
6. Both wrists are ulnar deviating (unhinging).

Figure 33.11   Figure 33.12

The arms have changed in many ways, but the greatest change is in the wrist and forearm movements. From an overhead view, you can clearly see the wrist differences.

The arms and the body work together. The body has rotated and is side bent into a new position; the arm changes balance those movements. You will achieve the arm movements described above if, when you practice your impact position, your hands are roughly in front of where your sternum is pointing (and your body is in a good merry-go-round position).

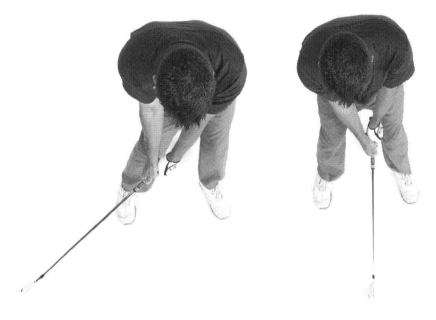

Figure 33.13   Figure 33.14

Most amateur golfers are surprised when they see impact from overhead. Impact location for the club head is not directly in front of the chest, like at set up. It is actually behind your body, about 20–30 degrees to the right of it.

I like to show my students what happens to the different club locations from set up to impact if I just change my arms but not my body. It really highlights the spatial location of impact compared to the sternum. It makes clear that the sternum needs to point a few feet down the target line at impact.

From overhead, if only the arms are in impact position, then "impact" is not where the ball is. The arms are slightly behind the body, with the club much more behind it and the club face more closed to the shaft than you would imagine. The merry-go-round drill is great for showing how the body moves that arm position to impact.

Impact is so important. Take a second to really digest these pictures. Imagine how it all fits together. This impact position is what enables you to produce the good flat and wide spot. You can't create those if both of your arms are straight at impact.

Figure 33.15

As we discussed in the brush location section of Chapter 20 the different body and arm positions complement each other. If the body is facing the ball, the arms will be straight. If the body is facing down the target line, the arms will be bent.

Recap: Linking the Secrets of the Stock Tour Swing

Impact is an important checkpoint to clearly understand. Comparing the positions of the club and body at set up to impact will reveal that almost every part of the body has changed.

The club handle is closer to the target than it was in set up, and since you have shaft lean, the club face will be more closed to the shaft. The arms are slightly more bent than they were at impact and you will typically have more side bend and rotation, especially with the driver. The lower body will be closer to the target than the upper body, and even more so with the driver than the irons. The wrists will also change from set up to impact (in order to close the face to the shaft). The lead wrist will be more flexed and the trail wrist will be more extended. The Stock Tour Swing impact position is important for building that all-important flat and wide spot after the ball.

CHAPTER 34

Follow Through

The body

Figure 34.1

Figure 34.2

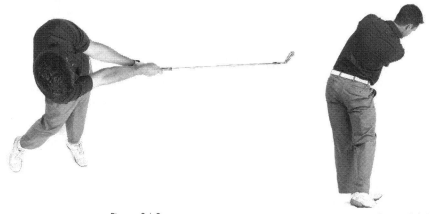

Figure 34.3

Figure 34.4

Observe the changes from impact to follow through. It appears that I keep my spine angle and straighten my arms, but there is more to it than that.

In my opinion, the follow through position is officially the end of the swing. As such, it's an important position to train. Even guys with funky follow throughs like Arnold Palmer or Tommy Gainey look fairly similar at this checkpoint. Their weird moves happen as they move toward the finish and are usually just the way they safely slow down the fast-moving club.

Most amateurs fly through the follow through position with little thought about its importance. Many have a hard time stopping at the follow through position when cued to do so.

On the range, many pro golfers practice swings that end by holding the follow through position. They hold the position comfortably, analyzing each little detail. This is a common end point for punch shots and short iron swings, so it is a useful move to take to the course.

From impact, the follow through position develops as you continue rotating, side bending, and extending (the trio of moves we refer to as bracing), as the arms extend and the lead arm rotates. You will learn in the transition section of Chapter 36, that much of the arm extension move is triggered from bracing during the release, but it's something to start thinking about here.

> If you have a hard time stopping at the follow through, it means you are bending your arms or rehinging your wrists through impact. Golfers with a good wide brush location can almost always stop at the follow through position without any problem. For this reason, it's a great diagnostic for revealing the intention of the arm movements near impact.
>
> *Insight*

From impact to the follow through, the upper body shows more extension, much more side bend, and is much more rotated than at impact. For the full swing, the key movements between impact and follow through are:

Rotational parameters

1. Continue rotation to close the gap between the pelvis and the upper body (each should have the same amount of rotation).
2. Achieve maximum side bend (upper and lower body).
3. Keep extending—the extension continues during the entire release (up to 30 degrees).

Linear parameters

1. Achieve maximum lift for both the upper and lower body.
2. The upper body works slightly away from the target as the lower body continues toward the target.
3. Achieve maximum differential between the location of the upper and lower body (a difference of up to 8 inches with driver).

The body plays a large role in creating the wide and flat spots. During the release, you'll learn to complement the body movements by moving the arms correctly. To create the flat spot, the body braces (extend hips, keeps side bending, keeps rotating, and the upper body moves slightly away from the target). Again, the good thing about this position is that you've already hit the ball—if you are hitting less than full shots, you can simply hold it.

Many people find it odd to experience maximum difference between the upper and lower body, at least at first. But great drivers tend to have a greater distance between their upper and lower body at follow through. If you try this and hit it either very heavy or off to the right, your arms are getting involved too soon and your club face is open.

If you get into the follow through position and feel any back pain, it usually indicates you are not using your glute muscles to create the motion. See a qualified coach or therapist to help you work through any back pain; it's a tough problem to fix by self-coaching.

The arms

Figure 34.5   Figure 34.6

Notice the rotation of the forearms. The extent of rotation that is visible on video depends on what the shoulders have done, but almost everyone rotates their forearms.

The arm movements between impact and follow through reveal key information concerning their movements at impact. In the Stock Tour Swing, three key checkpoints are:

1. Arms extend/elbows closer
2. Left forearm supinates/trail forearm pronates
3. Shaft orientation compared to the body

Function of the key arm movements

1. Arms extend/elbow closer—this moves the wide point later, makes the path shallower.
2. Left forearm supination—this move is the best way to absorb speed while extending the arms.
3. Shaft orientation—this checkpoint is a great indicator for identifying your overall path.

Remember the importance of identifying your path and face relationships? One checkpoint for analyzing the swing path is the shaft orientation when it is parallel to the ground in the follow through. Where the club handle points at the body can help reveal the swing's direction.

For a right-handed golfer, the more the club head points left of the target line, the more likely the path was an outside-in strike (unless you hit down on the ball an excessive amount). The more the club head points at the right of the target line, the more the path was likely in-to-out or to the right.

| Figure 34.7 | Figure 34.8 | Figure 34.9 |

The follow through position is a critical checkpoint for your swing. It can reveal the movements you make through impact and where you will have trouble in a full swing.

The follow through position is the end of the swing. By that I mean it is the point at which you are finished with all the critical movements. The rest of the swing, and the finish position, are just ways to absorb force in a safe and economical way.

> Momentum is what finishes the swing after the follow through position. Be wary of any tips you hear regarding a particular finish position; contact issues can arise for golfers who try to force a finish position.
>
> *Insight*

The follow through position allows you to monitor several critical things: the right side bend, extension of the pelvis/spine/rib cage, and the extension of the arms before the wrists release.

The right side bend will continue from impact

It is not until after the follow through position that you should start to stand up (left bend) out of your side bend. This delayed stand is what gives the appearance of maintaining a spine angle.

The spine extends and the pelvis posterior tilts, or tucks

Make sure you are using your hips (glutes) to initiate the total body extension, rather than the lower back. The combined tucking of the hips and extension of the midback creates the look of the classic "reverse C" pose.

The desired hip and spine movements create a stable platform for your arms to accelerate away from through impact.

The arms extend before releasing the wrists

Some schools of thought refer to the angle of the wrists as the "flying wedge" and regard the wrist angle as key to controlling the low point. From my years reviewing 3D data, I tend to find that the space between the elbows is even more important for the low point (and even more so for the widest point). Consistently narrowing the elbows between impact and follow through is very important for building that flat spot of the arc.

At follow through, the elbows should be as close together as you can get them without rounding (protracting) your shoulder blades. Closing the elbow spacing typically involves straightening each elbow and rotating the left forearm. If you try to get most of the rotation with the trail arm—especially the trail shoulder rotation—then the bottom of the swing tends to move backward and you will struggle with contact misses.

If you let your arms extend to the follow through position while your lower body resists against the ground in the bracing movement, you will typically feel a little tug from the club. If you have a buddy willing to help you, you can get this sense via an exercise I do with many students.

Bracing exercise (you'll need a helping hand)

Assume a good follow through position and have a friend give the club a tug on its head. Feel your arms give out just a little bit more—you want to experience this feeling in your swing. The club has a lot of momentum through impact, and I have heard a number of good ball strikers describe the "tug from the club" just after the ball as a sign of a free release. If you don't feel a tug, you probably have too much arm tension and are not letting your arms extend through impact.

Now that you have a sense of the key positions to monitor (set up, impact, follow through), let's dive into the movements that blend them into one unified swing.

Recap: Linking the Secrets of the Stock Tour Swing

The follow through position marks the end of the swing's active elements. In the full swing, you will fly through that position with speed, but in training, when taking less than full swings, it is a good checkpoint to monitor.

Compared to impact, the body movements that carry you to the follow through position are continued rotation, side bend, and extension. The hips move slightly toward the target and the upper body slightly away from it.

The most important arm movement is the extension between impact and follow through position. As the arms extend, the forearms will continue rotating in order to absorb force, and square the face (which we discuss in the release section (Chapter 36).

The shaft orientation to the body at follow through is a good checkpoint for your overall path tendencies.

CHAPTER 35

Movements

Positions are great checkpoints to train. But if you rely too much on positions, your golf swing will lack "wholeness." A good golf swing is a symphony of movements that blend together to produce a rhythmic, fluid action.

Imagine the swing as a basketball team. In that game, it's not always the best player that wins the title, but rather the best team. Some teams might have one great player, like Michael Jordan or LeBron James. But if that team is to win a championship, it needs good role players.

In the golf swing, a golfer with very skilled hands will have the most success if the body doesn't try to do too much (like a role player trying to be the hero). Conversely, a golfer with superb body awareness who creates great speed and club head path needs "role" contributions from the arms if she is to satisfactorily square the face and time the arm extension.

While a great team could feature one superstar, the best teams typically balance a few great players. Similarly, some good golfers might have one area of their body that is supremely coordinated, but the best golfers tend to have adequate ability with their body as well as their arms.

A lot of good amateurs never reach their potential because they have one area (their body or their arms) that works well and a bunch of other areas that sabotage the swing.

In this section, we discuss the movements of the body and how the arms work with the hands—each in isolation and together. Working on your weaknesses can be frustrating and difficult, but is critical for long-term progress. Long-term training starts with understanding where your swing is now and what movements you need to add to move it in the right direction. Let's dive into the key movements of each phase, starting with the backswing.

Backswing

The body

Figure 35.1   Figure 35.2   Figure 35.3

Notice the body pivot and arms. Like a loaded gun, they look set and ready to fire. In this chapter we cover the moves of the backswing that produce a similar look.

The backswing is the windup that prepares for the downswing. It has two main goals:

1. To create distance between the hands and the ball.

2. To achieve a body position capable of powerfully pushing against the ground.

As we highlighted in Part 2, tour golfers have a centered pivot look during the backswing. They achieve that look by properly using the ground, not by restricting the upper body's movement. Let's look at how the body has changed compared to the preceding reference frame—the set up.

Body movements during the backswing

Rotational parameters

- Rotate upper body 90 degrees and lower body 45 degrees

- Side bend away from target—upper body 40 degrees and lower body 10 degrees

- Reduced flexion of the spine

Linear parameters

- Minimal lateral shift—either away from the target with the driver (1–2 inches away) or toward the target with the irons (1–2 inches towards)
- Slight drop of upper and lower body
- Minimal shift of the upper body toward the golf ball

The backswing pivot is relatively simple to train. It should remind you of the loading pattern in other sports. Whether it's throwing or striking, the engine is the same—you want to use your hips and legs against the ground to create force. To do this, you have to load (stretch) the glute muscles during the backswing. You also must avoid overly shifting your upper body over your trail leg.

Try this simple drill to experience all of the backswing's body movements. Swing your arms across your chest and point your lead shoulder in the general direction of the ball.

How to feel the body movements in the backswing

| Figure 35.4 | Figure 35.5 | Figure 35.6 | Figure 35.7 |

Each golfer will feel the basic body movements of the backswing differently. Some feel crunched. Some feel loaded or coiled. Some feel centered. The key is to be in a good position to start the downswing's key movements.

Set up
With your arms across your shoulders, get in your golf posture with a golf ball in normal ball position.

Execution
Make a backswing pivot, trying to get the lead shoulder to point just outside the golf ball.

Focus and questions
Where do I feel it in my body? Can I do it without arching my lower back? With out swaying?

Two errors to monitor

Keeping the trail leg bent. Contrary to what golf instruction historically pushed, for most golfers, the trail leg will straighten a bit during the backswing. Trying to keep your knee exactly the same flex as set up can make you more likely to sway. You may feel like the knee doesn't change, but if it actually doesn't then you are in the minority of tour pros. You don't want to lock out the knee at the top. But as the hip turns, some natural knee straightening typically occurs (usually less than 10 degrees).

Arching the lower back to stay centered (left tilt). Staying centered is a byproduct of a good pivot, if you do it correctly. Some golfers arch their lower back to finish the backswing, but doing so can cause back pain. Also, arching your back typically moves your pelvis above your trail foot, which can upset your foot pressure pattern. Remember, to create speed, you need the foot pressure to be far from your center. A proper pivot makes that possible.

Now that your body has experienced a good pivot, let's discuss the arm movements that prepare you for transition.

Arm movements during the backswing

1. Left arm slightly lifts and the lead forearm rotates
2. Left wrist hinges
3. Right arm lifts/rotates
4. Right wrist extends
5. Right shoulder blade slightly retracts

DRILL - BACKSWING JUST THE ARMS

Figure 35.8   Figure 35.9

The backswing's basic arm movements look simple when you take away the movement of the body. Practice just the arm movements when training your backswing.

Set up
With or without a club, face a mirror

Execution
Hold an object or club and bend your trail arm, cup the trail wrist and let your hands drift outside your trail shoulder

Focus and questions
Did my arms rotate? Can I control the movement with either the lead or the trail arm?

There really is no "top of backswing" position, since the backswing should fluidly transition into the downswing. It's similar to the transition from load to fire when throwing a ball overhand.

In golf, the backswing's gradual end overlaps with the beginning of the downswing. I bring this up now because as you'll see in Chapter 36, some of the arm movements continue until you finish transition and start the release. The backswing's arm movements will make a lot more sense once you understand the downswing's arm movements.

One of the most important movements of the backswing is the rotation of the arms. Many amateurs try to hold their arms in front of their body the same as during set up, but almost no tour pros do that—and the ones who do have a major flattening move during transition (Jim Furyk, Ryan Palmer).

Insight — Any advice to "keep the hands and arms the same as set up" is a misguided attempt to keep the club face square during the swing. As you saw in Chapter 11, square does not mean the same thing at the top of the backswing as it did at address.

Your arms should rotate to create a good swing plane. They either rotate a lot in transition (like Jim Furyk), a lot in the backswing (like Ray Floyd), or gradually in both (most pros). Without arm rotation in the backswing, you won't be able to rotate your body with a good shoulder plane; you also won't be able to rotate the body open in the downswing without the club head path getting too steep.

To better digest the backswing's movements, we can break the backswing down into two phases—the takeaway and setting the club.

Backswing part 1—the takeaway

The takeaway is a simple movement, but one that is easy to perform incorrectly. A good one-piece takeaway involves turning and side bending the thoracic spine. The takeaway should feature equal amounts of side bend and rotation. There will be a good shift of pressure to the inside of your trail foot. The wrists usually won't change much during the takeaway, but the shoulders should have started to rotate to balance the left tilt of the body and keep the club working on plane.

To ensure the club head doesn't get too far off plane during the takeaway, use the shaft parallel position as a checkpoint. The shaft alignment should be roughly parallel to the target line at this point.

Backswing part 2—setting the club

The second half of the backswing features continued rotation/side bend of the body. New movements in this phase include extending the spine, lifting the arms to load the shoulders, and rotating the trail arm.

The extension of the spine first appears during this part of the backswing to help you push your trail leg against the ground and start the change of direction. The arm movements should take place as a result of the arms being somewhat relaxed and the club head being thrown passively upward by the body movements. Instead of the arms actively lifting to put the club in position, they will react to the movement of the center of the body. If the arms are too active, you will likely mess up your tempo and disrupt the loading of your lower body.

Two weird movements occur during the second half of the backswing. First, your body begins to extend as you use the ground to push yourself toward the target. Second, the arms rotate, which helps set up the arm shallowing movement during transition. Rotation is due to the lead forearm pronating and the trail shoulder rotating externally. A checkpoint for proper trail arm rotation is the location of the trail elbow at the top of your swing. It should be more in front of your chest than behind your body.

Recap: Linking the Secrets of the Stock Tour Swing

The backswing is the swing's first movement. While it is usually experienced as one movement, it can be broken down into two phases. The start of the swing, called the takeaway, is largely a body movement; the arms change only slightly. The core muscles primarily control this one-piece takeaway. During the takeaway, the pressure in your feet shifts to the trail foot and readies your body for the downswing.

The second half of the backswing is called setting the club. During this phase, your arms will rotate and set the club with the wrists. At the same time, to keep your spine angle, your body will rotate, side bend, and extend. If you do this correctly, your lead shoulder will point roughly at the golf ball (or a little bit outside of it); your arms will extend away from your body; and your trail elbow will be more in front of your chest than around the side of it.

CHAPTER 36

Movements of the Downswing

Before we dive into the details of the downswing, I want to issue a slight disclaimer. Training the downswing has higher short-term risk/reward, but also higher potential leaps in improvement compared to training set up, backswing, impact, or follow through. Downswing movements can be challenging, if you do them incorrectly it can disrupt performance worse than anything you've tried before. However, training downswing movements can also herald some of your biggest Eureka! moments and propel your swing to the next level.

The goal of the downswing is to achieve a fluid athletic motion. As you get into the details, know that the first dozen tries may be uncomfortable and require patience.

> **Insight**
>
> When learning a new movement, make practice swings without a ball. Simply try to brush the ground before you try it with a ball in front of you.

It always bothers me when the downswing is described as something that should happen naturally. In reality, the backswing has many detailed steps to practice.

The downswing was taught to me as either "swing out to right field," "swing smoothly," or "cover/trap the ball." These vague descriptions were probably due to the technological limitations of the time. Video lacked the frame rate to analyze the downswing, while the backswing was easier to study because everything moved slower. In fact, understanding the downswing was challenging until the advent of 3D motion analysis.

> **Insight**
>
> Good ball strikers have found a similar way to swing the club, and those similarities are greater on the downswing than they are on the backswing and set up.

In this section, the downswing is broken down into two phases—transition (the building speed phase) and release (the transferring speed phase).

Transition—building speed in the handle

Figure 36.1

Figure 36.2

Figure 36.3

Figure 36.4

Figure 36.5

Figure 36.6

The transition marks the blend from backswing to downswing. The body creates speed in the handle and the arms are poised to transfer that speed to the club head.

The transition is the first phase of the downswing. Its main goal is to build as much speed in the handle as possible, as quickly as possible, so you have more time to transfer that speed to the club head. While building speed it is important to start creating a path with a balance of steeps and shallows. You also want to start squaring the club face to the path. Create speed. Develop the path. Start closing the face. Get those three things right and the rest of the swing is much easier.

The timing of the transition is a little tricky. We commonly think of the swing as having two parts—a backswing and a downswing. This implies that the backswing ends all at once, and then the downswing begins. In reality, the backswing blends into the downswing, and I refer to that blending phase and early downswing as transition.

Blending means that the lower body changes from the backswing to downswing direction before the shoulders and the arms do, and that they all change direction before the club head. There is a sequence to it. A slow transition, or pause, is often a sign of a good swing.

The body must make a couple key moves when you start transition so you can sequence movement from the ground up. The two moves are a slight hip bump and slight left tilt/regain flexion of the spine. While the body builds speed, the arms shallow and we start to close the club face to the path.

Remember from the power section, Chapter 24, that the transition phase is our only chance to build speed. This means that our big muscles should create speed in the handle by working through the arms. We are best served when we use our big leg and core muscles, while the arms focus on getting into position in a relaxed way. In order for the lower body to use the ground to create a force before the delivery position, it will start to change direction much earlier than you think.

The lower body will start pushing toward the target mid-backswing, and keep pushing throughout transition. The pushing helps create speed and give the lower body the right platform.

Transition crunch (regaining flex)

Many amateur golfers avoid the transition crunch—when you regain flexion and slightly increase left tilt during the early stages of the downswing. The transition crunch creates the look of retaining posture during transition.

When amateurs omit the transition crunch, they look like they are "standing up" during the downswing. Standing up makes sense for amateurs because standing up is a major shallowing movement of the club, and most amateurs have steep arm movements that need to be balanced. Without the "bump and crunch," amateur golfers have difficulty creating a good flat spot or creating speed early enough to transfer it during the release.

Jackson 5 (hip bump)

When you change directions from backswing to downswing, shift your weight to the lead foot by pushing off the trail foot. The trail foot should push toward the target instead of toward the golf ball. Visually, this is easier to see in the hip than in the feet—on video, it looks like a hip bump in which the hip leads the body laterally toward the target. You can see a subtle inward roll of the trail ankle, but the hip bump is more visually pronounced. Shifting your weight is best done by sequencing the movement from the ground up. While the weight is shifting, do the transition crunch. When you add the transition crunch, make sure that it is triggered from the core, not from the neck/shoulders.

The body moves of transition

From the backswing section to mid-downswing (transition), here is how the body changes.

Rotational movements
1. Left shoulder very slightly side bends during the early shift
2. Spine flexes forward
3. Pelvis rotates back to face the golf ball, while the thorax (chest) remains slightly closed
4. Trail ankle rolls inward by pushing off the inside of the foot

Linear movements
1. Upper and lower body move lateral towards the target but lower moves more than upper (1–3 inches each)
2. Pelvis moves away from the ball (no early extension)
3. Upper and lower body drop closer to the golf ball (1–2 inches)

This probably sounds complicated and parts may sound counterintuitive. But in reality, it's only two movements to train—the left tilt/flexion move (transition crunch move), and the weight shift (the Jackson 5 move). If you get those two movements right, your body will have a solid, tour-like transition.

Figure 36.7   Figure 36.8

Figure 36.9

The two key movements of transition are the lateral bump (the Jackson 5 move) and the regaining of flex of the spine (left tilt or transition crunch). These two moves get you in a good position to use the body to trigger the release. The top image shows the Jackson 5 move. The middle image shows the transition crunch move. The bottom move shows both combined.

Figure 36.10   Figure 36.11

Set up

Get in your golf posture with a club across the front of your hips.

Execution

Keeping your spine perpendicular to your pelvis, bump your hips toward the target while keeping your upper body centered. Then add rotation.

Focus and questions

Did you stand up? Did your trail ankle roll inward?

Executing these body movements will make the swing will feel athletic, but you won't hit great tour shots without complimentary arm movements. In the next section, we will look at what the arms do during transition. But first let's discuss a hot topic related to the transition—the head drop.

Understanding the head drop—does it threaten your swing?

The spine is a flexible rod of a fixed length. Extending your spine to the top of the swing lengthens its height. Then, during the transition, make movements that will lower your head. The two major head-lowering movements are the transition crunch and the Jackson 5. The transition crunch rounds the spine (which makes it shorter) and the Jackson 5 tilts the spine away from the target (which lowers its top). Both of these moves lower your head.

Dropping your head is not what causes bad shots, regardless of what the guys on TV say. Yes, Tiger drops his head more than most, but so does Rory. That head drop is not the sole reason that Tiger has struggled off the tee, nor does it explain why Rory is one of the best drivers the game has ever seen.

Insight

All good ball strikers drop their head some, but golfers who were skinny as kids tend to drop it more. They didn't have the body weight to help them push against the ground, so they had to use more of a vertical drop to leverage the ground and create speed. If you know a young golfer with a head drop, don't coach it out of them! At the very least, wait until they finish growing and can create speed with their whole body instead of just their legs.

Arm movements of transition

| Figure 36.12 | Figure 36.13 | Figure 36.14 | Figure 36.15 | Figure 36.16 |

The two arm movements look complicated, but students are usually able to get a feeling for how the two movements work together in just a couple swings. It frequently feels athletic and easier after only a few hundred balls. The left image shows arm shallow. The middle image shows the motorcycle. The right images shows a combination of both.

Now that we better understand how the body creates speed in the handle, let's move on to the arms and their movement in transition.

Arms extend/elbows get closer

Left forearm supinates/ trail shoulder externally rotates

Flex left wrist flexes/extends right

Initiate the wipe movement

> The arm movements during transition are among the best indicators of a golf swing's skill level and can clearly differentiate elite golfers from high handicappers.
>
> Insight

Elite golfers shallow the arms and start closing the club face to the path. Higher-handicap golfers steepen the arms and keep the face open.

Some golfers find the combination of "shallow and closed" strange. This is commonly the case if your arms are really tense at the top of your swing. If the arms are tense, then the shallow move will feel forced. *Do it anyway.*

With time, the arms will learn to relax into the shallow and closed movements. If the arms are relaxed (about the same tension as throwing a ball), then when the lower body starts the downswing, the arms will shallow as a result of the sequencing—but only if you let them by having relaxed arms.

The arm shallowing move narrows the distance between your torso and the club head. It is the opposite of the amateur casting move, which widens that space. Bringing the club head closer to you allows you to rotate faster (like a figure skater pulling in her arms) and creates the space to side bend so you can widen the path at the bottom of the swing.

To narrow the distance between your chest and the club head, bend your trail elbow very slightly (or at least delay it straightening). Extend (or cup) your right wrist and flex (or bow) the left wrist.

These arm movements narrow the club head path, but what about the shallowing move? As we discussed in earlier sections, we want the club head weight to be on a shallower path than that of the hands. To do this, you need a bit more of the right arm rotation that began during the backswing. The shallow movement is key because the body movements (transition crunch, shifting left, rotating left) steepen the club path. You have to balance those steep movements somewhere; your two options are to stand up (see Chapter 47 on early extending in Part 6) or shallow the arms. I recommend shallowing the arms, as that's what almost all tour pros choose to do.

The arms' two key movements in transition are the motorcycle and the arm shallowing move.

THE MOTORCYCLE

Figure 36.17   Figure 36.18

Drill - Motorcycle

Set up
Hold your hands in the delivery position.

Execution
Flex your lead wrist to close the face or extend your trail wrist to close the face. Make sure the shaft doesn't steepen.

Focus and questions
Moving from the backswing to delivery position, can you feel the motorcycle and shallow movements happening naturally? Can they be a reaction to the lower-body movements or do they need to feel active at first?

The motorcycle is a key movement for setting up the rest of the downswing. It involves rotating the shaft to close the face. Since the wrists are hinged, the face is closed in this part of the swing by flexing the lead wrist and/or extending the trail wrist. You can do either, but more golfers flex the lead wrist.

The important thing is to start this move before the release. But since transition describes a chunk of time, you have some variability. Some golfers feel the motorcycle to end the backswing. Other golfers feel it after they have started the club back down. Which you prefer doesn't really matter. Some golfers like to get it set at the top and then just hold it. Others like the fluid feeling of the soft wrists making the movement during transition. Play around with the timing and figure out what works best for you.

Figure 36.19   Figure 36.20

Drill - Arm Shallowing

Set up
Hold the arms out in front of you, then rotate your arms to the right to move the club.

Execution
Make a backswing, and feel the same movement as you start down. It should feel like the hands stay high and the club head drops behind them.

Focus and questions
Does it feel odd to have the club head weight under the hand path? Does it feel weak?

The forearms and shoulders rotate to flatten the plane and to balance the steepening movements of the body. A big problem for novice golfers is standing up with the body, and steepening the arms. We want to do the opposite, flatten the arms and steepen the body. This movement of shallow arms and staying in your posture with your body are two key pillars for building a solid swing. Very few high-handicap golfers do it this way, yet almost all tour pros do.

Release starts immediately at the end of transition. We can use a position here mid-downswing as a reference—I call it the *delivery position*, which occurs at the end of the build phase.

Delivery position

Figure 36.21

1. Trail arm up and bent
2. Trail wrist extended and extending
3. Lead wrist flexed and flexing
4. Lower body slightly closer to the target than the upper body
5. Body flexed forward
6. Pelvis square but upper body closed

This should feel like the halfway point in a throw, between the step and the twist and arm motion. In golf, this delivery position is the ready position for the arms, which are loaded and ready to fire during the release. To achieve delivery position simply execute the arm shallowing and the motorcycle.

In the next section, we will explore what the arms and body do from delivery position to follow through. But remember from the tempo section (Chapter 28), just like any other movement, our goal is to connect these pieces into a symphony of movement. Like different notes joining harmoniously to create a beautiful song, each movement should connect to every other movement to make a smooth, athletic swing.

Also remember to avoid trying to feel all of the different movements when you swing. They are intended to serve as a reference for the things you want to train, or if you have fallen into a slump and need something to help you get back to form.

Recap: Linking the Secrets of the Stock Tour Swing

Transition takes place when you shift from turning away from the target to toward it. It is essentially marks the start of the downswing. Transition is a challenging movement in which the body creates as much speed in the handle as it can, but still gets you in position to transfer that speed to the club during the release.

Transition features two key body movements. One is the lateral shift toward the target (the Jackson 5). The upper and lower body both shift, but there should be slightly more shift from the lower body than the upper body. The other key movement is to have the spine return to flexion (the transition crunch). This can be viewed as a continued left tilt as you change direction.

Transition also features two key arm movements. One is to shallow the path so that the club does not get too steep when the upper body regains flexion (arm shallow). The second is to start rotating the clubface closed (the motorcycle). These four moves create a lot of speed in the handle, but also put you in position to execute a release that will produce a good brush location and flat spot.

Release

Figure 36.19   Figure 36.20   Figure 36.21

Figure 36.22   Figure 36.23

Figure 36.24   Figure 36.25

The release starts from the end of transition and continues until follow through. The ball will simply get in the way of the club face if you do it correctly.

The release is the movement between delivery and follow through. It's one of my favorite topics because golf instruction has historically lacked detail describing this phase. That will not be the case here, as we break down its key arm and body movements in great detail.

The goal of the release is to transfer as much speed as possible to the club head, and to do so on a path where the club head's sweet spot strikes the ball with a face-to-path relationship that curves the ball the way you want.

The two basic movements of the release are the body bracing and the arms extending through the ball. The arms extending through the ball is preceded by an important trigger move I call the wipe.

The wipe

When we are in delivery position, the arms make what initially seems like a funny move. They drift or wipe slightly toward the target instead of toward the ball. I call this slight move across your body **the wipe**. This move happens to varying degrees and at slightly different times, but golfers who use the entire body to swing the club tend to wipe more. Golfers who swing with just the arms tend to wipe less.

Think of it this way. At the top of the swing, the hands and arms are to the right of the middle of your body. But as you approach impact, you want them to get closer in front of your sternum. At around delivery position, the arms will start working across your body (in front of the ball) before the arms start to really extend. If the arms extend immediately from the top of the swing, you will have trouble getting enough side bend to achieve a good flat spot. As the arms make this wipe movement, the wrists will help rotate the face more closed.

Extend the arms

The second key movement is to fully extend the arms. This is a passive complement to the bracing movement. The arm extension is critical to developing the flat spot and late wide point. The arm extension also creates the rotation of the forearms that many tour golfers have described as a key release move. The trick is to time the arm extension so that it is a release movement, rather than a transition one.

The arm extension is critical to developing arm/forearm rotation. The arms rotated during the backswing and the transition. Then, when you extend your arms, with speed they want to unwind to neutral. When the forearms extend with momentum and speed, the weight of the club head encourages continued forearm rotation. The rotation helps the gradual closing of the face to the path that was initiated by the motorcycle move in transition.

Bracing

At delivery position, the body is poised to transfer the energy it has built in the handle down to the club head. The transfer should be initiated from the lead foot as it starts to brace and push toward the target.

When you push the ground away from you, the lower body continues to shift slightly toward the target, while the upper body stabilizes and moves slightly away from it.

Some of you probably consider the upper body moving back during the release as a "death move." This isn't the case. It's actually needed for a good flat spot. It is also needed to safely handle the speed of the club head. As with all the key movements of the swing, I've named them—the general term for the body movements during the release is the brace.

How the brace and the wipe relate

The brace move should start with the lead leg pushing slightly away from the target. At this point, the upper body will be slightly more flexed forward than it was at set up—this is because of the transition crunch move. If there is no transition crunch, the wipe is nearly impossible. Also, if there is no transition crunch, the hands will be higher and the arms will have to straighten before impact (instead of through impact) just to get the club head down to the ground.

You have a choice of combination to train. Option one is to brace (with side bend) and wipe. Option two is to cast and stand up (with no side bend or rotation).

Golfers who choose to brace with a good wipe move tend to be more consistent than golfers who cast and stand up. This is because it is hard to build a good flat spot without side bend. If the thought of the body bracing and going into right side bend triggers fears of hitting it fat, then you likely need two things—more wipe move and a later arm extension. My experience is that it is better to train the arms before the side bend.

Figure 36.26

The bracing move through the ball includes side bending and continued rotation as the arms extend (and rotate). The left rotation of the arms is more a result of the arm extension starting from a right-rotated position. Straightening the arms through impact is a key component to getting the wide point well after the ball. If you stall the rotation of your body through the release, you will have a hard time getting the wide point well after the ball.

Body movements of the release

Figure 36.27   Figure 36.28

Rotational movements
1. Side bends away from target
2. Upper body starts to extend
3. Left leg triggers release
4. Upper body continues to rotate

Linear movements
1. Upper body starts moving away from target
2. Lower body keeps sliding forward, but slower
3. Lower body raises 1–2 inches
4. Upper body doesn't raise much higher than where it started
5. Upper body moves away from the ball very slightly

Now that you have a good image of the body movements of the release, let's dive deeper into the **wipe and extend** of the arms.

Arm movements of the release

Figure 36.29   Figure 36.30

The wipe before the arm extension is key to developing the flat spot. Most amateurs extend and then wipe.

| Figure 36.31 | Figure 36.32 | Figure 36.33 | Figure 36.34 |

The wipe can be done with either the trail wrist or the lead elbow. Try both and see which feels more natural to your swing.

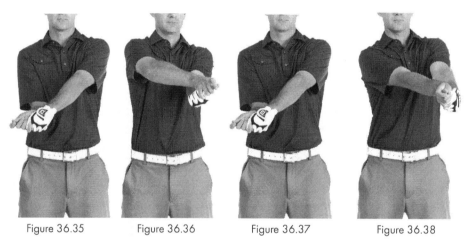

| Figure 36.35 | Figure 36.36 | Figure 36.37 | Figure 36.38 |

The second half of the release is an extension and rotation of the forearms. The rotation can be tricky. The first set of pictures shows the amateur method, which should be avoided. I rotated my shoulders to move my hands. The second set shows the tour pro method; note how I rotate my forearms without rotating my shoulders.

1. Lead arm abduction/trail arm adduction
2. Lead arm bends early—arms straighten late
3. Elbows move closer together
4. Both arms supinate (right arm palm up)
5. Both wrists unhinge and then maintain it past impact

The arms do a lot during the release, but it should all feel athletic and coordinated into one feeling, as opposed to a manipulated sequence. You might have to work your way through it, but if it doesn't feel fluid after a week or so of practice, double check to see what you're missing.

As discussed earlier, the arm movements of the release are broken down into the wipe and the extend. The wipe is the early part of the release. It involves a feeling that has been described as "stabbing the target" with the butt end of the club, or as the arms drifting across the body instead of out toward the ball. The two body parts that control the wipe are the lead elbow and the trail wrist. Doing the wipe movement helps with the feeling of "swinging out to right field." Omitting the wipe moves your hands toward the ball early and then makes the club swing more left through the ball. The wipe is a subtle positioning move that starts at the delivery position.

After that little drift or wipe, the arms will extend and the elbows will get closer. The first part of the extension is to unhinge the wrist. The second is to extend and rotate the arms through the ball. The elbows get closest (the furthest wide point) by having the lead forearm supinate. Even though the forearm supinates), it is actually more pronated at impact than at set up because of the arm shallowing move.

I believe that the forearm rotation is more the result of extending the arms from a rotated position. It is not that tour pros try to roll their arms over one another. They are trying to extend. It is also critical that the rotation stems more from the trail forearm than from the trail shoulder. If the trail shoulder internally rotates, the arms will typically bend and the wide and low point will move the wrong way (backward).

Just as we are sequencing the body, we need to sequence the arm movements so the shoulders move first (wipe of lead arm). The elbows extend next, and the wrists unhinge (ulnar deviation), and finally the forearms rotate.

For many, the wrist movements will feel like they happen *after* impact, as opposed to before. Delaying the wrist timing achieves the desired look at impact of the left wrist flat and the right wrist cupped. **The wrists are not actively held back**. Rather, the proper sequencing of the arms and the position of the sternum create that look.

Rotating the lead arm is the best way to safely decelerate. Rotating the lead arm rotates the club face during the release. This sounds scary for most amateurs, but feels more repeatable once you experience it.

> Some golfers do better by combining the wipe and extension into one feeling, but others are very sensory and need it broken down. If you combine them, you will likely feel the arms swinging out in front of the ball (around 30 degrees down the target line for an iron; around 15 degrees for a driver). Another way to think about it is to imagine standing at the center of a clock face. If the ball is at 12 o'clock, your arms will extend towards the 10 (driver) or 11 (iron). This move has been described as swinging "through the ball" instead of "hitting it."

Insight

Now you know the secret to swinging through the ball. There needs to be a little wipe before the arms extend. I know of no better way to learn the tour release than practicing the single arm releases. If you are a higher handicap, or have a wrist or elbow injury, it may be better to skip the individual arm release drills and just practice the open trail hand.

Figure 36.37   Figure 36.38

To combine the wipe and the extension into one move, get in delivery position. Extend your arms out in front of the ball a few feet down the target line. If you do this move correctly, you'll achieve the look of the release.

Figure 36.39   Figure 36.40   Figure 36.41

Set up

Assume a normal grip and ball position, then take your trail hand off the club.

Execution

Hit a 9–3 shot, focusing on getting the left wrist flat and rotating/pointing down, out, and away.

Focus and questions

Did you lose contact with your shoulder? Did the club head ever rotate over?

Figure 36.42   Figure 36.43   Figure 36.44

Set up

Assume a normal grip and ball position, and take your lead hand off the club.

Execution

Hit a 9–3 shot, focusing on getting the right wrist to hit the ball on a penetrating trajectory. The arm will extend more across your body, with your wrist working after your elbow.

Focus and questions

Did your upper body drift forward? Is the club following the same path with the left- and right-hand versions?

DRILL - OPEN TRAIL HAND

Figure 36.45   Figure 36.46   Figure 36.47

Set up
Assume a normal grip and ball position, and open your trail hand.

Execution
Hit a 9–3 shot (or full swing), keeping contact with the trail hand on the club.
Focus and questions
Is the club following the same path with the left- and right-hand versions?

We have covered a lot in Part 3, and you may feel a bit overwhelmed. Let this section serve as a reference guide for understanding why you hit the ball well sometimes and poorly other times. Knowing what the club is doing and how the body does it best will ultimately help you simplify swing objectives to one or two keys. Chapter 37 covers the most powerful combinations of movements that give golfers the big leaps in technique.

Recap: Linking the Secrets of the Stock Tour Swing

The release is the second big group of movements of the downswing. During the release, the golfer's goal is to transfer speed from the handle to the club head, as well as to direct the path to the ball while controlling the face-to-path relationship.

The body will brace to transfer speed and to trigger the right side bend. You need sufficient side bend to create a flat spot after the ball, and to create the late wide point. The brace consists of the front leg pushing against the ground, as well as the upper body side bending and moving slightly away from the target.

To side bend and not hit it fat, the release should include a wipe across the body before the arms fully extend. When they do, the arms should be rotated mostly from the forearms, not from an internal rotation of the trail shoulder.

CHAPTER 37

Putting Part 3 Principles into Practice—How to Break Through Using Stock Tour Swing Movements

I f the images and descriptions in Part 3 left you feeling overwhelmed, don't worry. While every swing is somewhat different, from a practical standpoint there are just a handful of key movements to train in addition to three key positions (a quality set up, a quality impact position, and a solid follow through).

Feeling every little *micromove* in your pattern is not necessary (or advised!) to play great golf. Rather, if you get stuck with one part of your swing, I want you to know how to investigate the problem. Your own personal breakthrough on a key move could come from understanding one little piece. So if you don't have great success the first time you work on a key movement, it doesn't mean the movement is ultimately not important for your game. Train the following key movements, as these will have the biggest impact on your swing shape. Learning these often lays the foundation for breakthroughs.

1. *Motorcycle—trains transition face control*
   - This is especially important for golfers who get too steep and too out-to-in. Learning to close the face earlier removes the reward for an outside-in swing and allows body rotation to power the swing.
   - To practice, hit shots where every ball curves with a slight draw. Keep the same amount of curve and try to change the start line by changing the club head path. The most common ways to move the path more inside-out are the arm shallowing move or the Jackson 5.

2. *Jackson 5/lower-body sequence—trains club head path control and helps with flat spot*
   - Suppose you already have pretty good club face awareness, but struggle with a steep angle of attack, especially when hitting with the longer clubs. Your next

big concept to practice is the amount of axis tilt in the downswing. This drill allows you to train the lower body to lead the downswing. Once the lower body is comfortable leading, you can experience big breakthroughs in arm extension and the flat spot in the follow through.

3. *Arm shallow move—trains club head path control and transition sequencing*
   - This is a bit of a tricky one, especially for higher-handicap golfers. Shallowing the club further opens the face, so if you already struggle with club face issues, I would generally attack the club face first. However, if you are in the 5 to 10 handicap range and struggle with shaft lean at impact, early extension, or lots of toe contact, the arm shallow move could be the big breakthrough you need.

4. *Arm extension—shallows turf contact and builds the late wide point*
   - Too many golfers achieve a great-looking delivery position, but break down during the release, either because they never unhinge their wrists in the release or because the arm movements are too steep. These golfers compensate by stalling the body rotation and flipping/scooping to stop the face from closing too much. This compensatory move typically makes it difficult to get arm extension through the ball and a late wide point.

5. *Bracing and wipe/arm extension timing—trains the club head path and club face control during the release*
   - If the upper body drifts on top of the ball during the downswing, it can cause angle of attack issues. An overly steep angle of attack causes major problems with the longer clubs. Learning to brace and extend the arms through the ball is key to producing consistent contact. Bracing can only work if you do the wipe move. You can train it in either order, but I usually have more success training the wipe move first, then adding bracing.

6. *Centered pivot—path control guards against contact issues*
   - The centered pivot idea is my catch-all for when the sternum moves excessively. Excessive movements of the sternum create inconsistency and show up in swing patterns in ways such as loss of posture, forward lunge, early extension, and sway (we will cover these in Part 6). All of these can cause contact issues that a swing powered more with body rotation doesn't have. Often, improving your awareness of the location of your body can significantly improve your consistency.

Work on each of these movements for at least 4 weeks before trying to combine them. That said, after you have trained each movement in isolation, combining a couple of them in a single practice session can yield huge improvement gains.

Reconsider how you perceive odd swings

These key movements can become a sort of checklist for understanding the swing's critical pieces. Let's study some of the more unique swings on tour and see if our criteria for a good one holds up to this checklist.

Jim Furyk

Does he extend his arms through impact and build a good flat spot? Yes, he has one of the best arm extension patterns through the ball.

Does he shallow the club in transition? Yes, his upright backswing makes his transition shallow move stand out. He appears to do it all from the forearms and not much from the shoulders, but he definitely flattens with the arms.

Does he power the swing with his whole body? Yes, he expertly sequences the downswing.

Does he square the face early in the downswing? Yes. To delay his arm extension as long as he does, he has to close the face early. He has some of the best arm extension through the ball, and I think that's part of the reason he is such a consistent striker.

Does he stay centered? Yes, even though he has some interesting timing moves. His pivot stays in the bubble to allow for each of these other key pieces.

Bubba Watson

Does he extend his arms through impact and build a good flat spot? Yes, his arms fully extend, and beautifully so.

Does he shallow the club in transition? Yes, he has one of the best arm shallowing moves.

Does he power the swing with his whole body? Yes, as well as anyone. His foot action highlights his sequencing.

Does he square the face early in the downswing? Yes, his delivery position is as classic as it gets.

Does he stay centered? Yes. Even though he has some interesting timing moves, he too stays in the bubble.

Matt Kuchar

Does he extend his arms through impact and build a good flat spot? Yes, his arms fully extend.

Does he shallow the club in transition? Yes, even though his arms are incredibly flat at the top of the backswing, he still flattens them in transition.

Does he power the swing with his whole body? Yes, he has great sequencing and arm extension timing.

Does he square the face early in the downswing? Yes, his delivery position is solid.

Does he stay centered? Yes, other than slightly flat arms in the backswing and a funky finish move, his swing represents all the key movements of an elite ball striker.

As you start to recognize these relationships, you will see the similarities among the best ball strikers, and the stark differences among golfers who struggle with ball striking. In Part 4, we will dig into why a golfer like Phil Mickelson can hit the ball so accurately with his irons, but struggles with his driver.

Balancing the power-path-face conundrum

Another way to summarize these moves is to reiterate that the goal of the Stock Tour Swing is a three-way balance of
1. Controlling the club head path
2. Organizing the face to the path
3. Creating speed

Training the golf swing would be easy if we could just add a move and be done with it. Unfortunately, as the great golfer Grant Waite once said, "Nothing changes in a vacuum." When you tweak one area, another area will change. However, knowing what *should* happen and how to read feedback makes it less frustrating when unintentional changes happen—and trust me, they will.

Suppose you are trying to get a bit more power. If you try to swing your arms a little faster, the path will typically steepen. Using your legs a little bit more may cause the path to shallow. If you are prepared for how a movement will change the face or path, you can better anticipate what might go wrong when implementing a change. This program is designed to present you with options so you can self-correct—you will be able to choose the combination of movements that balance the power-path-face conundrum best for you.

Recap: Linking the Secrets of the Stock Tour Swing

Key movement combinations that significantly impact your game include:

Backswing—the arms stay in front and rotate, and the body center pivot keeps the club on plane and sets you up for a powerful transition.

Transition—the body pulls on the handle with a shift of the body and left tilt, while the arms shallow to prepare for the release.

Release—the body starts to brace and triggers the release. The body starts going into right side bend/extension to help shallow out the path. At the same time, the arms extend across the ball as the upper body continues to rotate.

Part 4

Shot Shaping and Adjusting the Swing
for Different Clubs

Most golfers just want to build one swing they can trust day in and day out. Few realize there's a problem with this perspective. In Part 4 we discuss how the ideal swing for an iron (seven iron to wedge) is slightly different than that of a driver. I say "slightly," but after experiencing both swings, many golfers describe them as "drastically" different.

Many golfers will try to tell you that the only difference in the swings is some simple set up changes. But I have yet to hear a good answer when I ask how a world-class golfer like Phil Mickelson can hit great wedges/irons, but struggle immensely with accuracy and consistency off the tee. Are they suggesting he can't make a simple set up change?

Also, have you ever noticed in your own game how your best iron days and your best driver days are rarely on the same day? There is a reason, and in this section we will discuss how to fine-tune the Stock Tour Swing to fit different clubs or shots.

Understanding the driver–iron spectrum will allow you to use daily feedback even more effectively. Let's say you are warming up for a round; you are hitting your driver great but hitting your irons a little thin. By the end of this chapter, you'll have a few go-to solutions to help you avoid hitting thin irons all day.

One goal in golf is to develop skills that allow you to play different shots. The goal of swinging the club is not to be a robot and make the same swing every time. The goal is to have the flexibility to adjust your stock swing for the shot at hand.

CHAPTER 38

Swing Bias and Club Spectrum

t's important to realize there is no one magic swing that will work for every club. It's also important to know that your natural swing will be biased toward either a short iron swing or a driver swing. Knowing your personal bias can help you pick what to practice and what strategy to employ on the course.

> If you have an iron-biased swing move, you likely power your swing with more of your upper body—and have a tendency to get too steep. This can cause face alignment and angle of attack issues with the longer clubs. Therefore, those with typical iron-biased swings should be cautious about swinging hard on narrow tee shots.
>
> On the other hand, those with a driver-biased swing likely power the swing with their lower body—and have a tendency to get too shallow. This can cause contact issues with wedge shots. If this sounds like you, make sure to leave yourself 40-yard shots off a tight lie.

Insight

Knowing your swing bias helps you make smart changes and practice skills that will help you learn to adjust and manage your natural swing.

As I've mentioned, I have a driver-biased swing. I tend to get my lower body overly involved—my typical error is a swing that is too shallow, with the low point behind the ball. This bias creates difficulty with less-than-full wedge shots from 40–80 yards.

Since I know this is my tendency, I try to put myself in tough 40–80 yard shots during non-tournament rounds to practice. But if I'm playing in a tournament and I don't feel sharp with the wedge low-point control, I will intentionally leave myself 100 yards or more into short par 4s and par 5s. This way I can at least hit full wedges, where my weakness shows up less.

In practice sessions, I address the natural shortcomings of my swing bias by spending more time on short irons and wedges.

Iron bias versus driver bias

I like to listen to how elite players describe their movements. They may not always accurately portray what makes them great, but they often reveal the type of feedback to which they are paying attention. One example is how elite golfers describe the full swing compared to the short game. The short game is frequently described as an "underhand toss" and the full swing is described as "throwing a ball" (overhand or sidearm). Let's investigate this revealing analogy.

In an underhand toss, most of the power comes from the shoulder girdle and upper back. The body shifts weight to add some speed and provide rhythm. In general, all parts of the body move together in the underhand toss.

Contrast that with an overhand throw. In this throw, there is a whiplike sequence. The legs shift weight, the core rotates and transfers speed to the shoulders, and the arm amplifies speed at the end of the throw.

> **Insight**
>
> Think of the driver swing like an overhand throw (a total body action), and the iron swing like an underhand toss (more of an upper-body action). The cutoff point for each swing bias is about a six or seven iron. Either swing works with the middle range of clubs. But if you find yourself struggling with either the long irons and woods or the short irons and wedges, study this chapter in detail.

Many golfers fall on the iron-bias end of the spectrum. A result of that bias has been the creation of hybrids over the last 15 years. Hybrids can work better for an iron-biased swing than the long irons. If you want to play well right now and you have an iron-biased swing, consider trading out your long irons for hybrids.

While the lie angles, lengths, and lofts change slightly from one club to the next, comparing the specs at each end of your set reveals that they typically change quite a bit. You need a shallower swing with the longer clubs. To shallow the swing, get the lower body involved to help create side bend and to delay the arm extension timing. Wedges, on the other hand, don't require as much of a total body motion and can be viewed as more of an upper-body swing.

Let's go through some conceptual differences for what makes a good short iron swing and what makes a good driver swing.

Figure 38.1

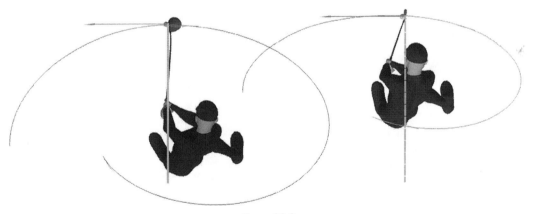

Figure 38.2

These images show the same tour golfer hitting an iron and hitting a driver. The golf ball is in the same horizontal location on the page in the top set of images. Notice how much farther behind the golf ball the driver swing is, and notice how much more the shoulders are pointed down the target line. In the second set of images, I added a line to highlight where his head and hands are compared to the golf ball.

In this third set of images, you can clearly see how much farther behind the ball the tour golfer is when hitting a driver. While the hands have a very similar release pattern, because of this body difference, they show up with different shaft angles at impact.

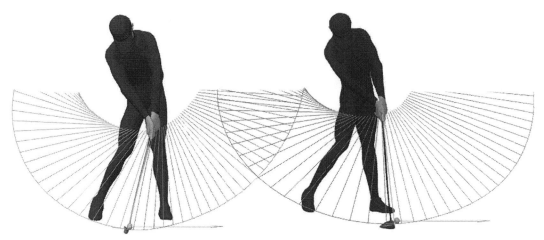

Figure 38.3

Here you can see the low and wide points of the two different swings. While the driver's low point is before the golf ball (instead of after, as with the iron) the widest point is roughly in the same spot after the golf ball.

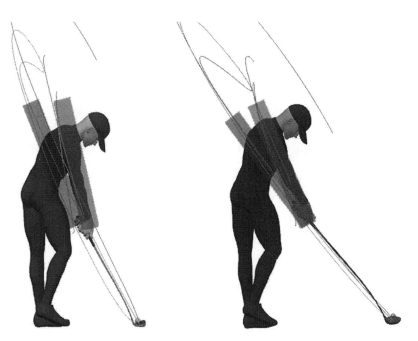

Figure 38.4

There is a more pronounced shallowing movement of the arms with the driver swing. If your tendency is steep with the arms, you may be able to hit good iron shots, but you will likely struggle with the driver.

Iron swing

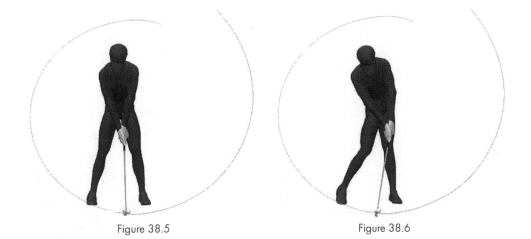

Figure 38.5   Figure 38.6

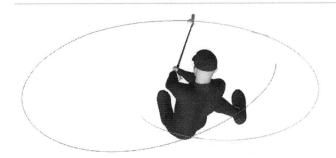

Figure 38.7

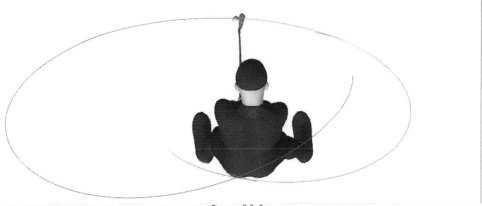

Figure 38.8

Power-path-face

Power of the swing—whole body, but upper body is more active than in the driver swing

Club head path—more left and more steep

Club face—more of an open club face

Simple set up changes

Ball position—more centered

Stance width—more narrow

Grip strength—more of a weak grip, especially trail hand

Movement changes

Centered pivot—you can get away with more of a reverse pivot or upper body moving toward the target in the backswing

Lead arm motion—more of a chop across the rib cage

Swing faults that help (or at least you can get away with)—forward lunge, lift, and cast

Timing of face rotation—can be later in the downswing

Driver swing

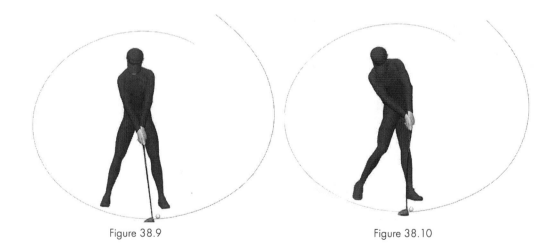

Figure 38.9   Figure 38.10

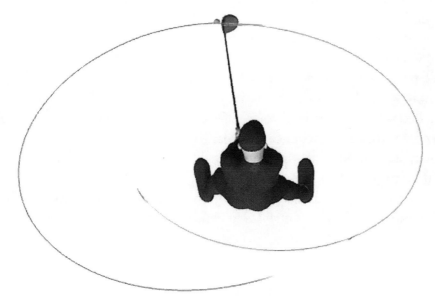

Figure 38.11

Figure 38.12

Power-path-face

Power of the swing—whole body, but lower body more active than in the iron swing

Club head path—more right and more shallow

Club face—more of a closed club face

Simple set up changes

> Ball position—more forward, can be ahead of left shoulder
>
> Stance width—more wide
>
> Grip strength—more of a strong grip, especially the trail hand

Movement changes

> Centered pivot—you can get away with more of a hang back style pivot
>
> Lead arm motion—more of a lift off the rib cage
>
> Swing faults that help (or at least you can get away with)—sway and early extension
>
> Timing of face rotation—better to close earlier in downswing

You now may have an idea of why you struggle more with one area of your game. Instead of getting frustrated and shouting, "Why can't I just do the same thing I do with the wedge with a driver!" you can use the limitation in one area as a diagnostic. You can leverage your awareness of your swing bias to manage your practice time and focus.

Ball shaping: Short-term option—tweak the club face

The Stock Tour Swing program produces a neutral path that errs slightly on an in-to-out path or draw bias. But not every golfer likes a little draw. If you don't want to draw it and prefer a fade, or if you are behind a tree and need to deliberately curve it, then this chapter will help you see the variables at play.

Even if you like a soft draw as your stock ball flight, you have to be able to shape shots if you are to get to a certain level of golf. If you can't shape shots, your on-course shot selection must accommodate that limitation. This section will give you options for making the ball curve. Remember from the section covering ball flight (Chapter 7) that the curve is created by the angle difference between the club face and club head path.

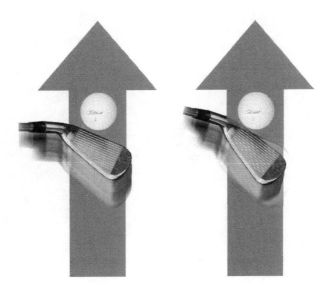

Figure 38.13

Remember that a golfer typically has a consistent path, and it is the face that changes more.

For long-term training, I like to work on the path. For short-term options, it's all about the timing of face control.

So you have a key decision to make when it comes to shot shaping. Are you going to play your normal path and just change the face, or are you going to adjust the path?

Draw golfer, trying to hit a fade?

Draw Hook → **Push Slice**

Figure 38.14

Figure 38.15

The easiest way to curve a shot to the right is to simply open the face to the path. The risk is that the ball may launch higher than you want and/or may not have as much curve as you want.

If you, a draw golfer, keep your in-to-out path the same and open the face, then you will play a push fade, which starts right and goes right. When you set up, you will need to imagine the "target line" to the left of where you really want to hit. Also, keep in mind that the push fade will typically go higher than normal (like a flop shot). So, if you need to hit a fade shot with low trajectory, you'll have to take a very low lofted club and hope for the best.

Fade golfer, trying to hit a draw?

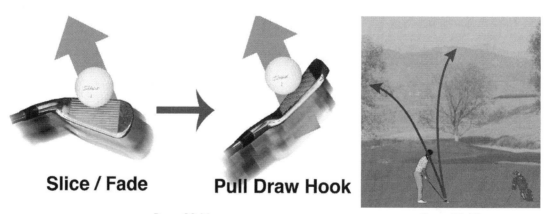

Slice / Fade → **Pull Draw Hook**

Figure 38.16

Figure 38.17

The easiest option to curve a shot to the left is to simply close the face to the path. The risk is that the ball may launch lower than you want and/or have less curve than you want.

If you, a fade golfer, keep your normal outside-in swing path and just close the face, you are going to hit a pull draw, which starts left and curves left. When you set up, you will need to imagine the "target line" to the right of where you really want to hit. Pull draws tend to fly very low and have a fair amount of roll. This is great for punching out of trouble, but hard to get to hold a green.

Ball shaping: More challenging but more versatile adjustments (path and face changes)

If you are an advanced player and trying to shape it for a different shot, here are your options.

To hit a draw

You don't have to change everything to make a shape change. Usually one or two small changes will be enough to make the ball curve differently. But if you want a *lot* of curve, you'll have to change at least a few of these. Also, when you experiment with these on the range, you may find that some are easier to implement than others. Options can be scary at first but are useful as you progress, so here is a list of set up and movement options that will shallow your club head path, make it more inside-out, and close the face-to-path.

Set up options (and path or face influence)
Ball back in stance (path more right)
Strengthen the grip (close the face to the path)
More axis tilt (path more right; great for longer clubs, but be careful with shorter clubs—you could hit fat shots)
Closed stance (path more right)

Movement options
More arm shallow (path more right)
More motorcycle (closed face-to-path)
More Jackson 5 (path more right)
Keep your back to target longer in transition (path more right)
More lift of arms during follow through (path more right)
Roll lead arm (more face closed)

To hit a fade

Again, you don't have to change everything; a subtle change can get the ball to curve more or less. Here are the set up and movement options that will make the club head path steeper, more outside-in, and open the face-to-path.

Set up
Ball forward in stance (path more left)
Weaken the grip (open the face to the path)
More shoulders level (path more left, but careful with longer clubs)
Open stance (path more left)

Movement options
Steeper arms (path left but be careful, body may shallow)
More of a "hold off" release—a deliberate chicken wing (open face and path left)
More forward lunge (can steepen path *a lot*—careful with longer clubs)
More upper-body rotation (move path left)
More chop of arms during follow through (path more left)

Recap: Linking the Secrets of the Stock Tour Swing

Your Stock Tour Swing will produce a standard shot for your body. This shot may be a slight fade or a slight draw. You will probably have more success with the longer clubs than the short clubs, or vice versa. It's natural to have a bias one way or the other, and knowing your bias can help you make decisions on the course and in practice.

If you hit your short irons well but struggle with the driver or three wood, your swing is most likely upper-body dominant with a steeper path (iron swing). You may set up with the ball position more in the middle of your stance, and you may have a weaker grip or a narrow stance. You may close the face later and your arms may straighten earlier.

If, on the other hand, you hit a driver/three wood well but struggle with the short irons, then your swing is most likely lower-body dominant with a shallower path (driver swing). You may set up with the ball position more forward in your stance, and you may have a stronger grip or a wider stance. You may close the club face earlier and your arms may straighten later.

To curve your normal swing, you can either keep your club head path the same while changing the face relationship to that path. Or you can try and change both the face and path.

If you normally hit a fade and want to hit a draw, it may be easier to just close the face and hit a pull draw. The risk is that the ball may launch too low and on some shots have limited spin. If you normally hit a draw and want to hit a fade, you could just open the face and hit a push fade. The risk is that your launch may be too high to stay under tree limbs when hitting a recovery shot.

One of the best drills for calibrating your personal face-and-path relationships is the **9 shot** drill presented below.

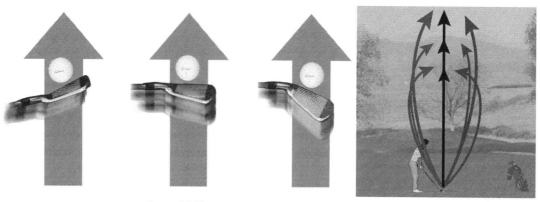

Figure 38.18   Figure 38.19

The drill requires three face-to-path relationships with a high, normal, and low trajectory. It helps you dial in your personal club face and club head path tendencies.

Set up
Alignment stick and target.

Execution
You need to hit three trajectories (high, medium, low), for each trajectory you need to hit all three curves (draw, straight, fade). You can either try to hit multiples of each in a row, or try to hit all nine in succession.

Focus and questions
What are your easiest shot combinations? Which are your hardest? Does it matter what club you use?

CHAPTER 39

Putting Part 4 Principles into Practice

As a general rule, good players will benefit from deliberately curving the ball in practice. Even if they are going to hit their normal shot on the course, learning to control the amount of curve helps them monitor and calibrate their club face-to-path relationship. This helps you build a range of face-to-paths your brain can use. Having a larger range helps develop your precision.

Warm-ups to the course

Experimenting with face-to-path can also be helpful during the warm-ups, when you take inventory to see what shots you are hitting well that day. For instance, if in warm-ups you are hitting quality fade shots but having a hard time drawing it, you have a choice: You can either try to force draws when needed, or just play your fade on every shot. If you are more concerned with your score for that day, play the fade. However, if you don't really care about your score and are more focused on long-term training, it can be rewarding to work on correcting your swing on the course. We will discuss this in depth in Part 5, but the course is a great place to test skills you're learning. For many golfers, "tests" feel more real on the course than they do in simulations on the range.

The Stock Tour Swing program—recap

By this point, you have a solid understanding of what the club head needs to do (Part 1) and how the body can best perform it (Part 2). You are familiar with the details of how the Stock Tour Swing works (Part 3) and how it can be adjusted to specialize in either the irons or the driver, or a particular shot shape (Part 4).

Remember that our initial goal was to answer three questions:

What do I want the club to do?

How does the body best perform that task?

How can I train it?

In Part 5, we will discuss how to train it. You are in the closing stretch of understanding the golf swing, but you still have a long way to go in terms of training a swing that will hold up during a key round. With proper training, you can be proud of your swing and experience a level of control that makes the game enjoyable on whole new levels.

Part 5
Training Your Swing

Thus far, we have focused on the golf swing from a purely mechanical point of view. In Part 5, we discuss the process of building a golf swing that will hold up on the course. This topic can easily be a book on its own! First, let's establish that there are three ways to improve your score when playing golf:

1. Improve your technique.
2. Improve your practice habits to turn techniques into dependable skills you can transfer to the course.
3. Improve your on-course mental game so your brain can access your trained skills.

You can fail to live up to your potential if you don't improve in all three areas.

CHAPTER 40

Building a Skill from a Technique

There is a big difference between *technique* and *skill*. Techniques are learned quickly, while skills take time to develop. I can teach you to shallow out your swing with either your arms or your body in five minutes, and you will know the technique for doing so. But until you put in hours of training, you will lack the skill to do it consistently and the precision to adjust it for different shots on the course.

Most golfers want to just learn more and more technique, but the real art to playing good golf is learning to turn a technique into a skill. Nurturing a new skill takes developing precise movements and becoming flexible regarding the range of movement needed to produce different outcomes.

Most golfers think a golf swing is something to be built, step by step, and once built it cannot be lost. This is a frustrating and even dangerous way to look at golf. The best professional golfers are lucky to have their *best stuff* for a month or two. *A month or two. For the best in the world.* After living in the zone for a month, something gets a little off and they typically have to tinker a bit to get it back.

The golf swing is a powerful athletic movement that requires high levels of precision. Power and precision are a challenging combination to train in unison.

Many former pro athletes often talk about how hard golf is compared to basketball, football, soccer, and other sports. These athletes are accustomed to a certain level of consistency in their performance that is rarely experienced in golf. You—all of us—will have good days and bad days. The key to consistent golf is understanding your swing to the point where if you hit a few bad shots, you can take steps to get it back.

It is completely delusional to think you will never lose your swing. It is completely realistic, however, to think you can develop the skills to quickly find a lost swing. Once you know your pattern and how to own your swing as best as you can, you won't be scared of bad shots. Moreover, you'll feel proud of the good shots because you will actually know what produced them.

Adjusting your practice mindset

So you now know that the goal of training your swing is not to memorize a movement pattern. This likely changes how you decide to practice. Just because you can perfectly hit 10 seven irons in a row on the driving range doesn't mean you "have it."

You will "have it" when you can put your game to any test and it holds up. The bigger the test you pass, the more you know you have it. The ultimate test happens on the course, with something on the line and a bunch of people watching you—when you have just one swing, one chance to prove your game. That is the gold standard test, but it is hard to recreate when practicing.

Try to make your practice more challenging than what you will encounter on the course. On the course, strangers will observe you. You will have a couple minute delays between shots. You will have uneven lies and visual stresses. You will have to find that mental state where you can get out of your own way and let the swing you've built materialize. Anything you can do to make practice more like these situations will help you on the course.

Here are some ideas to amplify difficulty in your practice session.

Do you normally hit five balls a minute? If you get a good groove, try hitting five balls in 10 minutes and see if that swing thought holds up. Do you normally hide on the corner of the range and practice when the range is empty? If you get a good groove, move to a highly visible part of the range and practice when the range is packed with golfers. You can even call over a friend and have them watch you hit a few shots. Try hitting balls out of divots instead of good lies. The options are endless, but the message is simple. Practice is all about overcoming a challenge. The secret to quality practice is to challenge yourself the right amount.

The purpose of practice is to develop a skill by creating a detailed picture of the movements (and their ranges) that create a good shot. In no way does making the same swing over and over develop the skill. Repetition without thoughtful challenges will make you more aware of your stock shot, and it will help you build some confidence when you do test the skill. But it doesn't build the type of recall you need when playing on the course.

CHAPTER 41

Performance Versus Arousal (the Yerkes-Dodson Law)

I have benefitted from a curious personality and the good fortune to be able to ask as many questions as I could of every smart person I could find. I've had some insightful conversations with sports psychologists about the golf swing, which helped me understand the barriers to training a technique into a skill. I don't pretend to be a sports psychologist, but I want to share what I've learned (and personally experienced) about how to train the proper state of mind for elite performance.

The art of letting it happen versus forcing it to happen

There is a famous curve in sports psychology called the performance versus arousal curve (the Yerkes-Dodson Law). Basically, we humans have a hot spot for performance. Complex tasks thrive in a calm state; simple tasks thrive in an aroused state. Hitting a golf ball is a complex task, so it tends to be done optimally with lower excitement.

When you hit a good shot, you are in a certain state of mind. It's neither absent (bored) nor overly focused (stressed). It's generally somewhere in the middle, like Goldilocks and her porridge that was just right. Rarely are golfers too bored on the course. Most golfers get too excited, and their performance suffers as a result.

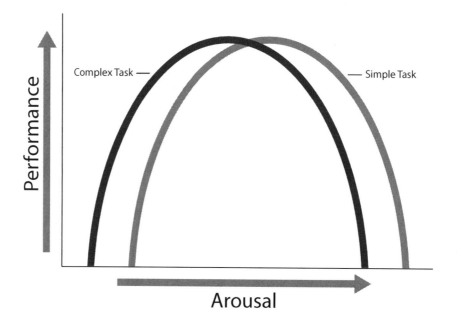

This is a common problem among former athletes who were successful in other sports. Since most sports are simpler tasks, athletes are used to succeeding with higher arousal. They could get *jacked up* and it would help them succeed.

It may sound counterintuitive, but if you focus too much (or get too excited/aroused), your performance will suffer the same way as if you cared too little.

I have coached many golfers who reached technical breakthroughs after important rounds, trips, or tournaments. What happens is that prior to the trip, the golfer was grinding mentally and overfocused because they desperately wanted to play well. Their arousal level put them farther to the right on the graph and their performance suffered in the key round.

Then, after the key round, they relaxed and their intensity dropped, which allowed them to perform at a higher level. I typically see the ramp up starting about three weeks before the important event. I call it the "three-week freakout" and I now prepare golfers for it about six weeks prior to the important event.

This situation can also happen within a round. Many golfers have experienced the following situation, which is shared by a student of mine:

I had a good lesson and practice session early in the week to get ready for playing with a buddy on Friday. It was a big round for me because my buddy played in college and almost always shot in the mid-to-low 70's. If I played really well, I could give him a decent match.

When I get to the course on Friday, I know I want to play well. I try to focus on the range during my warm up, but I hit a bad shot. A minute later, another bad shot. The harder I focus, the more the bad shots come. I start to panic. In my panic, my mind spirals to the point where all I can think about is embarrassing myself with bad shot after bad shot.

I can fix this if I just focus harder. I am totally in my own head on the first few holes, in a bad way. I get a little frenzied even, and my swing loses its fluidity and rhythm—my swing doesn't line up anymore, my timing is so off. I hit a number of bad shots before I finally give up. It starts to sink in, "This is just not my day." After I give up, my worries and panic subside. Somehow, out of the blue, I start to hit some really good shots. I play well for a series of six or seven holes. It's amazing how my day turned around, and suddenly I realize that I'm close to shooting my lowest round ever (even with the crummy start). So of course I start focusing again to finish the round strong. I really want that record, and I start getting in my head again. And just like that, it's gone. I lose my swing again and fail to finish the round strong.

This experience will sound familiar to many amateurs, and even some pros. While talking about their round at the 19th hole, they will frequently say, "Why couldn't I play like that good section the whole time? What changed in my swing?"

If we videotaped the swing, we could see some technical errors. But the mental issue took place before the technical issue. His technique didn't break down—his ability to access the skill did.

This is why technique is but one of the three ways to improve your score. There is much more to hitting a good shot than just beautiful technique.

If managing your arousal level is so important, you must be wondering—*What's a practical way to identify my arousal level?*

> It's hard to adjust your emotional state, since once you start thinking about it, the state has already changed. But try setting a benchmark or baseline for your emotional state next time you're hitting it well on the range. Most players will find that their focus level isn't extremely high and that the swing is "easy" or "effortless."
>
> *Insight*

The next time you are struggling on the course, try to identify your level of focus and intensity. If it is really intense, you are likely going to perform worse. Simply bringing down your focus and intensity may be enough to improve your game.

There is an art to finding the right state of mind. If you set a baseline when you are playing well (or even hitting it well on the course), never go above that. Especially if you are a Type A personality, you will almost always perform better by lowering your intensity, not raising it.

There are lots of other programs that can help you achieve this state of mind. *Vision 54* has games to get you to experience this level of intensity. *The Fluid Motion Factor* has some good strategies and exercises as well. Or, you can ask yourself questions to bring your intensity back down. *Fearless Golf* and other golf psychology books can help you ask yourself the right questions.

Chapter 42

How to Practice with a Productive Process

Trillium Rose is a brilliant golf instructor, highly skilled in the process of learning. She gave a talk in 2014 that inspired this chapter—if you enjoy it and want to know more, please check out her material.

During her talk, Trillium described how learning to swing the golf club is the same as learning to draw a shape—say, a heart. Imagine you have two students trying to draw a heart. Student A takes a stencil and traces a heart 100 times. Student B uses a stencil to draw the heart 20 times. He then traces it 30 times with no stencil, and then 50 times on his own.

Which process is more successful for drawing a heart from scratch?

When most golfers practice, they try to do the same thing over and over—but they never really test their skill to check its status. They think if they hit 10 balls in a row really well, they've got it. But there are steps to the process of practicing—take a look.

Step 1: Make a movement plan

Establish a clear image in your mind of what you are currently doing and what you want to do differently. Then make a movement plan. It must be specific, but it doesn't have to be highly technical. It can be as simple as saying, "I am currently standing up, and I want to stay in my posture through the release."

If you understand this program's core concepts—ideas related to steep/shallow, what opens and closes the face, and what influences brush location—then you should be able to predict your likely miss pattern when you try something new.

The "something new" doesn't have to be technical. It could just be, "I'm going to swing smoother" instead of "I'm going to ulnar deviate as I side bend earlier."

When forming the plan, ask yourself, "If I commit to this plan, what are my likely shots?"

Suppose I'm working to create more side tilt and to stop lunging my upper body in front of the ball. If I side bend and don't lunge, I am likely to have fat misses and hit more pushes, because the low point will move backward and the path will be more in-to-out (unless I balance the swing path with more upper-body rotation). If I hit the ball well, this should feel more effortless and have a little higher launch with the driver compared to my normal drives. If I hit a ball that is a low pull cut, I know that I couldn't possibly have executed the move I planned.

Step 2: Execute the action

Once you have a movement plan, your goal is to execute the action and stay present with the plan. As we covered in Chapter 41, you don't want to be so aroused to create anxiety, but just be engaged with the attempted movement. I like to describe this as "being aware of the movement" rather than being "hyper focused." For many, framing it as "being aware" creates the right intensity level to maximize performance.

Step 3: Evaluate the movement in relation to the plan

Did you do it?

This sounds like a simple question, but it's critical to the process.

Did you do what you were trying to? This is usually the missed step for most golfers. If you did it and it produced a likely shot pattern (not necessarily a great shot), then mentally reward yourself and put in reps until you feel ready for a test. If you didn't do it, then try to identify where you felt like things got off track.

Most golfers have a hard time with this step and only want to focus on how well they hit the ball. But elite golfers are able to separate the two objectives and focus on the movement they are making.

> *Teaching scenario: My swing is over the top and I'm spinning my upper body, so I need more of the Jackson 5 move. How do I actually work through implementing the Jackson 5?*
>
> *(Student hits a ball.)*
>
> *Coach: How did you do with your plan of moving your hips?*
>
> *Student: Terrible. I felt my arms scoop and I hit it on the toe!*
>
> *Coach: Were you able to pay attention to your hips at all?*
>
> *Student: Sure, they were fine but I scooped it!*

This example highlights how golfers waste practice reps. It's a bold word, but yes—it can be a waste if you fail to focus on one thing at a time.

The golf swing is tricky because it needs multiple elements to working together if it is to perform like clockwork. It is similar to how playing a beautiful song on the piano requires one to integrate two hands and ten fingers. First you learn one hand, then the other. When you try and put them together, you are focused on putting them together, so that still counts as "one thing" to focus on.

In the above example, the scoop may be a sign that the student didn't do the Jackson 5 move. Or it could be a sign that that the student did the Jackson 5 move and was trying to avoid hitting it fat. Only reading the feedback, or looking at video, would make it clear. *If you are putting in reps without clear feedback, you will have a hard time making progress with your game.*

Some are surprised to learn that it is not muscle memory and repetition that builds a skill—it's something called deliberate practice.

Deliberate practice, according to Trillium, involves "solving a problem through experience and thoughtfully evaluating each repetition. It requires effort and feedback." It requires you to be aware. It requires clear feedback. It requires effort.

If you are only focused on contact with the ball, you will need multiple things to work at once. When your solution requires multiple factors to simultaneously function, it challenges the requirement of "clear feedback." Wishy-washy feedback impedes true learning.

Part of the reason this program started with so much background about the club is to help you develop the clear feedback required to evaluate your practice and allow you to change your overall pattern.

Consider the following example of why it is important to understand cause and likely effect.

I was working with a 25 handicap golfer who had a steep arm movement in transition. As a result, he often shifted in toward the golf ball on the downswing. Basically, he stood up and scooped. Obviously it took a few movements for him to correct the stand up and to rebalance the pattern. The question is, where do we start to rebalance his pattern? Do we try to first correct the stand up or the steep arms?

I asked him what he thought. At first he said the legs, because he always wanted to get onto his lead foot and not hang back. I helped him work through the thought process by asking the following questions:

Me: If we don't stand up, what would steep arms do to contact?

Joe: They will slam into the ground.

Me: …And that won't feel good. What if we shallow the arms first?

Joe: I'd hit it thin?

Me: Yes, you may even whiff or top it, but at least that won't hurt. Why don't we start there?

We ended up starting with the arms. Even though he had a bunch of topped shots, after two weeks of working on the arms shallowing, he shot his best front nine holes ever with a 40—don't ask about the back nine.

Most golfers want to make one change and hit it perfectly. And that can happen once you've learned how to swing, but you'll first go through a period of uncomfortable misses. As long as you can predict and understand your misses, you will stay on track and make great progress toward your goal.

Feedback

A good shot doesn't always mean you are making progress; it could just be good timing with the old move. So, contact by itself isn't wholly reliable. Since we can't entirely rely on contact, you have to design drills, either at home or at the range, that offer clear feedback.

There are two major kinds of feedback: intrinsic and augmented.

Intrinsic feedback is what your body actually experiences.

Augmented feedback is information from outside your body.

Ultimately, intrinsic feedback is all that you will have on the course, so it is the most important.

Intrinsic feedback can be:

Visual—sight

Auditory—rhythm

Proprioceptive—muscles/joint positions

Tactile—skin/touch

Olfactory—smell

With intrinsic feedback, you know you hit a thin shot because of the vibration in your hands after contact.

Augmented feedback is everything else—everything outside your senses:

What your coach (or a buddy) says you did

What you see on video

What your divot looks like or where you see a ball imprint on your club

With augmented feedback, you know you hit a thin shot because of the mark on the club, the lack of divot, and the way the club appeared to contact the ball when observing video.

Augmented feedback helps build your intrinsic feedback's sensitivity and reliability. With accurate intrinsic feedback, you'll be able to make better adjustments on the course.

It's important that the drills you practice are designed to help build your memory bank of internal feedback. As Trillium said, "If you want to improve your play, a good goal is to be able to recognize and detect errors, otherwise you will be in trouble when you go to the course." This is why it's critical to be clear about a drill's purpose—so you can tweak it to enhance either your awareness or the feedback you receive.

Internal versus external focus

Internal focus is when you are most aware of a specific movement or section of movement. Focusing on a specific movement is great for training your swing, but not for execution on the course. Conversely, external focus isn't great for training your swing, but it is pretty good for execution on the course.

Suppose you are working on transition and trying to develop the Jackson 5 move. Internal focus means trying to feel that movement during the swing. External focus means focusing on a specific outcome, such as how you want the ball to fly or how you want the club to brush the ground/ball.

The internal focus would be the Jackson 5 move, while the external focus would be trying to get the club to brush the ground (which is aided by the Jackson 5 move). When you take your new skill from training to the course, the external focus (brush the ground) will likely perform better than the internal one (Jackson 5 move). But to build the muscle memory, you had to use internal focus to train the precision of the Jackson 5 move.

Internal focus can help quickly improve your swing pattern on the range. But success on the range is a double-edged sword on the course. On the course, golfers frequently overdo the movement that worked on the range. The result of trying harder is increased arousal and decreased performance.

> Find an external focus for playing on the course (feeling the weight of the club head brush the ground or feeling the club face alignment). External focus tends to keep the swing as a whole movement and keeps arousal down. This is especially important if you are not sure of a precise internal key. The worst thing to do on the course is to think of a movement instead of recalling a feeling that you developed during training.
>
> *Insight*

Internal versus external focus summary

If you have an internal focus that works really well in practice, you can test it on the course as long as it doesn't overly arouse you. Otherwise, use part of your practice to find an external focus that reproduces the same mechanics created by the internal focus.

Think of external focus as a general feeling that ties everything together in your swing. Those thoughts are much "safer" to play with on the course. Use internal focus sparingly and only when you have a feeling that has been confirmed to work well in random practice and games.

Arranging a practice session

You can't just practice technique and expect it to immediately transfer onto the course. This is not about muscle memory—it's about training the brain. In that sense, not all hit balls are equal—hitting 10 balls in a row the way you want is not the same as executing one shot in a row with a long break before it, 10 times.

All forms of practice can work to some degree, but some are better than others. The three basic forms of practice are:

Blocked—doing the same thing over and over again. This is great for the early stages of learning a technique.

Random—changing at least one thing each event. This is great for turning a technique into a skill.

Games/tests—a style of random practice that has consequences for bad shots. These are great for revealing potential on-course problems with your swing.

There is also a fourth category when it comes to golf. It's really just a form of random practice, but I usually have to point it out for my students. It involves going out with a few balls and practicing on the course, a couple shots at a time (I tend to get fewer dirty looks for playing multiple balls if it's late in the day). Practicing on the course is excellent for keeping expectations realistic and overcoming the struggles of adjusting techniques for different lies. It's also one of the best ways to turn a technique into a skill.

A good practice session will include more than one of these forms of practice. It will often begin with a blocked station to work on fundamentals. Starting with a blocked station utilizing internal focus with external feedback can establish great swing thoughts to test later. If you are a beginner, this could comprise up to 80 percent of your practice. If you are more experienced, blocked practice should take up less than 25 percent of your practice.

The next stage of practice should be random practice. This includes changing clubs and targets after each ball. For each swing, run through a scenario as if you were on the course. See if you can use just your pre-shot routine to dial in your swing (as opposed to rapidly firing balls to dial in your swing, as in blocked practice). Random practice is excellent for switching from internal focus to external focus.

Lastly, test your pattern with a game or a test. Make your practice feel closer to an important round by invoking scenarios in which you have to focus and worry about making a mistake.

For example, let's say your goal is to work on iron contact. You have been hitting your irons fat and thin and think a better brush location would help.

Phase 1—A blocked station with long irons. This helps us feel where the club is brushing the ground if we have better arm extension timing or direction. We may come up with an internal focus that enables better ground contact. After working on technique with some blocked practice, we move on to random practice.

Phase 2—A simple random practice. We play some pretend holes on the range. We visualize each shot and go through our full pre-shot routine. This is the perfect time to shift to external focus. We go out to play holes on the range. If we hit a good drive, we get a pretty good lie on the range; if we hit a bad drive, we get a bad lie on the range (either out of a divot or rough, if you have access to rough at your range).

Phase 3—A game to test the skill. We hit five shots in a row to a green. If we miss the green more than once, we have to start over. We have to complete this game with one short iron, one mid iron, and one long iron before we can leave the range.

When we come back for the next practice, we can truly test the skill by trying the game again without the blocked or random phases first. It's a slight gamble to test it with no warm up.

On the one hand, if we do well with the test, our confidence will receive a big boost. On the other hand, if we do poorly or we get frustrated, we may feel discouraged.

Know yourself and strategically choose your tests. If you don't want to start the second practice with a game, start with blocked practice and work through the stages again.

If you arrange your practice in phases that feature progressive activities that use a movement plan, you will more likely see good practices yield good scores on the course.

Assessments

If you are not sure what to practice, try looking at statistics for your rounds. If you don't have statistics, do a skill assessment to get an idea of where you're at. Most skill assessments are for the short game, but you can do them for the full swing as well. When scoring your assessment, make sure to use a fair grading scale. If you have a 25 handicap, it is not fair to use tour pro benchmarks.

Skill assessments can help calibrate reasonable expectations. Frustration sets in when there is a big gap between your ability and your expectations. Being frustrated makes you more likely to move into a higher level of arousal and underperform. Poor results make you even *more* frustrated, and thus the cycle goes around and around.

Golfers who start with unreasonable expectations tend to give up on their movement plan and revert to what "they've always done." Usually, reverting to your comfort zone decreases arousal, which makes it even more comfortable to stay at the same level and to give up on evolving your game. Managing your expectations is key to long-term success.

Insight

Suppose you are practicing and experience a big drop-off at the end of the session. You are either experiencing information overload or are simply fatigued. If a big drop-off happens, switch to another task or walk away and try again after a break, or at the next practice session.

CHAPTER 43

The Process of Playing a Shot

n this section, we discuss the process of playing a shot. This should include the pre-shot routine, the execution, and the post-shot routine. Other than monitoring your arousal level, constantly following a routine on the course is the best way to access the skills you have trained.

If you read any "mental game" golf book, you will encounter a common process for executing a shot. It includes three distinct phases. Let's look at each of those phases to see how we actually play with this swing we're developing.

The Stock Tour Swing mental process

1. *Pre-shot routine*—prepare for the shot. Establish a clear image or feeling of the shot in your mind.
   a. Evaluate the factors and decide on the shot you want to hit.
   b. Fully commit and trigger the execution phase (a tempo, a visualization, or a feel are all great triggers).
3. *Execution phase*—execute the shot, keeping arousal low. Strive to achieve the feeling of being in the zone.
   a. Keep a single-minded focus on the shot with an optional general awareness of the technique. Focus intensity should be low to improve performance.
   b. Execute the shot with a "see ball, hit ball" attitude and let the ball get in the way of a graceful swing while staying focused on the target.
3. *Post-shot routine*—this is the time to evaluate the shot. Either imprint the shot or try to learn from it.

        i.   If you hit a quality shot, imprint it.

       ii.   If you hit it poorly, learn from it.

  b.   Finally, let it go and move on to the next shot (repeat 60 or so times a round, hopefully).

I'm sure you can imagine what average golfers do, but let's take a look.

Consider the typical process for your average golfer. Let's call him John Q. Duffer:

1. Pre-shot routine
   a. John Q. Duffer optimistically grabs a club with which he can barely hit the full distance required for this shot.
      i. Cautionary tale: John Q. Duffer doesn't know how far each club really goes.
   b. John Q. Duffer forgets to factor in subtle factors like slope, risk vs. reward, and comfort level with a shot.
      i. Cautionary tale: He is genuinely surprised that the ball didn't go the same distance as his best shots on the range.
3. Execution phase
   a. John Q. Duffer stands over the ball and runs through an elaborate swing checklist.
      i. Cautionary tale: He should have run through mechanics in the pre-shot routine phase, not the execution phase.
   b. John Q. Duffer swings "at the ball" with a lot of tension and mechanical thoughts.
      i. Cautionary tale: His mechanical thoughts are arousing and internally focused, both of which challenge his ability to perform.
4. Post-shot routine
   a. Two options: Either
      i. John Q. Duffer hits it well, tells everyone in earshot how easy the game is, and that he's finally got it; or
      ii. John Q. Duffer hits it poorly and concludes his swing isn't working.
         1. Cautionary tale: His solution is to play golf tip roulette and try whatever random swing advice he recently read in *Golf Digest*.
   b. John Q. Duffer is more emotional over bad shots than good shots.
      i. Cautionary tale: His mental process slowly conditions his brain to hit more bad shots than good ones.

This gives you an idea of what *not* to do. Now, let's break down the phases of what we should do. We are going to use some terms that I learned from Dr. Bill Campbell—the **Caddy Zone** and the **Player Zone**. To these I've added the **Interview Zone**. These concepts aren't unique—almost every mental game book uses some form of the language. In *Vision 54* it is "Think Box/Play Box." In *The Fluid Motion Factor* it is "Universe 1/Universe 2." Whatever you call it is fine, so long as you recognize the different phases involved in hitting a good shot.

Caddy Zone: Pre-shot routine

1. Assess all the factors of the shot.
   a. What shot am I most comfortable with in this situation?
   b. What are the on-course factors that will influence the shot?
      i. wind (what direction and what intensity?)
      ii. lie (Is the ball sitting up, down, clear? Will it come out fast or slow?)
      iii. slope—both of the lie and the landing spot (uphill/downhill/side hill)
      iv. hazards (Any water or out of bounds to avoid?)
   c. What is my swing shot shape today? (Am I in control of my ball or should I be more conservative? Is it curving more than normal today? Does my normal curve fit the shot at hand?)
   d. Distance (Which club will hit my landing spot?)
   e. Trajectory or shape I want to hit (Is it different from my normal? Is this a shot I can pull off better than 50/50? What are the consequences of a bad shot? Is the reward worth the risk?)
2. Choose the club for the shot you want to hit and fully commit. It is better to commit to a lower-percentage shot than to hit a high-percentage shot with poor commitment. Amateurs mess up the right shot with poor commitment, while professional golfers pull off the "wrong shot" because of full commitment.
3. Take your practice swings (if you do so) with a general awareness of the technique for the shot, but with a clear focus on an external focus (the intended shot shape, the landing zone, or my favorite, how the club is brushing the ground.)
4. Fully commit and start the execution sequence.

Player Zone: Execution

The mental state of a good execution is similar to a meditative state. Some golfers experience vivid sensations while others "go blank" and remember nothing. The goal is to reach a state of automation similar to the mental state you have while tying your shoes or brushing your teeth.

The last thing you want is to have words floating around your mind while you hit the ball. The place in the brain that controls movement is not where self-talk occurs, so if you talk to yourself over the ball, you are using the wrong part of your brain during the execution. If you normally talk to yourself over the ball, break that habit in your transfer practice time (random practice and games).

A lot of golfers like to have one clear swing thought. But it's important that these thoughts not be words. Saying words to yourself uses one part of the brain, however the feeling or sensation should trigger another. A good swing thought should be either a feeling or sensation in one part of your body (such as, "I feel my arms relaxed as they start the swing"). Or they could be a tempo ("I feel smooth and balanced"). Or they can be an image of the shot with no sensation in the body ("I see the picture, and I will recreate the picture").

For this reason, I like to call them swing *sensations* rather than swing *thoughts*. They can help you get into the zone, just as having a single focus (like a mantra, counting your breath, or focusing on a candle flame) can help you meditate.

Execute the shot while in this athletic zone state, then move on to the post-shot process.

The Interview Zone: Post-shot routine

If you are committed to being a process golfer (a term you'll learn shortly), you have two options after a shot. Either you hit it well and imprint that shot in your memory bank, or you hit it poorly and learn from it. In the event of a bad shot, resist all temptation to condemn yourself. Condemning yourself is an outcome-focused response and can have major long-term consequences.

What if you hit a good shot?

If you hit a good shot, imprint the shot and take a moment to reflect. You can hold the finish longer, tap your sternum and say "good shot," or reaffirm yourself and say, "That's the real me." Or, you can do what I stole from Mark O'Meara and Tiger Woods, and spin the club.

I didn't think in these terms when I started spinning the club, but doing so was my way of imprinting good shots. After bad shots I wouldn't spin it, and since I thought spinning looked cool, it became a little extra mental motivation. "If I hit a good shot, I get to do the club spin!"

In one of the videos I made a while back, a colleague of mine actually called me out for spinning the club on a practice swing. In my mind, I made a great swing and thought it deserved a spin of the club. Even though I didn't hit a ball, I subconsciously rewarded the good swing.

What if you don't hit a good shot?

If you don't hit a good shot, decode the feedback to find out where the process went wrong. Start with the most critical piece of information—either you were in a good mental state (free from distractions and had a good level of arousal) or you weren't.

If you hit a bad shot despite the fact that you were in a good state (mentally free from distraction) and had a low level of arousal, read the objective feedback and deduce what mechanical error you made. If the error becomes a pattern, you can address it in your next practice session. On the other hand, if you weren't mentally free from distractions, ignore the mechanical feels and investigate what prevented you from fully committing to the shot.

Examples of thoughts that prevent such commitment include:

— Physical distractions (*"Something just didn't feel right"*)
> — You may not notice the ball is below or above your feet, or your balance is off.
> — You may not notice excess tension in the arms before a specific shot. Your arms are tense and this changes the timing or club face orientation.

— Visual distractions (*"Something just didn't look right"*)
> — You may not be prepared for the ball to be sitting down in a bad lie and your brain freaks out.
> — You may not be able to stop looking at the water hazard. You tell yourself to stop it, but your brain asks why? You don't answer it and so you hit where your brain was focused—the water.
> — You saw something move out of the corner of your eye. By the time you shifted your focus back to the ball, the swing was already off.

— Mental distractions (*"I just didn't focus on the shot"*)
> — You may be thinking about outcome while standing over the ball, but swing anyway.
> — You may rush your process because you are worried about slow play. As a result, you hit a shot in the wrong state of mind.

Once you identify the interference, figure out how it was first allowed into your mind. It's somewhat like dog training. You have to issue the correction before the dog bites, not after. For example, you may see the dog's ears go back and correct his attitude then. If he's already biting, it's too late for the correction. With your golf game, you want to look for the first sign that you were going to have interference. Once you identify the first sign, you can build a strategy to prevent it next time.

Recap: Linking the Secrets of the Stock Tour Swing

There are three ways to improve your game on the course:

1. Improve your technique.
2. Improve your practice habits to turn that technique into a skill.
3. Improve your mental game so your brain can better access your trained skills.

Make sure your practice habits reflect all three ways to improve; avoid spending all your time working on technical aspects.

The mental intensity you bring to the course greatly affects your game. This can be looked at via the performance vs. arousal curve. Simple tasks like sprinting are better performed with high intensity, but complex tasks like the golf swing are better performed with a lower level of arousal.

To really train a skill, practice smart. Don't try to hit 50 good shots in a row. Make sure your practice features challenges and obstacles. Remember to think of learning like tracing a heart versus drawing one with no stencil. If you only know how to do it with the stencil, your game will break down on the course.

The three steps to practicing with a realistic process are:

1. Make a movement plan.
2. Execute the action.
3. Evaluate the movement in relation to the plan.

This process requires that your feedback be specific to your drill. Stay focused and try not to get distracted by something unrelated to the movement plan.

Feedback can be intrinsic or augmented. Intrinsic feedback is what you can sense with your body and eyes. Augmented feedback is what helps calibrate your intrinsic feedback, such as a coach or video of your swing. Intrinsic feedback is the most important, and ultimately all that you have on the course.

To arrange a practice session, use three types of practice:

1. Blocked practice—when you do the same thing over and over.
2. Random practice—when you do something different each time
3. Games/tests—random practices in which the performance has a score or consequences.

If you are not sure what to work on, use in-round statistics or a game assessment to illuminate your weaknesses.

Finally, playing a shot generally has three phases:

1. Pre-shot routine—think about the shot and plan the swing you want to make.
2. Execution—clear your mind and let the swing go.
3. Post-shot routine—nonjudgmental self-reflection that reinforces the process.

CHAPTER 44

Putting Part 5 Principles into Practice "You Can't Serve Two Masters"

I once overhead James Sieckmann share the following story in a clinic, and it's a perfect summary of what I see in my students. In golf, and in life, there are two masters you can serve. One is the "process" and the other is the "outcome." As a golf coach, the students who improve the fastest and experience the fewest setbacks are the ones who serve the process. The golfers who struggle more typically serve the outcome.

> Golf is a hard game. You can do everything right, but still end up in trouble thanks to a funny bounce, misjudged wind, or another factor outside your control. Since there are so many of these, do what the best golfers do—commit to the process and spend time working on what you can control.
>
> *Insight*

Why the outcome master is misguided

We all want to hit good shots. But if we focus on hitting good shots, it makes it hard to stay in the moment. Also, focusing on the outcome tends to generate too much excitement/arousal. When you hit well in practice, you rarely feel pressure for results. Who cares if you hit a bad shot? You can just take another ball.

Those who serve the outcome master get more excited on the course than in practice. Doing something different on the course is a recipe for on-course letdowns.

In golf, it's better to have a clear plan (which we will cover in Part 7) regarding your improvement. A first step is to decide on a clear plan. Most of the time, golfers who are committed to the outcome don't truly understand what they are working on or why the work will help. They thus have a hard time staying on track. They can commit to working on one area as long as it's going well. But at the first sign of adversity, many jump ship. They usually aren't averse to putting in the time and working at their game. But because they lack a real long-term plan, they bail before they have a chance to make real improvement.

Here are two typical examples of conversations I have with students. The first is with someone who serves the process and goes something like:

Me: How's your game?

Process student: Struggling a bit. I can do the move I'm trying to make on short swings or slow swings, but when I try to add speed it falls apart.

Me: How have you been practicing? And how have you been trying to problem-solve it?

Process student: I've been hitting 9–3 shots and I can do that pretty well, but when I try to go to the full swing I can see on video/feel myself lunging at the top. I think I'm struggling with transition. If I slow it down I can hit it better on full shots, but I can't really play with that feeling.

Me: Great feedback. Can you do it in a full swing without a ball and by just brushing the ground?

Process student: I don't know. I've never tried that. I'll do that next practice. I think I would hit the ground behind the line on a full swing. But on the 9–3 I think I could do it pretty well.

Me: Well, sounds like there is something getting you out of position in transition. If you think you are at a place where you can add more, we can discuss what you are doing. Or if you think you need more time to work on your impact drills, we can stay there for a bit. You can hit more of a punch shot on the course if you play this week.

Process student: I think I can handle more. We can try it, and if it is too much I can always back off and use my impact drills. But I want to keep moving and I think that transition is a big reason why I'm having trouble doing it in the full swing. This isn't easy, but it's fun and I can see how big this will be for my game—I'll keep working on it.

This second conversation is typical of those who serve the outcome master:

Me: How's your game?

Outcome student: It's a wreck,

I practiced for X amount of time (which really isn't that much on a learning timeline but sounds like a lot to this golfer). I haven't gotten any better. I think we are on the wrong track.

Me: How have you been practicing? And how have you been trying to problem-solve it?

Outcome student: I tried the drills and feeling it in the full swing, and it's not working.

Me: How were you monitoring whether you did the drills correctly?

Outcome student: I tried to do them and thought about it in my swing, but I was hitting the ball all over the place.

Me: Well, why do you think it's not working? Are there any times you can do it correctly? 9–3? Pump swings? If you hold your follow through position like we did in the lesson?

Outcome student: I don't know, but this isn't working, I'm not hitting good shots.

These two archetypes illustrate how your approach can influence the extent to which you improve. Every high-level golfer I have talked to sounds like the process student. The key self-reflection here is which one you aspire to be. The process student or the outcome student?

The outcome student has not internalized what the club is doing and what it should do differently. He's just hoping to find the magic swing tip, but this leaves him no wiggle room to troubleshoot during practice.

A lot of golfers simply try to think the new swing move. But to train it correctly, you have to come up with a drill or thought where you can get clear feedback. Then you can train it by putting in the reps in the different practice stages.

If you don't understand what you need to train or why it is important, you're playing *golf tip lottery*, and it's unlikely that putting in reps will help you.

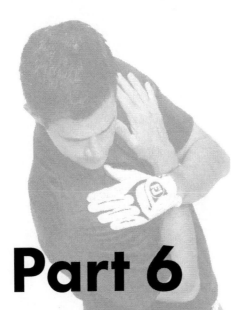

Part 6

Common Problems Faults and Fixes

We are in the closing stretch of the Stock Tour Swing program. By this point you should have:

- a clear image of the golf swing's ideal shape (and maybe a fuzzy image of your own swing pattern);
- a solid understanding of how the body produces the shape (both high-level ideas and important details of the key phases); and
- a basic understanding of how to train a swing you can trust on the course.

In this section, we tackle the all-important question—what are the common mechanical pitfalls to avoid?

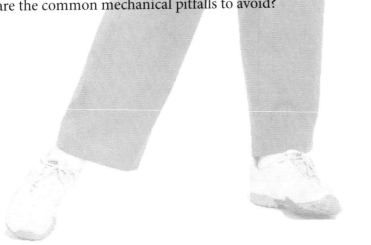

CHAPTER 45

Swing Pattern Influences

t's easy to identify the goal of the golf swing and to visualize the ideal swing shape (once you know it). But actually producing the ideal swing is another issue entirely. Even if you know all the movements, two people doing the same thing won't look identical because of different limb lengths, muscle attachment sites, muscle fiber blends, previous sports experience, and more.

This section is designed to help you navigate common problems with the swing. Know there will be struggles but don't sweat them—struggles will likely be predictable misses based on the path of the club. Since the misses are predictable, so are the solutions!

When it comes to movement, we are creatures of habit. As a result, you likely have swing issues that consistently plague your game. Numerous tour pros have stated they continue to battle the same swing issues they faced in junior golf. Movement patterns are established when you are very young, so it's very easy to fall back onto your natural tendencies.

For example, I was a tennis player and a basketball player before I was a golfer. As a result, I have a very active lower body. If I'm not careful, I can fall into an early extension/slide pattern. Also, because of tennis, I have a tendency to use my right arm on top of the shaft during the release. This causes the club face to close and the arms to get a bit steep. The lower-body action balances the right arm on top of the shaft for my long game, but I tend to struggle with wedges. When I'm playing well, I feel centered in my body, especially over the shorter clubs and half swings. When I get lost, I have my key four or five drills that get my transition and release back on track.

My goal for you is to be able to clearly say the same about your golf game. Your description of yourself should reveal your own tendencies, limitations, and drills you rely on. You may even create a theory about why or how your swing tendencies initially developed.

Before we discuss what I call **swing faults**, know that no swing fault is completely wrong. All swing faults solve a problem, but we call them faults because they usually aren't the best way to solve the problem.

Swing faults develop in the early stages of a golf career—usually the first year, because it involves so much trial and error. Don't view a swing fault as necessarily bad. Regard it as revealing with which movement combinations your brain is most comfortable. When first looking at a swing I always ask myself:

"Why would a reasonable brain do this in the swing?"

Asking yourself that single question can change the way you look at swing faults.

Suppose a beginning golfer takes a few swings, mostly with his arms, and hits the ground before the ball. This doesn't feel good, so he tries to fix it. His brain has an idea, so he makes a change (standing up, lunging forward, turning more, and so on) to improve contact. Most golfers don't consciously know what change they made, but they know they changed something. After taking more swings and hitting the ground in a better place, golfers start to imprint the solution into their swing. However, the solution to hitting the ground (in this case, by standing up or bending the arms) is usually not the best long-term fix.

The same thing happens when a new golfer tries to hit the ball straight. It usually flies off to the right (a slice). After some trial and error, the golfer learns that if she stands up at the right time and flips her wrist (early extension to close the face with a cast pattern), then the ball goes more straight (especially with the seven iron that she practices with the most). While this solution works for the shorter clubs, she notices it tends to still slice a lot with the driver.

The stand up/cast pattern sometimes works, but not for getting a straight ball flight with all clubs. Eventually this leads to a swing that is built around the timing and extent of standing up, and further ingrains the pattern. Over the years, the swing has a handful of integrated key movements. If this golfer were to apply the solutions in this book, there may be only one or two major patterns to reprogram if she wants to improve. But if the golfer lacks a *clear solution with predictable misses*, then she will frequently get lost trying to reprogram the pattern.

One good thought exercise is to investigate the struggles you faced during your first six months playing golf. These complex puzzles are like peeling an onion. If you discover the core disturbance at the center of the onion, you can save yourself a lot of time fixing layers that aren't the real problem.

With proper direction and information, you can make a lasting swing change. All it takes is to understand the core pattern and focus on the moves that will correct it.

Physical influence

I'm going to let my personal trainer background creep in here. Your body is affecting your swing. To be clear, I don't think there are any physical restrictions that directly cause a swing fault. But there are physical situations that can significantly contribute to certain swing patterns.

I tell my students that we can train most of the key movements correctly, without training the body. However, if you want to speed up the process, you should work out with a qualified trainer to improve the parts of your body that influence your swing fault.

For this swing fault section, I will suggest physical areas that may be contributing to a swing fault. If you work with a trainer, show them this section and discuss whether a physical restriction is involved in your swing pattern.

We could elaborate on corrective exercises here, but since this is an instruction book I won't go into much detail about exercises for each scenario. Instead, I explain the movements and concepts that are more likely the cause than the body. While you are learning to swing better, you and your trainer can also work on your body to accelerate your progress.

It's worth pointing out that almost every swing fault can be linked to problems in the T-spine (thoracic spine) and hips. In fact, one of the tour stereotypes of a program from a certified Titleist Performance Institute trainer is that everyone has a *tight T-spine* and *weak glutes*. In addition, almost everyone is told to reinforce their weak shoulder blade stabilizers and core muscles.

If everyone has the same physical restrictions, then that universal diagnosis (a tight T-spine and weak glutes) can't possibly correlate directly to swing faults, since there are many types of those. This raises the question: **Are all swing faults just different ways to compensate for these common physical dysfunctions?**

While a physical limitation may contribute to a swing fault, simply fixing the physical dysfunctions does not necessarily fix the related swing fault. To truly fix a swing fault, you must understand what the swing fault does that is helpful for your swing. That's right: *a swing fault actually helps your swing in some way.*

To replace a swing fault, you must identify what the fault does that is helpful and what would be a good replacement.

CHAPTER 46

Backswing Patterns

Loss of posture

Figure 46.1   Figure 46.2

Loss of posture results from a lack of left tilt in the backswing. The shoulders look flat and the head raises from the set-up position.

What is loss of posture?

Loss of posture, simply put, is when the upper body rises in the backswing. This happens either because the upper body actually rises, or more commonly, there is a lack of side bend in the backswing.

Loss of posture makes it harder to use your lower body to start the downswing, since the hips are not in a **loaded position**. Without the hip bump (the Jackson 5 move) leading the downswing, the body tends to be steeper during the release, which limits production of the flat spot.

There are very few tour pros who have the loss of posture pattern, but one is Kenny Perry (he developed his loss of posture move as a result of an injury).

How do you know if you have loss of posture?

On video, loss of posture is easy to see from the down-the-line view of a golfer. It will look like the head is elevated in the backswing. Many well-meaning partners see a golfer do this and say, "You picked your head up." As a result, it's common for golfers to try to keep their head down.

Unfortunately, when most golfers think, "Keep your head down," they try to stay more flexed forward instead of adding more side bend. In actuality, staying flexed forward will usually worsen a backswing by causing the upper body to shift off the ball and the arms to bend.

Figure 46.3   Figure 46.4

Typically loss of posture is followed by a pronounced chop or crunch on the way down. Loss of posture can result from using a chop move to power your swing instead of rotating your body.

How can loss of posture help? What do you need to replace it with?

Golfers receive two benefits from loss of posture. It helps create power in the trunk (chop move) and/or prevents fat shots. The power part is usually easy to solve—just learn to create speed from your legs. Learning to not hit it fat is a little trickier and requires us to explore the different root causes of loss of posture.

Lack of side bend. Loss of posture is simply a change in elevation or posture during the backswing. This gives the impression of standing up, but when your buddy says you are doing this, please interpret it to mean you are really lacking side bend toward the ball. Many golfers have been told to rotate their spine, but this fails to focus on the key difference between standing up and not standing up. It isn't forward/backward; it is in side bend. To make a good pivot, review the backswing section and the backswing shoulder plane drill (Chapter 35). If you do it correctly, you won't stand up, and you will feel load in your trail hip even though your weight may feel more over your lead hip.

Lack of arm rotation. The second half of the backswing involves some spine extension as the arms rotate into position. Players who omit the side bend often fail to rotate their arms at all. Rotating your arms can challenge your upper back muscles, so if you feel a strain in your back at the top of the swing, strengthen this area.

Grip. A third common reason to stand up is when the grip is too much in the palm—this prevents hinging (or setting) the wrists. If you can't set your wrists, standing up can help create arm load and height.

Power. If you create speed in the downswing based around a crunch-and-chop movement, standing up in the backswing will make chopping more effective. If you want to change your loss of posture in the backswing, and your swing is based around a crunch-and-chop movement, you would first need to work on the way you power the swing in the downswing.

What physically contributes to loss of posture?

While there are other reasons for a lack of side bend, what follows are the common physical restrictions to look for if you are trying to manage this swing pattern.

Thoracic spine (T-spine). Side bending requires the rib cage and the hips to be flexible. Many golfers avoid side bending because they lack the flexibility to side bend and rotate.

Trail shoulder. Poor trail arm shoulder flexibility can restrict your ability to externally rotate the trail arm. To support the weight of the club, you want your trail elbow (not your lead elbow) underneath the grip. If you lack shoulder flexibility, you will not side bend, since side bending requires more trail shoulder external rotation to attain that alignment.

Hip dysfunctions. Tight lead hip external rotation or tight trail hip internal rotation can cause a golfer to lose their posture. Also, weakness in the trail glutes can lead to standing up during the backswing (standing up avoids putting too much force into the hips).

Neck. If the neck is stiff, turning your shoulder under your chin can overstretch the levator scapula on the lead side. If you get a *kink in your neck,* it is probably because you are overusing the levator scapula muscle, which also could contribute to your loss of posture.

Mid-back. Weakness in the mid-back muscles challenges arm extension at the top of the swing. In this case, the club head usually feels heavy. This is a common issue for women, but can also plague men who have rounded shoulders.

How does loss of posture affect the shape of the swing? Can it be counterbalanced?

Loss of posture makes the club head path more like an actual circle instead of an ellipse with a good flat spot. It does this by raising the circle higher off the ground.

Lack of side bend at the top of the swing is a sign that a golfer is not loading their hips. This isn't a problem when they don't use their hips in the downswing (say, for a full wedge shot) but it is a problem for something like the driver, where you want to have a good flat spot.

If you don't come back down, your flat spot will be too narrow at the bottom. In addition, your angle of attack will typically be steep from the lack of axis tilt.

Since this is a backswing issue, it is possible to compensate in transition to get it back on track, but few are able to do that. It's really hard to get back on track from this lack of loaded glute position.

Keys to solving loss of posture and drills to train the solution

To fix the flat shoulder plane, point your lead shoulder more down (at the ball) as you rotate. This creates the look of keeping your spine angle. You will also need a bit of arm rotation. Golfers who lose posture usually have to overcome the fear that staying close to the ground will make them too steep and/or hit it fat.

Sway

Figure 46.5   Figure 46.6

There are two kinds of sways—an amateur sway and a tour sway. These photos show the amateur sway pattern.

What is sway?

Sway is a backswing issue in which the lower body moves laterally away from the target. Sway is characterized by one of two things:

The weight goes to the outside of the trail foot; and/or

The pelvis moves away from the target in the backswing.

A sway almost guarantees timing and club-to-ground contact issues, especially if the golfer's pressure shifts to the outside of the foot. The shift to the outside of the foot can disrupt the lower body's mechanics during transition and cause a host of contact issues. However, it can also help some golfers feel rhythm in the backswing.

Tour players who sway tend to rely on hitting many, many golf balls to stay sharp; they are usually labeled as *streaky*.

How do you know if you have sway?

On video, from face-on angle, see if the inside of the trail foot is elevated at the top of the backswing, and/or if you see the pelvis shifted laterally over the trail foot. It is OK to shift a little bit in the backswing, as long as you don't break those two rules. They both limit how well you are able to use your lower body in transition.

What does sway do that's helpful? What do you need to replace it with?

There are two types of sways.

Tour sway

One type of sway is a shift during the early part of the backswing. This is just a timing move and doesn't pose a major issue, unless the weight moves to the outside of the foot and stays there—or if the pattern shows up in your short game. A shift of just the pelvis but not the foot is known as the **tour sway**. A number of elite golfers employ this sway to help their rhythm and timing. As long as the pelvis doesn't shift too much, and as long as it starts working back toward the target well before the top of the swing, it only minimally affects the shape of the circle.

Amateur sway

The second type of sway typically happens later, during the backswing, when the arms and wrists set. A golfer with **amateur sway** frequently reaches max sway at the top of the backswing. The amateur sway is usually accompanied by either too much arching of the lower back (a reverse spine move), or, if the spine stays neutral, then all the sway is in the lower body and foot. This second sway is usually followed by an over-the-top move to start the downswing. While the second amateur sway pattern is bad for performance, the first (reverse spine version) is especially bad for the back. If you reverse spine, it's only a matter of time before you will experience low back pain.

> The sway is one of the easier patterns to fix once you become aware of it, but if your sway pattern doesn't go away after a month or two of practice, it is most likely tied to your power source. If you suspect this is so, then the downswing needs to be trained before you can permanently correct the sway.
>
> *Insight*

The amateur sway loads the lat muscle (latissimus dorsi)

A sway is often a sign that a golfer has a lat-dominant power source. Getting the hips more under the shoulders puts the lat muscle in a strong position to pull down on the club. However, this is a weak position for lower-body rotation. If you sway, it is usually a sign that you aren't taking advantage of rotation for speed during the downswing.

What physically contributes to sway?

Hip flexibility lead or trail. If you have a hard time rotating your hips, you will have a hard time rotating in the backswing. Since you can't rotate the hips, something else has to move—usually the feet and knees. Using the feet and knees frequently creates the amateur sway pattern and breeds inconsistency.

Thoracic spine (T-spine). To create depth (by moving the hands away from the target line) in the backswing, the body must rotate or the arms must work across your body. If you are limited in hip or T-spine rotation, you will usually just move your arms across your body. If your arms work across your body, then rotating your spine creates too much depth. To avoid getting too deep, most golfers stop rotation, which leads them to sway.

Ankle restrictions. If the ankle is stiff, it will be restricted the same as when wearing a ski boot. In a so-called ski boot ankle, the only way to shift your weight is to roll to the outside of the foot. There isn't much your lower body can do from the outside of the foot, so you will be left with an upper body–dominated swing.

Lat dominance. If you are weak in hip and core rotation, it is common to use your lats and upper-body pull as your main power source. If you do so, then getting into a loaded position will look different for you than a swing powered by the legs and core.

Wrist. Very late wrist set and limited wrist movements can prevent a golfer from feeling a complete backswing until late in the swing. Backswings of golfers with restricted wrist set usually stop the backswing at the point of tension in the lower back instead of the hips and core.

What does sway do to the shape of the swing?

It moves the circle farther away from the target. But since the sway doesn't move the circle up or down, it doesn't have to ruin the flat spot—but it can challenge your ability to produce it. Why? Because when you sway, it requires more speed and/or time to shift the circle toward the target in the downswing. Many golfers who sway will have a hard time waiting to fire their arms.

Keys to solving sway and drills to train the solution

Fixing sway is a matter of learning to push with the inside of the trail foot and keeping your core stable as you set the club. Golfers who sway will sometimes have to overcome the feeling that they will be steep without a shift in weight.

Golfers who use sway for timing need to find rhythm differently. Instead of having big body moves, they need to train the body to feel subtle rhythmic changes from shifting weight through rotation.

CHAPTER 47

Downswing Problems

Downswing patterns are trickier to change than backswing patterns. The downswing takes around .25 seconds to perform. That's it. It's hard to feel so many different movements in such a short amount of time. The good news is that solving the right downswing problem can offer your game the biggest technical leaps.

Early Extension

Figure 47.1   Figure 47.2

Early extension can be one of the more frustrating patterns because it creates a feeling of inconsistency—both in contact as well as ball flight curve.

What is early extension?

Early extension is one of the more frustrating swing patterns because of its inherent inconsistency. Golfers who struggle with early extension almost always complain about having both big blocks and big hooks, as well as having trouble making solid contact with irons off of the fairway. The early extension pattern is characterized by a standing-up move, or moving the hips toward the golf ball (instead of toward the target), during the downswing. This thrust movement is commonly accompanied by an early release of the arms and hands. Golfers who early extend will frequently describe themselves as a **picker** style of golfer. There are a number of issues that make early extension complicated, but it is possible to solve. Let's discuss each complication created by early extension.

Early extension is a difficult pattern to clearly define. It's typically described as the lower body moving excessively toward the golf ball during the downswing. But it can also be described as the upper body moving excessively away from the golf ball. But what exactly constitutes excessive?

Less than 2 inches of movement in either direction is a good goal. There are lots of tour golfers who move less than 2 inches toward the ball with their mid-pelvis, and less than 2 inches away from it with their upper body. But there are many amateurs who are in the 3- or 4-inch zone for both. If you see a dramatic movement away from the line drawn on your tailbone, you are probably in the 3-inch (or more) category.

Many tour pros do this movement to some degree, but rarely as severely as amateurs. As you'll see, a little of this movement is helpful because it aids all three factors in the power-path-face equation; too much, however, can cause dramatic inconsistency.

How do you know if you have early extension?

Looking at a down-the-line video, draw a vertical line on your tailbone (either at address or at the top of the swing). Look to see if your lower body moves off that line, toward the golf ball, in the downswing.

It can also help to draw a line on the forehead. Movement off the forehead line reveals a secondary form of early extension.

The likely miss pattern with early extension is an exaggerated in-to-out path. This usually results in blocks, hooks, or even snap hooks. It can cause shanks and heel hits. Early extenders also typically have more trouble hitting short irons and handling really tight lies.

What does early extension do that's helpful? What do you need to replace it with?

Early extension helps with all three of the swing's key drivers. It shallows the club head path, squares the club face, and helps create speed.

Path. Early extension is one of the best ways to move the club head path more in-to-out. Early extension is often a support move for an overly steep arm motion during transition because it creates an overly shallow path from the body.

Avoid fat contact. For many golfers, the first few golf swings are scary. Beginners typically freeze their body in an attempt to make solid contact. While this is a normal reaction, it leads to raising the upper body to prevent hitting the ground before the ball.

Face. Early extension is one of the fastest ways to create club face rotation through impact. If your club face is well open at shaft parallel to the ground, you will almost always use some form of early extension, and stall to close the face quickly down at the bottom of the arc.

Power. For many golfers who extend early, doing so makes them feel powerful and like they are able to hit the ball hard. A forward thrust of your hips/pelvis is associated with jumping and dead lifting (picking up a heavy object off the ground). These two movements are very powerful forms of hip extension. If you extend early as a result of power production, your toughest battle will be learning to feel rotational speed as a dominant force producer.

Pushing through the ground. This third mental barrier can be similar to the power production concept. When you extend early, you push through your feet like you are sprinting or jumping. That means you push the ground away from the ball and end up with more of your weight toward your toes. Most tour pros tend to work their way toward the left heel during the release. Even golfers who appear to get up on their toes (Bubba Watson, Laura Davies) do so from vertical force. When they do finally land, they are typically more in the heel than the toe.

To avoid shifting your weight into your toes, you should feel like you push the ground toward the golf ball. I have had a number of players do this movement and say, "How do you create power like that?" Measuring will confirm that the club head speed doesn't drop significantly. The fear stems from a mental barrier more than a real performance drop. Sometimes, club head speed will increase, even though it doesn't feel like it does.

Compensating for a square lead foot

If the lead foot is square to the target and you don't have enough hip flexibility to turn your body toward the target, you have just created a new problem. You have to pivot your lead foot, or avoid rotating through the ball altogether. The most common way to avoid rotating is to thrust upward and spin the foot to a new position while you are off the ground.

What physically contributes to early extension?

Glute muscles. If your hips do not drift forward, your hip extensors must work harder through the ball. Early extension can be due to a weakness in the lead leg's glute muscle. In response to glute weakness, golfers use the lower back during the downswing, causing the extension toward the ball.

Deep squat. If you ever solicit the services of a golf specialist, they will likely test you with the **overhead deep squat**. Chances are you will fail this test. Even if you don't fail, there is a good chance you might still extend early, since this movement has some positive elements for the golf swing. I have had more success improving early extending by clarifying the technical barrier than by improving the ability to deep squat. I think the link of early extenders to poor squatting is more correlation than causation. Most people can't squat. Most people extend early. Boom—you've got correlation.

Lead shoulder. This is a tricky one. If the lead shoulder is injured and limited in external rotation, the golfer will try to keep the arm in a safe position (like in a sling—shrug and hug) during the bracing movement. This position moves the low point back, so the golfer will frequently slide and extend early to compensate.

Lead hip/ankle. It takes a certain amount of lead hip and ankle flexibility to play golf well. The lead foot turnout test (see Chapter 32 in Part 3) reveals where you should set up to allow the hip and ankle to work properly. But there is only so much foot flare available. If your hip is severely tight, you might not be able to open your foot enough to adequately compensate for it.

What does early extension do to the shape of the swing?

Early extension disrupts the flat spot because the body typically doesn't drop enough in transition. Since the thorax moves farther from the golf ball with early extension, during the release the hands will work more high to low instead of slightly up. If you think you might have this issue, evaluating the height of the hands is easiest to see with a face-on camera angle.

Keys to solving early extension and drills to train the solution

Early extension is one of the trickier patterns to solve and requires patience. You must learn to shallow the path in with the arms (in transition), close the face earlier in the swing with the motorcycle movement, and to wipe the arms more across your body instead of extending at the ball (in the release).

Insight

A quick note on the slide: I have never seen someone who struggles with a slide who didn't also have issues with early extension. If you try to fix the slide, it doesn't fix the early extension; but if you fix the early extension, it almost always fixes the slide. Don't worry about your slide—fix the early extension if you want more consistency. If you find that you hit the ball fat when you don't slide, look at the wipe movement as it relates to your release.

Figure 47.4

The slide is almost never a problem by itself; it almost always shows up with early extension. Early extension is usually the problem to fix.

Cast (spin/throw)

Figure 47.5   Figure 47.6

The cast is an upper body–dominant downswing pattern. The cast pattern works really well with the short irons and wedges, but golfers who cast frequently complain of distance off the tee.

What is the cast?

The cast is an upper body–dominant downswing pattern in which the arms activate early in the downswing (often immediately in transition).

Casting is almost always described as an unhinging motion of the wrist (like using a hammer), but 3D doesn't show it that way at all. **On 3D you will see the trail elbow straightening early, the trail wrist flexing early, or the lead shoulder abducting early.** If you see yourself on video and it looks like you are casting, investigate the trail arm or lead shoulder, but forget about trying to increase the hinge of the lead wrist.

Sir Nick Faldo had a trail wrist cast move. He was a very consistent ball striker, but lacked distance. With the cast move, it is possible to create high club head speed, but that is rare. Like early extension, the cast pattern helps the swing in a number of ways that need to be replaced.

How do you know if you cast?

The cast can be subtle, but is recognized in two different ways on video. From the face-on view, you will see an increase in the angle between the club shaft and lead arm. If you are really good at using video, you will also notice the trail arm straighten or the lead shoulder pull away from the body. But remember—just because it looks like an unhinging of the wrists doesn't mean it is. Usually, it is a lack of trail wrist extension that gives the look of unhinging from the face-on camera.

The second way to see the cast is with the down-the-line camera view. From this view, you can see the club face in an open (or opening) position when the club shaft is parallel to the ground in the downswing. If you are skilled with video, you can compare the amount of trail wrist extension at shaft parallel in the backswing to shaft parallel in the downswing. In the Stock Tour Swing, there is more extension in the downswing. In the cast pattern, there is less.

The common misses for a cast pattern are pulls and slices and contact more toward the toe. A golfer with the cast pattern typically struggles with the driver, but is great with the short irons and wedges.

What does the cast do that's helpful? What do you need to replace it with?

The cast pattern helps all three components of the power-path-face balance. It helps with the feeling of power, helps close the club face with in-plane shaft movement, and helps shallow the club head path.

Strength versus power

For many golfers, the cast movement frequently feels more powerful than a lag-building movement. At least, it does before impact. To understand why, let's compare power and strength.

Power is best developed sequentially, from the deepest muscles to the more superficial ones. Strength, on the other hand, is best developed by activating everything at once.

If you are doing a pull-up, you want to activate your arms, legs, and core almost simultaneously. A pull-up represents strength. If you are throwing a ball, however, you want a sequence built from the ground up. Throwing a ball represents power. The cast pattern involves activating the arms and the body simultaneously to start the downswing, instead of keeping the arms relaxed and delaying their activation.

Golfers who previously played sports that feature skills dominated by big body movements (like basketball, football, or swimming) may be more likely to cast the club as a way to control the swing with their upper body. In golf, a balanced approach to creating speed is superior to one in which the upper body dominates.

Squares the face with the path

If you have an open face-to-path relationship, a leftward club head path helps point the face at the target. The cast pattern closes the face with in-plane shaft movement instead of with shaft rotation.

In-plane shaft movement is not the best way to square the face for the full swing. It is great for squaring the face with a wedge shot, but it can be disastrous with the driver and long clubs.

Not all casters slice the ball. If you hit down enough, or keep your chest closed long enough, the path could be right of the face and you could actually draw the ball with a cast pattern.

Shallows the club head path

When the arms extend, the club head moves farther from the body and shallows out the club path. Arm extension early in the downswing restricts the body's ability to side bend and encourages early extension.

To support the arms extending too soon, many golfers lunge their upper body toward the target (a move in this chapter called the **forward lunge**). The cast and the lunge work together by balancing the face and path, but typically create a steep angle of attack and limited flat spot. Both create issues for the driver.

Helps the short game

A cast is only bad when applied to the wrong shot. The ideal time to use a cast sequence is in the short game. If you are a good wedge player but struggle with the longer clubs, there is a good chance that you swing the golf club with a cast or upper body–dominant swing pattern.

What physically contributes to cast?

Trail shoulder external rotation. Trail shoulder external rotation shallows the club head path. If your external rotation is limited, you will typically shallow the club head path by straightening the trail arm. But straightening the arm widens the radius of the circle too soon, which messes up your flat spot.

Lack of body rotation also messes up your flat spot. The more body rotation you have at impact, the more trail shoulder external rotation you need to keep your path from getting too steep. (Without external rotation, the only way to avoid getting steep, if you do rotate your body, is to have a release like Jim Furyk.)

Tight or weak hips. Rotating and side bending from the hips can be challenging on the body, especially if your hip movements are tight. If your hips are weak, or tight, then pulling with your arms is the next-best strategy for creating power. But since pulling is a big steep movement, you have to shallow the club head path another way. Most people do so with two movements: straightening the arms earlier (cast), and early extension.

Thoracic spine (T-spine). With a lack of T-spine mobility, it is common for the shoulders to be weak and for the swing to be dominated by arm movements. When isolated arm movements dominate the backswing, the arms work around the body—swinging the arms causes the trail shoulder to get stuck behind the body. When this happens, the shoulder is less able to externally rotate. This backswing position causes the trail arm to internally rotate too soon (steep), which is then balanced by the cast (shallow).

What does the cast do to the shape of the swing?

A cast is problematic because it widens the circle's radius too soon. A wide radius makes it difficult to side bend during the release without hitting fat shots. Without enough side bend, you can't produce a good flat spot. This is great for a wedge shot (it allows you to use the bounce), but not for a full swing.

Keys to solving the cast and drills to train the solution

Learn to delay when the arm straightens and become comfortable hitting with more external rotation. Learn to power the swing more with the body and less with the shoulders. Learn to square the face with the motorcycle move. Learn the arm shallowing movement in transition.

Chicken wing

Figure 47.7

The chicken wing is an active bending of the lead elbow through impact—typically to close the face by moving the shaft backward and letting the club head pass the hands.

What is chicken wing?

The chicken wing is when your lead arm is bending at impact and continues to bend until follow through. There are lots of good golfers who have a bent arm at impact (in fact, almost every tour golfer's elbow is more bent at impact than at set up). So the chicken wing is not purely a bent arm.

Even if good golfers have a bent lead elbow at impact, their arm is straightening at impact—even if it doesn't always look that way on video. The error (chicken wing) is an active bend of the lead elbow through impact.

How do you know if you have chicken wing?

It is challenging to diagnose the chicken wing on video. An overhead camera angle shows it best, but unfortunately not every golfer likes to use a selfie stick to capture this view.

The next best option is to observe from down the line. From this angle, check your follow through. If just after follow through you chicken wing, you will see your lead elbow appear on the left side of your body before the club head.

From the face-on view, it is actually harder to see because it is masked by shoulder rotation. You can check if your lead elbow is fairly straight after impact. I usually look between shaft 45 and shaft parallel.

The miss pattern for the chicken wing is usually fat/thin and contact will usually be on the toe.

What does chicken wing do that's helpful? What do you need to replace it with?

The chicken wing does three key things. It helps square the face, narrow the arc, and distribute force through the whole arm/shoulder.

Square the face

Bending the lead arm helps square the face to the target (but not the shaft) by moving the path left. It also squares the face with in-plane shaft movement.

Narrows the arc

Bending the lead elbow narrows the swing's arc. This makes the wide point closer to the ball instead of well after impact. The chicken wing helps prevent hitting the ground behind the ball, but it is usually a compensation for failing to rotate the body enough.

Distributes force

Bending the lead elbow recruits more muscles than just the forearm to handle the speed of the club. If the body lacks a good bracing position, it will have difficulty handling the club's speed after impact. Bending the lead elbow can complement a lead shoulder shrug to handle the force of the club just after impact.

What physically contributes to chicken wing?

Lead shoulder external rotation. Limited lead shoulder external rotation can be a problem if it is severe, but that is rarely the case. The chicken wing is often a result of steep transition arm movements and poor transition sequence (body then arms). If the arms fire too soon, they create the need for the chicken wing.

Neck rotation. Limited neck rotation can restrict your ability to rotate your body open at impact and can result in a forward lunge pattern. The lunge pattern is almost always accompanied by a chicken wing movement at impact.

What does it do to the shape of the swing?

The chicken wing limits the flat spot and moves the wide point closer to impact location. This combination is great for chip shots, where you want the wide point, and low point, at the ball. But it doesn't work well for the full swing.

Keys to solving chicken wing and drills to train the solution

You can avoid chicken wing by getting the body more open at impact. Training usually requires working on shallowing the club with arms, squaring the face earlier with the motorcycle movement, and powering the swing more with the body and less with the arms.

Forward lunge

Figure 47.8   Figure 47.9

The forward lunge is a linear movement of the upper body toward the target. It steepens the club head path and decreases the flat spot, but it feels very powerful to some golfers.

What is the forward lunge?

The cousin of the cast, the forward lunge is an excessive shift of the upper body toward the target during the downswing. Of all the upper body–dominant power sources, the forward lunge typically feels the most powerful. The forward lunge uses body weight to speed up the club but leaves you out of position to use your legs to initiate the release.

The elite swing normally includes a slight shift of the upper body toward the target in transition, but the forward lunge is a greater movement than just the normal shift. As a result, the upper body ends up a few inches closer to the target than it was at set up.

How do you know if you have forward lunge?

Face-on video is the clearest vantage point for identifying the forward lunge. You will notice that your upper body is on top of or in front of your lower body during the release. It's normal to have the upper body drift a bit forward during the transition (not quite as much as the lower body). But during release, your upper body should move slightly away from the target with the irons and significantly away from the target with the driver.

The miss pattern for the forward lunge is typically a steep path. If you hit the ground, the miss pattern will be fat. If you chicken wing, your miss will be thin. Either way, the forward lunge typically results in low shots and struggles with the driver.

What does forward lunge do that's helpful? What do you need to replace it with?

It creates power! The forward lunge uses the upper body to pull the club linearly toward the target.

It also helps you avoid fat shots when accompanied by the cast pattern. If you cast and have a good pivot, you will hit the ground a foot behind the ball. When a golfer with a forward lunge is out of rhythm with their lunge, they struggle with fat (or thin) contact.

The forward lunge movement is especially common in athletes who have played sports that require more body adjustments than arm adjustments. Hockey, baseball (except pitchers), and football players (except quarterbacks and kickers) tend to be more prone to this kind of swing problem because they are skilled at controlling the details of their swing with body location rather than with the fine movements of their arms/hands.

What physically contributes to forward lunge?

Neck. When the neck is limited in rotation, it's very common for the body to lunge in front of the ball to restrict body rotation. But a forward lunge generally causes the angle of attack to be too steep and the club path out-to-in.

Shoulder. If the trail shoulder is tight, then rotating the body will be a challenge, unless you want to use more of a Jim Furyk method. Most people don't feel very strong with the trail arm bent and behind their body like Jim. A reasonable solution is to forward lunge instead.

What does it do to the shape of the swing?

The forward lunge moves the circle forward. But wait—don't we want to move the circle forward? Yes, we do. But too much movement of the upper body on top of the ball kills axis tilt and limits your flat spot potential. It steepens the angle of attack, which is hard to overcome with the driver. A forward lunge is not all bad. It is the best way to hit shots out of thick rough.

Keys to solving forward lunge and drills to train the solution

There are two key movements to fixing the forward lunge—the wipe and the hip bump (the Jackson 5). The supporting movements to the wipe and the Jackson 5 are to shallow the arms in transition, limit early extending, and use the motorcycle move to square the face.

Downswing summary

You may have noticed that almost all the downswing swing faults compensate for one or more of the following root problems:

1. Steepening with the arms in transition;
2. Using in-plane shaft movement instead of the motorcycle move as the primary face closer; and
3. Powering the swing more with the arms than the body.

The body is very skilled at coming up with compensations, but the majority of issues can be traced to these three root problems. They show up in different amounts, speeds, and timings for each golfer.

Solutions to downswing problems can take time to retrain. When you do retrain the root source of your issue, you will experience technical leaps in ball-striking proficiency that you only dreamed of.

CHAPTER 48

Contact Issues

Contact issues can exist independently of swing faults. You can either balance the swing pattern or address the contact issues on their own. There are no physical restrictions that make you prone to one contact miss or another, but there are definitely movement combinations that create them.

Shank

Figure 48.1

There are a few major causes of the shank. Leaving the club face open while bringing the club from the inside is a common cause—as shown here.

What is the shank?

A shank is when you hit the ball on the hosel of the club and it flies off the hosel sideways. It's one of the most penalizing shots in golf and one of the worst-feeling shots. As shown in the movie *Tin Cup*, players often think of shanks as more mental than technical. But as you're learning in this book, nothing in golf is impossible to solve.

If you've historically blamed shanks on your mental game, the good news is that there are a handful of major technical causes to consider. They are:

- Early extension—see the early extension section (Chapter 47)
- Overly open club face—usually accompanied by body rotation
- High forearm plane in the release—part of early extension
- Trail arm straight too soon (outside-in)—if you shank it from an outside-in pattern, you will likely have your trail arm fully straight at impact
- Hands moving toward the target line, instead of left, through impact
- Standing too close to the ball—this is really rare: one in 10,000 shankers struggle for this reason.

What is happening to the shape of the circle?

The hosel of the club is moving too much toward the golf ball.

Keys to solving shank and drills to train the solution

Become aware of the path of the club head down at the bottom of the swing.

Figure 48.2

Set up

Place two tees in the ground about half an inch on each side of the club.

Execution

Practice swings in which you make the club head pass between the two tees. After successfully doing so a number of times, place a golf ball (preferably on a tee) between the two tees and repeat a swing that passes between them.

Focus and questions

Can you identify with the path of the club head? Try to feel like you are swinging it through the tees, not guiding it. For a challenge, start in the middle and clip the inside tee—that may be "straight" for you.

Topping

Figure 48.3

Figure 48.4

A topped shot almost always stems from producing a low point behind the ball, so the club head rises up through impact and hits above the ball's equator.

What is topping the ball?

Topping the ball is when the golf club strikes above the ball's equator. It typically comes from path that is either too steep or too shallow.

From a mechanical view, topping the ball develops from two major issues in the downswing—either increasing the distance between the upper body and the ball (standing up) or shortening the radius of the circle (bending arms). Often, these two issues compensate for an overly steep arm path or an overly open clubface.

There is a simple two-part solution to topping the ball. If you keep your thorax the same distance from the ground, and if your arms extend through the release, you eliminate any chance of topping the ball.

What does topping the ball do to the shape of the swing?

The circle is either working up through impact or is never low enough. Either way, the low and wide points are not far enough forward, which leaves you a small margin of error.

Keys to solving topping the ball and drills to train the solution

Become comfortable with the upper body closer to the ground while also ensuring that the arms extend through the shot. You will often need to work on the amount of rotation at impact. Review the impact and follow through positions; train to make those feel comfortable. For a simple external focus approach, work on getting the club head to brush the ground. This yields quick and easy improvement for most golfers. If the club head brushes the ground near impact, it's almost impossible to top the ball.

DRILL - BRUSH THE GROUND

Figure 48.5   Figure 48.6   Figure 48.7

Set up

Without a golf ball, take your normal address posture.

Execution

Make a swing (either 9–3 or full swing) with an iron, and attempt to get the club head to brush the ground in the direction of the target for as long as possible, starting ahead of the middle of your stance.

Focus and questions

Can you repeat swings producing a soft and gentle brush, not a loud thud? A thud indicates a steep angle of attack. Make sure your upper body stays centered, and focus on the sound the club makes with the ground.

Fat/Thin

Figure 48.6

Figure 48.7

Figure 48.8

Figure 48.9

A fat shot and a thin shot can have almost identical swing paths, but with slightly different low points. Both shots are frequently caused by an early release of the trail arm and a low point behind the ball.

What is fat/thin?

Fat and thin both come from a swing path where the low point is before the ball, while the wide point could be either before the ball or after it. It's odd to think of a fat and a thin shot as part of the same pattern, but they are. Tour pros hit it close to the sweet spot because their club head path has a fairly tight dispersion near the ball. Amateurs tend to have paths that change a bit more, and as a result they more frequently struggle with the fat and thin shots.

Outside-in fat/thin

This version occurs when the wide point and the low point are before the ball. A chicken wing almost always accompanies an outside-in fat/thin miss. The chicken wing avoids slamming the club into the ground. It's almost impossible to have this miss without relying on either a cast and/or a lunge; for corrections, refer to those sections in Chapter 47.

Inside-out fat/thin

This version occurs when the wide point is before the ball but the low point is after it. Arm extension is not the problem; it is usually early spine extension (raising the sternum) that forces the path to swing too low–to-high and makes it hard for the club to consistently brush the ground.

Keys to solving fat/thin and drills to train the solution

The motorcycle
Because the low point is before the ball, one of the most common causes of fat and thin for the full swing is to lose the motorcycle too soon (or to never do it in the first place).

> One of the most common ways golfers shift from average contact to solid contact is by working on the motorcycle move. It's one of the few real game changers out there.

The brush location

Part of the reason I harp on the brush location is because it is impossible to have a good brush pattern and a really bad club head path. Hitting the ball fat/thin is a path issue, and brush location is a big-picture way to look at path. If the club head approaches the ground like an airplane landing gently, and if the club head brushes the ground in a consistent spot, all you have to worry about is the club face working with that path and brush location. A good way to monitor your brush location is with the famous line drill.

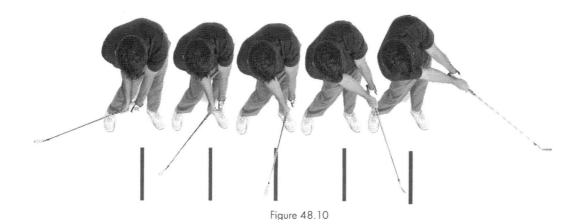

Figure 48.10

Set up

Use chalk, paint, or a tee to put a straight line on the ground. Using an iron, set up roughly perpendicular to the line, with the line in your normal ball position (or if you are a new golfer, start with the line even with your left ear).

Execution

Make swings (either 9–3 or full swings) with the golf ball on the target side of the line. Notice where the divot or brush mark occurs compared to the line.

Focus and questions

With smooth ground contact, how far forward can you brush the ground past the golf ball?. If the ball flies off to the right, then this indicates you will need to work on face-to-path relationship.

Recap: Linking the Secrets of the Stock Tour Swing

There are many ways a swing can get off track, but in general, there are predictable patterns. These include a backswing pattern or a downswing one, but frequently there will be problems in both of these swing phases.

The backswing patterns are loss of posture and sway. Loss of posture is frequently described as standing up. In our Stock Tour Swing model, loss of posture is really a lack of left side bend coupled with limited arm rotation. The sway is when the pelvis moves excessively away from the target. Some tour pros sway with their driver by moving their pelvis away from the target, but the pressure in their feet doesn't move to the outside of the trail foot. This is the real problem of the sway and typically results in poor contact consistency.

The downswing patterns are early extension, cast, forward lunge, and chicken wing. Early extension is an excessive thrust of the lower body in toward the golf ball, or when the upper body moves too much away from the ball. Basically, it looks like the golfer stood up in the downswing. Early extension is caused by too much lower-body action and is used to shallow out the swing and help square the face. The cast, forward lunge, and chicken wing are all upper body–dominant swing patterns. They typically all include straightening the arms too early, which makes it harder to create the flat spot.

There are also contact patterns that exist independently of swing patterns. The worst contact miss is the shank, which involves hitting it on the hosel. Golfers also frequently struggle with fat and thin contact. It's important to recognize that fat and thin misses typically have the same swing pattern but slightly different low points. A topped shot is an extremely thin shot where the club is typically moving up through the hitting area and makes contact above the ball's equator.

Chapter 49

Putting Part 6 Principles into Practice

After learning the swing patterns, students often ask, "Should I change my swing?" or "Should I own it?" My response is always a series of questions.

"How bad are your poor shots?"

This is my way of asking, "With your current pattern, can you score the way you want and hit the shots you want?"

"What are your goals?"

If you are a competitive golfer, consider how much time you have until you need to play well. If you are lifelong-journey golfer, it's a no-brainer. Working on your swing pattern will provide long-term joy.

The goal of these questions is not to talk you out of making changes. The goal is to help you acknowledge that changing your swing is your project. You don't have to change your swing, but change is your only choice if you are tired of the predictable misses built into your pattern.

Some swing patterns are easier to solve than others. Some golfers have an easier time working through the changes than others. Contact misses are usually solved with external focus. As a result, contact misses are relatively easy to improve and should almost always be worked on—especially the shanks. If you have the shanks, fix them now. They are a miserable miss to fear while playing golf.

The movements can be a little more challenging. But if you are tired of your current misses, or excited about the thought of reaching your potential, then working on your swing pattern is the only option.

How to plan for a swing change leads us to Part 7, where we review the GSA Mastery Flow Chart. The goal of the chart is to walk you through the process for laying out a long-term plan. It is a proactive approach to prioritizing and organizing your game. No plan will eliminate the ups and downs inherent in golf, but having a long-term plan keeps things moving when the slumps inevitably set in.

Part 7

GSA Road to Mastery

If you're like most of my students, you've probably had a handful of promising Eureka! moments while reading this program. You know that there is real hope for your game, but figuring out where to start may seem daunting. Do you start with set up? Backswing? Downswing? Or do you just work on your brush location and forget the details for now?

The truth is that there are a few reasonable options, and in Part 7 we discuss my flow chart for applying a logical process to managing your game.

Even if you don't make big changes to your game right away, hopefully the golf swing will make more sense when you watch TV, read magazines, or play a round. Maybe you will see a slow-motion analysis on TV and notice these key movements. You'll start to ignore the things that look quirky and instead focus on the things that define the elite tour pro swing. Or maybe you'll read a tip and be able to connect it to other parts of the swing.

CHAPTER 50

Putting It All Together

When you hear a tip in the future, how do you know if you should try it or not?

There is a three-step process to decoding the value of a tip:

1. Read a new tip.
2. Translate the tip to a core concept in the GSA system.
3. Consider ramifications—are any complimentary changes needed to make the tip work for your swing pattern?

Suppose you see a drill suggesting that you stay centered in your backswing. That idea makes sense and you want to try the drill. But since you can now see the big picture, you realize that this tip only works if you shallow your arms in transition; otherwise it could cause your club path to be too steep to function.

Thinking in this way gives you ownership over your game.

When training, there is really one important question to answer: "What are we doing here?" In other words, "Why am I doing this drill or why am I playing this game?" What will this do for my game if I train it? If you can answer that key question at any time, you are on track with your game.

This chapter outlines the process described in the "Mastery Flow Chart". The flow chart can be downloaded at http://golfsmartacademy.com/stocktourswingbook.

GSA Road to Mastery - Planning your training focus

Step 1: Identify your swing pattern??

3 Factors

1. Club Path? (outside-in, inside-out, shallow, steep, etc)
2. Power Source? (Legs, core, shoulders/arms, forearms, cast vs loaded, etc)
3. Club Face? (Look at top of backswing and release. Do you close the face starting early in transition or late in release? How do you close the face (with the shaft rotation in-plane shaft movement)?

Your swing pattern reveals your:
- ball flight pattern (fade, draw, straight)
- feared misses (tops, shanks, slices, pulls, hooks, etc)
- favorite shots (driver, wedges, bunkers, short rough)

Note: Usually you will find you have the same swing pattern through the bag, but it is possible to have a distinct swing pattern for your long game, mid game, and/or short game.

You are consistent – find your pattern!

Know your pattern? Skip Step 1 and move on to Step 2: Train your pattern

3 ways to identify your pattern

1 - Read Objective Results (most beneficial way)
- Contact with the ball
- Contact with the ground
- Ball Flight
  - Curve
  - Starting Direction
  - Height
- What are your Misses?
- What are your Strengths?
- What shot do you most fear?

If you can identify your pattern by reading feedback, then you can use it on the course and make quick corrections to save the day.

Properly reading feedback could be the most important golf skill you develop

To download the complete, updated version of the flowchart please visit golfsmartacademy.com/stocktourswingbook.

Step 1: Do you know your pattern?

Knowing your own personal swing pattern is by far the most useful starting point for answering the question, "What are we doing here?" Keep in mind that identifying your pattern doesn't require you to change anything in your swing. You could identify your pattern and simply use it to build your course strategy and enhance your shot selection.

Knowing your pattern can help you make on-course decisions such as:

- Which risky shots to attempt and which to pass up
- When you should play conservatively
- When you should attack a pin
- When you should challenge a dog leg
- When you should play for the fat part of the green

The simplest way to define your pattern is to analyze your club head path tendencies. Later, if you wish, you can add layers to your pattern. These include how your major power source creates that path and what methods you rely on for controlling the face-to-path relationship. Of course, one of the biggest reasons to decode your pattern is to help you prioritize your practice time.

How to identify your path and face pattern

The best way to determine your path pattern is to use contact and ball flight feedback.

On your own, identify the pattern of your path and face alignments based on a number of questions:

- Which shots can I do easier than others, and which invoke fear?
- What are my typical misses?
- Do I take divots before the ball, after it, or do I not take divots at all?
- Where do I make contact on the club face?
- When I hit a good shot, where does the ball start? How does it curve?
- Would I prefer to hit a driver or a short iron?
- Do I prefer the ball above or below my feet?

All of this information helps you identify your global pattern.

How do I control the path?
How do I control the face?
How do I create power?

Using objective data—either on your own or with a coach

Another way to identify your global pattern is to use technology. Trackman, 3D, and even high-speed video can help. In fact, video and 3D can highlight your pattern at different parts of the swing.

Figuring out exactly in which swing phase your swing shifts too steep/shallow or too open/closed can lead you to breakthroughs faster than simply knowing your general ball flight and contact pattern. Identifying your path tendencies at different parts of the swing can help you zero in on key movement combinations to either train (if you want to balance your swing) or to manage (if you want to own your swing).

For example, if you have an outside-in ball flight pattern (slices/pulls/worse shots with the driver than short irons), is it because of what you do in transition or the release? Or does your backswing cause the trail arm to get stuck behind your body?

The problem-solving approach—why you have the pattern and how to fix it—takes trial and error. But as long as your solution logically balances your swing issue, it is likely to help your performance immediately.

> **Insight**
>
> If the solution balances your swing, then it will help your performance immediately.

If you know your pattern, you can move on to step 2. But do not skip identifying (and understanding) your pattern.

Step 2: Own your swing or improve it

Just because you know that your swing isn't perfect doesn't mean you have to change it right now. There are lots of reasons why it might be best to schedule working on a change later, in the right time of the year.

If you put off improving your pattern, then owning your swing will also help you decide which shots to avoid hitting on the course. For example, if you have an outside-in path, and you need to hit a draw on the course, then the smartest choice is to hit a pull draw. That way you can keep your normal swing pattern and simply close the face more at set up.

It is very common in other sports to focus on understanding yourself and your pattern. This enables you to maximize your strengths and minimize your weaknesses. Take football for example—if you know you are a running team, then you will draft players and build your team differently than if you run a West Coast offense. Or take tennis—if your opponent hits a poor lob shot to your backhand and you have a strong forehand, a great option is to run around your backhand to take advantage of your strength.

If you struggle with the driver because your pattern is steep and out-to-in, you could always hit three wood off the tee until you have time to work on your club head path. Or you could set up with the ball more forward and just play a big fade. It might not go as far, but you can still score well over the rest of your game. Golfers often say, "But I hit it short and I need all the distance I can get." If you are steep and outside-in, then hitting the three wood likely won't cost you distance anyway.

At the 2006 Masters, Phil Mickelson was a great example of how to strategically minimize weaknesses in a game. He knew his swing and came to the course with two drivers—one to fade it and one to draw it. Knowing your pattern helps you make all kinds of smart strategy decisions and do the best to score at any given time.

How to own it and how to improve it

Once you know your pattern, you could either work to own it or work to improve it.

To own it, make minor changes (usually set up only or strategy only) and let your swing just repeat its pattern. You won't change any phase of your swing, with the possible exception of the set up. You can still work on brushing the ground and things like tempo that have a high carry-over effect to your scores on the course. You can also still practice different clubs and shots, but mostly to identify what you have in your tool box at the moment.

> Speaking generally, it is usually a bad idea to attempt a swing balancing change during a pre-round warm-up. Instead, take inventory to see which shots you are feeling and which are difficult to pull off. Small set up changes and/or consciously focusing on club-to-ground contact will help you swing what you have that day and more consistently score at your best.
>
> *Insight*

The second option is to try to improve (or balance) your swing. That's not to say that having a perfectly straight shot is the goal; rather, shoot for the ability to adjust your swing for different shots. For example, a shallow body move is better for the longer clubs, but if you can't adjust how you shallow the club for the short shots, you will have a hard time scoring.

If you are in an improvement phase of training, you can do drills—to change the shape of your circle, your flat spot, and your impact position—so you can hit more consistent and effective shots while your swing is evolving.

Balancing your swing is the more mentally challenging task and that's why most of this book covers the subtleties to reading feedback, freeing you to confidently make technical changes to your swing.

The keys to improving your swing are knowing how to read feedback and knowing what to change during each swing phase. When you understand the golf swing as a whole, it's easier to commit to changing one or two key things that cause your pattern.

I consistently tell my students that knowing what you want to do is just the first step. You still have to put in the reps over a series of weeks or months before changes will feel natural on the course.

Step 3: Make a plan

Regardless of whether you choose to own your pattern or work to balance it, the final step is to write down a plan. This is necessary to play like a champion. The backbone of your plan should be built around when you have scheduled your most important rounds, trips, or tournaments. It is also important to decide whether your priority is just to have fun or to reach your full scoring potential.

Another key factor in designing your plan is your current level of patience/frustration. It is a challenge to work intensively on your swing all year round. If you just finished a few months of working hard on your release, it's a good idea to throttle back the intensity of your practices and let the new movement solidify before adding more technique.

Think about when you want to play well and what your goal is. Can you mentally handle the road ahead? Your answers will inform when you decide to pursue intensive changes (which might take months to feel comfortable) or simpler changes (which might only take a practice session).

Consider your short- and long-term plans. This is common in strength and performance training and can be helpful in golf as well. Designing a year-long golf training program could be a book in and of itself, but we can highlight the important components of the process.

Your short-term plan should cover what kinds of practice you will do each week and what your focus will be. Laying out the long-term plan takes more thought.

Own your pattern

You may decide to own your pattern. In this case, you will briefly work on dialing in your mechanics in warm-up before you practice, and then spend the majority of your practice time on techniques that will transfer to your on-course game—techniques like random practice or playing games. You may decide to spend your practice time on the course—not keeping score, but practicing in the environment in which you play. The safest things to work on are set up, tempo, brushing the ground, and, possibly, follow through.

But keep the big picture in mind. Make sure you spend time practicing the parts of your game that will have the biggest impact on your score. Suppose you are terrible at bunkers and iron contact. You may spend a lot of time working on bunkers but find that you only hit from bunkers once or twice a round. Your iron play, meanwhile, you typically use on every hole. A small improvement in your iron play will probably help your game more significantly than a big improvement in your bunker play.

Train it

On the other hand, if you are going to train your pattern, you may structure your practice sessions to work on mechanics. You may test those mechanics with a game then finish by jumping back to mechanics. You may also decide to spend most of your time on the downswing, since that is where the greatest potential exists to improve both contact and ball flight.

After putting in time on the mechanics, test your new skill before taking it to the course. For example, avoid practice for a day. Then, in your next practice, start with a challenging game to see if the new mechanics have stuck.

Blend the plans together

Change the focus of your practice throughout the year. When you have a break of at least a couple weeks, target train your swing. When you have less than two weeks of regular practice (at the range or at home), it is very risky to tackle a new concept. With less than two weeks, work to own what you currently have.

The one exception is that you can often revisit things you have worked on previously. For example, if you worked on the motorcycle for a month or two earlier in the year, it is very easy to focus on it again later in the year for a practice session or two and suddenly have your swing click. Improvements may come very quickly when focusing on something you have previously trained.

A simplified approach to the year-long plan

- In-season: If scoring is your main goal, work on playing your game. Your only swing changes should be small or continued practice on things you started in the off-season. If you don't care about your score and just want to work on technique, identify important rounds on your calendar and use those to intentionally schedule breaks from your technique work. You can't work on technique nonstop and expect continual progress. It is mentally fatiguing and you'll lose the necessary precision. It's better to work on something for a few weeks then let it settle for a bit before moving on.

- Off-season: Work on balancing your pattern by improving your mechanics. This is the perfect time to work on movement fixes that change your path or power source. Tweaking your path control, face control, or power source can significantly change your shot pattern and long-term consistency. However, expect to have major performance fluctuations when engraining them.

CHAPTER 51

Putting Part 7 Principles into Practice

I've noticed there are a few different groups of people who study the golf swing: competitive golfers, lifelong learners, coaches (or parents), and casual fans. I have a few suggestions for how to apply this system to each kind of game. I enjoy coaching anyone willing to listen. Hopefully, this book helps your game as much as it's helped my own.

Competitive golfers

Your path differs from most golfers. Every fraction of a stroke is significant to reaching your goal. Two common pitfalls that you might make when laying out your plan are (i) chasing a destination; and (ii) failing to switch from "working on my game" to "owning my game."

The first problem is easy. You will never have a *perfect* swing. You want a game that is bulletproof, but every golfer—even on their best days—has shots that don't fit their natural swing. By owning your pattern, you can choose wisely. As you work on your weaknesses, remember to spend time maintaining your strengths. If you leave your strengths unattended for too long, they will become your new weakness.

The second problem is more challenging. If you struggle with one area of your game, you will tend to downplay progress. You will tend to believe that nothing has changed, when in fact you are making subtle progress. When enough progress has been made in your swing, you will have a hard time letting go of the belief that your swing is *broken*. This is a normal phase. Your swing will need constant maintenance, but when you are in this place, you will have all the tools to repair your swing after a poor round. You may struggle to let go of the belief that each poor round requires a complete swing overhaul. Trusting in the physics and isolating the phase you need to tweak is the fastest route to regaining flow.

Lifelong learners

For you, golf is a spiritual journey. You have the patience to troubleshoot swing problems. For you, the key is having clear focus. As you work through the different areas of the swing, you will naturally gravitate toward the release. The release is the crux of the golf swing, and you will find great joy in understanding its subtleties. I have trained two lifelong learners who each spent over a year with single arm release training. The single arm release drills have a Zen-like quality and nothing holds a swing together consistently like a good release.

You may have breakthroughs in the backswing or in transition, but for you, the magic of golf will come from training your release.

Coaches (or parents)

It takes more patience to coach someone through learning the golf swing than it does to actually learn the golf swing. Early in my career, I would shift focus more quickly than the student was ready. I would see progress and immediately jump to a complementary movement.

With years of coaching, I have learned to let a golfer *get bored with success* before I suggest a new area of focus. If the student asks for more, that is one thing. But if they are content at a certain skill level, it is a disservice to shift them to something new unless it will absolutely help quickly. My minimum time working on one area is three weeks. Transition or the release require a minimum of six weeks. If you try to speed things up, you will actually hinder progress for your students.

The other key skill is to recognize frustration level. If the student gets highly frustrated, focus their attention on the club brushing the ground or reacting to feedback.

Casual fans

As a casual fan, you are similar to the frustrated golfer. The details of Part 3 may be a challenge to feel at this point, so you will do best refining your skills brushing the ground and reacting to ball flight. I have had casual golfers experience great improvement to their scoring by focusing on nothing but reading feedback and adjusting with simple corrections.

While it is true what many golfers say, that you will score better from working on your wedge play and putting, nothing will be more satisfying than learning to strike the ball solidly consistently. Nothing will help your ball striking consistency like learning to brush the ground consistently.

Chapter 52

Parting Thoughts

I can still remember the first time I went to hit golf balls. My grandfather took my brother and me to the course and gave us some basic advice on how to hold the club and stand. I could have stayed on the range all day. When my first real technical struggles came, I wasn't able to work through them on my own, as I'd been able to do in other sports. It bothered me, but also provided opportunities. I grew and matured while searching for a solution. Golf has taught me a lot over the years, and I hope this program helps you and those you share it with to enjoy this magical game.

Golf is complex and requires a slew of different skills. For most students, the joy comes from hitting the ball well. The full swing is a mystery for amateur golfers, but one that tour pros have mostly solved. Like revealing the secret behind a magic trick, I wanted to create a program to remove the mystery. That said, there are many components to scoring well not included in this book that are critical to playing well. Some of these were touched upon, but not to the same level as on my website:

- Finesse wedges—shots around the green
- Distance wedges—shots from 30–100 yards
- Bunker—shots from the sand
- Putting—shots on the green
- Trouble shots—shots from funky lies
- Course strategy
- Mental game

One of my favorite sayings is, "*A good gardener does not leave a patch for weeds.*" In that spirit, a good golfer cares for their game by keeping weaknesses under control.

When I first set out to share my studies with the world, I created a training program at http://golfsmartacademy.com which is designed as an interactive reference for passionate golfers and coaches. To see the moves we discussed in action, or to work with us on implementing the strategies, please check out our programs and videos.

I appreciate your investment in your game and hope you found this program illuminating. I hope it helps you develop your swing based on the key fundamentals for success. We are on the cusp of a great era in golf instruction, and I'm proud to help get the message out there. With the help of golf science, there is always hope for your game.

Happy golfing,

— Tyler Ferrell
Golf Smart Academy (GSA) Team

Acknowledgements

I would not be here without the loving help of my parents, John and Jan, and my brother Brian. Thank you for supporting me while I pursued my dreams.

This book would have been a completely different product had it not been for the help of my key supporters: Lauri Scherer, Brian Ferrell, Nick Taylor, Wes Waddel, Michael Anderson, all the proofreaders, and my business partner Lawrence Lee.

My professional journey has led me to many brilliant people in the world of golf training, and I wouldn't be where I am today without them. A complete list of everyone who has influenced me, and this book, would include almost everyone that I've known and conversed with, or whose books I have read. Let me apologize in advance to those who I have forgotten in this less-than-comprehensive list.

My first boss and mentor, Dr. Greg Rose, (cofounder of the Titleist Performance Institute) was instrumental in helping propel me to where I am now. His general advice was critical to the areas I decided to study; he advised me to question everything that I heard or read (even from him) and to look outside the golf industry for inspiration. He also inspired me to push myself to become a lifelong learner. He taught me it wasn't weird to read a textbook just for fun. He was a great subject to observe during my early years of coaching, but his most influential role was a key conversation during which he talked me out of trying to be a player and instead to become a coach.

One of my biggest influences outside of the golf industry has been Janet Alexander and her husband and partner Chris Maund. Janet is one of the best in the world at designing long-term exercise programs. She grew and tested my creativity and understanding of the body. I saw how working on one area could train another—for example, how training the pelvis could also train the neck. This philosophy has influenced the way in which I coach the golf swing. Some of the connections in this book would have never been made had some of her creativity not rubbed off on me.

As a golf fitness trainer I was influenced by Dr. Bobby Duvall, Lance Gill, and my fellow trainers Allison Kirsch, Jason Meisch, and Kyle Anderson. But while I was studying fitness and the body, part of my brain was always trying to solve the problem of the golf swing. I had a great foundation in understanding it with the help of Bob Dolan, Wayne Defranscesco, Bernie Najar, and my real first coach and high school teammate, JohnScott Rattan. I also benefitted from really smart instructors off of whom I bounced ideas—Brendon Post and Ryan Chaney.

However, over the last few years, one coach—Chris Como—has really influenced the questions that I ask and made me feel more secure in my understanding of the swing. There is a very small world of golf science experts, and Chris is one of the few who can read all the graphs but also relate them to the coaching process. We discuss what we would love to measure as well as the limitation of every system. He has helped streamline my focus, and the content of this book would have been very different had we never crossed paths.

I would also like to thank those who supported me either emotionally, physically, or professionally. I am deeply thankful for the help of Dee Tidwell, Corrie Tayman-Myers, Dr. Mindy Clark, Edo Zylstra, Scott Herrera, Dan Hellman, Dr. Ryan Dunn, Dr. Evan Katz, Trevor Montgomery, Heidi Gastler, and Dr. Guy Voyer.

For making golf science cool, I want to thank those who have helped create the measurement systems responsible for the data I use to form my theories. These scientists are the unsung heroes in golf science: Dr. Phil Chetham, Dr. Young-Hoo Kwon, Dr. Mike Duffy, Dr. Sasho Mackenzie, and Dr. Rob Neal.

For the software to create the images of the 3D models in this book, I want to thank Michael Neff of GEARS. If someone in your area has a GEARS system, I highly recommend getting suited up to see some really amazing visuals.

For my big break and my exposure to coaching at the tour level, I am forever in debt to Grant Waite, Charles Howell III, and Jeff Leishman.

Lastly, there are two huge groups of people who would take too long to list individually. To all the trainers, coaches, instructors, and biomechanists whose works I have read, classes I've attended, or simply been fortunate to have conversations with—thanks. The second is my students. Every key breakthrough has been shaped by your experiences. Most of the simplicity of explanation has come as a result of the question that you've helped me understand from other perspectives—"...and what is that experience like for you."

About the author

Since 2002, Tyler Ferrell has studied under leaders in golf research using groundbreaking 3D technology, a key to the explosion of golf science.

He has two main purposes for this book. First, to share the movement combinations that he has refined during 15 years of coaching using 3D motion measurement technologies. Each key point and movement recommended in this book is backed up by data collected from thousands of golfers.

His second goal is to share the problem-solving philosophy that he and his students have found to be the most efficient way to evolve a golfer's game and to keep golf fresh over a lifetime. He hopes this book will help golfers who are willing to put in the work develop an improvement plan that builds the right skills to evolve their game.

Made in United States
Orlando, FL
13 July 2024

48912345R00191